Gerald Corey
Michelle Muratori
Jude T. Austin II
Julius A. Austin

Counselor Self-Care

AMERICAN COUNSELING
ASSOCIATION
6101 Stevenson Avenue • Suite 600
Alexandria, VA 22304
www.counseling.org

Counselor
Self-Care

American Counseling Association

6101 Stevenson Avenue, Suite 600 • Alexandria, VA 22304

Associate Publisher • Carolyn C. Baker

Digital and Print Development Editor • Nancy Driver

Senior Production Manager • Bonny E. Gaston

Copy Editor • Kay Mikel

Cover and text design by Bonny E. Gaston.

Library of Congress Cataloging-in-Publication Data

Names: Corey, Gerald, author.
Title: Counselor self-care / Gerald Corey [and three others].
Description: Alexandria, VA : American Counseling Association, [2018]
  Includes bibliographical references.
Identifiers: LCCN 2017052640 | ISBN 9781556203794 (pbk. : alk. paper)
Subjects: LCSH: Counseling psychologists—Mental health. | Counseling
  psychologists—Job stress. | Counselors—Mental health. | Counselors—
  Job stress.
Classification: LCC BF636.64 .C67 2018 | DDC 158.3023—dc23 LC
  record available at https://lccn.loc.gov/2017052640

* * *

To my grandchildren, Kyla, Keegan, and Corey,
who remind me to be in the moment.

—Jerry Corey

To the memory of my father, Edmund Muratori,
and in gratitude to my mother, Vera Muratori,
and my extended family.

—Michelle Muratori

To our parents, for their love, patience, and sacrifice.

—Jude and Julius Austin

* * *

Table of Contents

$\mathcal{P}reface$

The topic of self-care for mental health professionals is increasingly in the spotlight. When we attend professional conferences, there is not even standing room in the audience in sessions on self-care. The four of us have a keen interest in self-care for counselors and decided to engage in this collaborative project. We are convinced of the motivational value of presenting these ideas to students and professionals, and we hope you will take an honest look at how you are caring for yourself and providing care for the clients you serve. We offer diverse perspectives on self-care with the objective of encouraging counselors and counselor trainees to evaluate their present level of self-care and consider specific changes they want to make in attending to all aspects of wellness in their personal life. We are all engaged in professional work in different settings and are at different stages in our careers. Individually and collectively we strive to offer a balance of challenge and support as you consider ways to enhance your personal and professional life through self-care.

Rather than providing a reference book focused on an exhaustive review of the empirical and scholarly literature on counselor self-care, our approach is to take you on a personal self-care journey. To speak to you in a personal way, the four of us set the tone by revealing our own self-care journeys, and you will hear our voices throughout this book. In addition we invited 52 guest contributors, from new professionals and graduate students to seasoned professionals, to share their experiences and thoughts about various aspects of self-care, including what challenges them the most. Our central purpose is a focus on relevant themes in self-care that stimulate thoughtful reflection and encourage discussion of practical and useful ideas. We present the ideas in a conversational and personal way and continually asked ourselves how we could inspire you to want to take positive actions that would lead to building on the resources you already possess and to acquiring a set of self-care practices that will work for you in all aspects of your life. No one person has the ideal formula for optimal self-care; we are unique individuals with varied life experiences. With this in mind, we invite you to take this opportunity to live vicariously through our and our contributors' struggles and triumphs with self-care. Some of these stories and ideas will strike a chord in you, lead to new insights, and inspire your growth (or determination to change). We imagine that the personal narratives included here may evoke a range of reactions including empathy, sadness, laughter, anger, and surprise—all emotions you are likely to encounter on a personal journey. We hope you enjoy reading *Counselor Self-Care* as much as we enjoyed creating it!

This book can be used as a supplement in a wide range of courses in the counseling field and related helping professions. *Counselor Self-Care* is an ideal supplementary resource for both master's and doctoral programs in counseling. It has been intentionally written to be a practical and personal book relevant not only for graduate students but also for professionals at all phases of their career. New professionals and seasoned professional alike must develop self-care practices that will enable them to carry out their professional roles effectively.

Overview of the Book

Chapter 1: Taking Care of Yourself offers a rationale for adopting self-care practices as a requisite for competent professional practice. Self-care as an ethical mandate is emphasized, as is taking active steps to acquire and maintain wellness in all aspects of living. The concept of wellness is presented as a life-long journey that has implications both personally and professionally, and therapeutic presence is discussed with a focus on wellness. A key message of the chapter is how caring for self is a must if you are taking care of others. Empathy fatigue and counselor burnout, managing empathy fatigue, preventing burnout, and happiness as a foundation of self-care all receive our attention.

Chapter 2: Seasons of a Career illustrates how and why self-care is essential at all the stages of one's career: graduate school, early career, mid-career, and late career. In this chapter, we each describe key experiences at the different stages of our careers.

Chapter 3: Self-Care in Graduate School is written largely from the perspective of Julius Austin and Jude Austin, who discuss their experiences in their master's and doctoral programs and what they learned from their journeys about self-care and becoming counseling professionals. Topics include committing to self-care, setting boundaries, coping with anxiety, reflecting on motivations for becoming a counselor, maintaining self-worth, and practicing self-care during the dissertation process.

Chapter 4: Personal and Professional Stressors addresses how counselors and counselor educators have been affected by and have navigated the personal and professional stressors they have experienced.

Chapter 5: Managing Stress in a Stressful World presents a wide variety of routes to stress management: meditation, mindfulness, relaxation, yoga, Pilates, tai chi, experiencing nature, sound nutrition, exercise, recreation, and service to others. This chapter is full of ideas for self-care from a holistic perspective. There is no one right way to practice self-care; many different strategies can be used to deal effectively with stress and to achieve wellness.

Chapter 6: Establishing Personal and Professional Boundaries focuses on our successful and unsuccessful experiences setting boundaries at home and at work. Creating healthy work–life boundaries is explored, and our contributors share their ideas on establishing good boundaries, both personally and professionally.

Chapter 7: Relationships With Self and Others focuses on self-compassion, embracing the self, finding ways to nourish oneself through solitude and connections with others, developing forgiveness for self and others, taking time to form meaningful relationships, and mentorship.

Chapter 8: Finding Meaning in Life highlights the relationship between meaning in life and self-care. The existential approach is given attention as a way of finding meaning in life. Several guest contributors describe ways they create meaning for themselves and how this is connected to self-care.

Chapter 9: Creating a Realistic Self-Care Plan highlights the importance of designing a realistic action plan to enhance your self-care practices. The emphasis is on making an honest self-evaluation of your self-care and then deciding how you can make key changes in living. Several guest contributors describe their personal strategies for designing and implementing self-care action plans.

Acknowledgments

Counselor Self-Care is the result of a team effort. It is a collaboration between four coauthors and our guest contributors and reviewers, who have brought their influence to the development of this book. We appreciate the work of Marianne Schneider Corey, who was a reviewer and consultant for us at various stages of development of the book. We also extend our gratitude to the people who read the manuscript and provided us with valuable feedback: Mike Aldrich, Ruth Burton, Jamie Bludworth, Craig Bray, Omar De La Vega, Riley Harper, Robert Haynes, Amanda Johnson, Kim Kabar, Nicholas Lazzareschi, Jeff Markow, Naomi Tapia, and Alyssa Theis.

Special appreciation goes to Carolyn Baker, the associate publisher at the American Counseling Association. Carolyn encouraged us along the way and contributed her expertise by reviewing the entire manuscript, providing insightful comments and suggestions, and offering support and guidance throughout the evolution of this project. A special note of thanks to the manuscript editor, Kay Mikel, who made sure the presentation was clear, practical, personal, and effective. Our gratitude goes out to the 52 guest contributors for their inspiring and honest personal stories about their experiences with self-care. You can learn more about them in the Guest Contributors section.

About the Authors

Gerald Corey, EdD, ABPP, is professor emeritus of human services and counseling at California State University, Fullerton. He received his doctorate in counseling from the University of Southern California. He is a Diplomate in Counseling Psychology, American Board of Professional Psychology; a licensed psychologist in California; and a National Certified Counselor. He is a Fellow of the American Psychological Association (Division 17, Counseling Psychology; and Division 49, Group Psychotherapy); a Fellow of the American Counseling Association; and a Fellow of the Association for Specialists in Group Work. He received the Lifetime Achievement Award from the American Mental Health Counselors Association in 2011, the Eminent Career Award from the Association for Specialists in Group Work in 2001, and the Outstanding Professor of the Year Award from California State University at Fullerton in 1991. He regularly teaches both undergraduate and graduate courses in group counseling and ethics in counseling. Jerry Corey is the author or coauthor of 16 textbooks in counseling currently in print, along with more than 60 journal articles and book chapters. His book, *Theory and Practice of Counseling and Psychotherapy*, has been translated into Arabic, Indonesian, Portuguese, Turkish, Korean, and Chinese. *Theory and Practice of Group Counseling* has been translated into Korean, Chinese, Spanish, and Russian.

Issues and Ethics in the Helping Professions has been translated into Korean, Japanese, and Chinese. With his colleagues he has conducted workshops in the United States, Germany, Ireland, Belgium, Scotland, Mexico, Canada, China, and Korea—with a special focus on training in group counseling.

The following are a few recent books Jerry Corey authored or coauthored, which are published by Cengage Learning:

- *Issues and Ethics in the Helping Professions,* Tenth Edition (2019, with Marianne Schneider Corey and Cindy Corey)
- *Groups: Process and Practice,* Tenth Edition (2018, with Marianne Schneider Corey and Cindy Corey)
- *I Never Knew I Had a Choice,* Eleventh Edition (2018, with Marianne Schneider Corey and Michelle Muratori)
- *Theory and Practice of Counseling and Psychotherapy,* Tenth Edition (and *Manual*) (2017)

These four books, authored or coauthored by Jerry Corey, are published by the American Counseling Association:

- *ACA Ethical Standards Casebook,* Seventh Edition (2015, with Barbara Herlihy)
- *Boundary Issues in Counseling: Multiple Roles and Relationships,* Third Edition (2015, with Barbara Herlihy)
- *Clinical Supervision in the Helping Professions: A Practical Guide,* Second Edition (2010, with Robert Haynes, Patrice Moulton, and Michelle Muratori)
- *Creating Your Professional Path: Lessons From My Journey* (2010)

• • •

Michelle Muratori, PhD, is a senior counselor at the Center for Talented Youth at Johns Hopkins University, in Baltimore, Maryland, where she works with highly gifted middle school and high school students who participate in the Study of Exceptional Talent and their families. She earned her MA in counseling psychology from Northwestern University in Evanston, Illinois, and her PhD in counselor education from the University of Iowa, where she developed her research and clinical interests in gifted education. Her graduate research on the academic, social, and emotional adjustment of young college entrants earned her recognition from the Iowa Talented and Gifted Association, the National Association for Gifted Children, and the Mensa Education and Research Foundation and Mensa International, Ltd. At the University of Iowa, Michelle Muratori also earned the Howard R. Jones Achievement Award, the Albert Hood Promising Scholar Award, and the First in the Nation in Education (FINE) Scholar Award.

Since 2005, Michelle Muratori has been a faculty associate in the Johns Hopkins School of Education and teaches courses in the master of science in counseling program. In 2014, she was honored with the Johns Hopkins University Alumni Association Excellence in Teaching Award. She regularly presents at national conferences in counseling and gifted education and is a member of various professional organizations including the American Counseling Association. When not engaged in professional activities, she enjoys writing, attending concerts, and spending time with her family and friends.

Michelle Muratori has coauthored (with Gerald Corey and Marianne Schneider Corey) *I Never Knew I Had a Choice* (Eleventh Edition, 2018), published by Cengage Learning, and (with Gerald Corey, Robert Haynes, and Patrice Moulton) *Clinical Supervision in the Helping Professions* (Second Edition, 2010), published by the American Counseling Association. In 2007, she authored *Early Entrance to College: A Guide to Success,* published by Prufrock Press. She has contributed to a variety of other publications in the counseling and gifted education fields.

● ● ●

Jude T. Austin II, PhD, LPC-R (Va), NCC, is an assistant professor in the Counseling and Human Services Department at Old Dominion University. He earned his MA in clinical mental health counseling from the University of Mary Hardin-Baylor, and his PhD in counselor education and supervision from the University of Wyoming. His current research involves exploring counseling students' development of therapeutic presence in session, counselor education pedagogy, political values in counseling, and counselor education faculty's relational dynamics. He teaches graduate courses in professional counseling and ethics, advanced counseling skills, and counseling theories. He has presented at state, regional, and national conferences, guest lectured at various universities, and has been invited to give a keynote address at the University of Mary Hardin-Baylor's Scholar's Day Research Symposium. He also contributes to the development of various content for textbooks by Gerald and Marianne Corey, as well as online textbook content for Cengage Learning. Before becoming a counselor educator, he was a collegiate and professional soccer player.

• • •

Julius A. Austin, PhD, PLPC, is a former collegiate and professional soccer player who earned his MA in clinical mental health counseling from the University of Mary Hardin-Baylor, and his PhD in counselor education and supervision from the University of Wyoming. He is currently an assistant professor in the Marriage and Family Therapy and Counseling Studies program at the University of Louisiana at Monroe. Throughout this book, he shares his experiences in his previous role as assistant clinical director in the University Counseling Center and adjunct professor in the Department of Psychology, Counseling, and Family Studies at Nicholls State University. In his clinical role, he provides individual, couples, and group therapy to the college population and faculty and staff members on campus. He teaches graduate courses in multicultural counseling, life-span development, and basic facilitative skills. His current research involves building collaborative relationships between graduate counseling programs and collegiate athletic programs and psychophysiological aspects of the therapeutic relationship. He has presented at state, regional, and national conferences, guest lectured for various universities, and has been invited to give a keynote address at the University of Mary Hardin-Baylor's Scholar's Day Research Symposium. Julius Austin contributes to the development of content for various counseling textbooks by Gerald and Marianne Corey. He is involved in developing the online platforms for these books with Cengage Learning.

• • •

About the Guest Contributors

Our guest contributors have added immense vitality and meaning to this book, providing a diversity of thoughts, experiences, and perspectives. The contributors include graduate students in counseling (both master's and doctoral level), counselor educators, licensed professional counselors, social workers, clinical and counseling psychologists, marriage and family therapists, psychiatrists, rehabilitation counselors, and mental health practitioners. We greatly appreciate their honesty, courage, and wisdom in sharing their experiences.

Clara Adkins, BA, is a second-year graduate student at Old Dominion University. She is a research graduate assistant and is beginning a clinical internship at a mental health clinic in the community.

Mike Aldrich, BA, is working as an MFT trainee at a local community agency while completing a master's of counseling from California State University, Fullerton.

Randall Alle-Corliss, MSW, LCSW, was a clinical social worker at Kaiser Permanente for 26 years and recently retired from this position. He is presently on the part-time faculty in the Human Services Department at California State University, Fullerton, and has a private practice as a clinician.

Jasmine T. Austin, MA, is a doctoral student in the communication studies program at the University of Oklahoma. She is a graduate teaching assistant in this department and an adjunct professor in the Department of Human Relations and African and African-American Studies at the University of Oklahoma.

Kent Becker, EdD, LMFT, LPC, serves as dean of the College of Social Sciences at Saybrook University.

Fred Bemak, EdD, is a professor in the counseling and development program and director of the Diversity Research and Action Consortium at George Mason University in Fairfax, Virginia.

Dana Blake, BS, received her degree in human services from California State University, Fullerton.

Jamie Bludworth, PhD, is a licensed psychologist, director at the Counselor Training Center, and clinical assistant professor, Counseling and Counseling Psychology Department, at Arizona State University.

Leah Brew, PhD, LPCC, is professor and department chair of counseling at California State University, Fullerton.

Kellin Murphy Cavanaugh, MA, is a first-year doctoral student in counseling and counselor education at Syracuse University.

Nancy Chae, MS, formerly a professional high school counselor at a public, magnet, International Baccalaureate World school in Baltimore, Maryland, is a doctoral student in counselor education at the College of William & Mary in Williamsburg, Virginia.

Angela D. Coker, PhD, LPC, is a visiting associate professor of counseling and human development at Johns Hopkins University School of Education.

Amanda Connell, MS, graduated from California State University, Fullerton. She is a marriage and family therapist intern and professional clinical counselor intern for two community mental health agencies.

Rhea Cooper, BS, is a second-year graduate student in the counselor education program at the University of Louisiana, Lafayette.

Jessie Darkis, MA, is a first-year doctoral student in the counseling and human services program at Syracuse University.

Norma L. Day-Vines, PhD, is a professor in and program lead of the counseling and human development program at Johns Hopkins University.

Omar De La Vega, BA, is a graduate student in counseling at California State University, Fullerton.

Debbie Joffe Ellis, MDAM (Medical Doctor of Alternative Medicine), is a licensed psychologist and mental health counselor and an adjunct professor at Columbia University in the Department of Clinical and Counseling Psychology.

Matt Englar-Carlson, PhD, is a professor of counseling and the director of the Center for Boys and Men at California State University, Fullerton.

Andy Felton, PhD, LPC, is an assistant professor at the University of Wisconsin–Stout.

Sandi Fulcher, MS, MFT, is a certified practitioner of yoga and Pilates in Idyllwild, California.

Shana Gelin, MA, is a doctoral student in counseling and counselor education at Syracuse University.

Aaron Hatcher, BS, is a marriage and family therapist trainee in the counseling program at California State University, Fullerton.

Robert Haynes, PhD, is a clinical psychologist who retired after 25 years as training director of the clinical psychology internship program at Atascadero State Hospital in California.

Marja Humphrey, PhD, is a lecturer in the counseling and human development program in the School of Education at Johns Hopkins University.

Thomas Jackson, MD, is a psychiatrist who works with a variety of patients with a wide range of problems at Desert Behavioral Health in Apple Valley, California.

Amanda Johnson, BS, is a graduate student in the counseling program at California State University Fullerton.

W. Brad Johnson, PhD, is a clinical psychologist and a professor in the Department of Leadership, Ethics & Law at the U.S. Naval Academy, and a faculty associate in the Graduate School of Education at Johns Hopkins University.

Jennifer Kordek, BS, is a graduate of the human services program at California State University, Fullerton.

Nicholas Lazzareschi, BA, is a first-year master's student in counseling at California State University, Fullerton.

Crissa S. Markow, MSW, LSW, works at the Summit View Hospice, in Reno, Nevada, and at the Davidson Institute for Talent Development, Reno, Nevada.

Michael Morgan, PhD, LMFT, is an associate professor in the counselor education and supervision program at the University of Wyoming.

Adrienne Naquin-Bolton, MA, LPC-S, is the director of the University Counseling Center and University Health Services at Nicholls State University.

Ed Neukrug, EdD, is professor of counseling and human services at Old Dominion University.

Ariadne Patsiopoulos, MA, is a registered clinical counselor in Victoria, British Columbia, offering private sessions and a variety of workshops and groups to clients.

Gerald Pennie, PhD, LPC, is an instructor of psychology at South Plains College and is the chief strategy officer for Impact Communications LLC.

Aparna Ramaswamy, PhD, EdD, is a visiting assistant professor at Johns Hopkins University and is a performing artist and a clinician.

Sonia H. Ramrakhiani, PhD, is an assistant professor in the Counseling and Guidance Department at California Polytechnic State University.

Stephanie Robinson, MS, LPC, and is a doctoral student in counseling at the University of Holy Cross.

Petra Schoning, MA, is a licensed marriage and family therapist and a board-certified master personal and executive coach.

Ashley Scott, LPC, is a doctoral student in counselor education at Sam Houston State University.

Danielle N. Sirles, PhD, is a counseling psychologist in the Counseling Center at Sam Houston State University.

Justyn Smith, MA, is a doctoral student in the counselor education program at Sam Houston State University.

Mark A. Stebnicki, PhD, LPC, is professor and coordinator of the Military and Trauma Counseling Certificate, Department of Addictions and Rehabilitation, East Carolina University.

Naomi Tapia, BS, is a graduate student in the master's program in counseling at California State University, Fullerton.

Alyssa Theis, BA, is in the master's program in counseling at California State University, Fullerton.

Patricia A. Thomas, PhD, LPC-S, is an assistant professor in the counseling program at the University of Holy Cross in New Orleans.

Judy Van Der Wende, PhD, is a licensed psychologist with a private practice in Simi Valley, California.

Brandon Wildish, MS, received a master's degree in counseling at California State University, Fullerton, and is a professional musician.

Susannah M. Wood, PhD, is an associate professor in the Department of Rehabilitation and Counselor Education at The University of Iowa.

Robert E. Wubbolding, EdD, is the director of the Center for Reality Therapy in Cincinnati and professor emeritus of counseling at Xavier University.

Mark E. Young, PhD, is professor of counselor education at the University of Central Florida and is a Fellow of the American Counseling Association.

Chapter 1

Taking Care of Yourself

• • •

It's not selfish to love yourself, take care of yourself,
and to make your happiness a priority.
It's necessary.

—Mandy Hale

• • •

Whether you are a student in the helping professions or a seasoned mental health practitioner, taking care of yourself is critical to your professional success. Incorporating self-care in our lives is a prerequisite to being competent mental health practitioners. Although we are indoctrinated with this advice early in our professional training, many of us say we simply do not have time to take care of ourselves. This begs the question, "Can we afford *not* to take care of ourselves?" To successfully meet the demands of our professional work in an increasingly stressful world, it is essential that we attend to our physical, psychological, intellectual, social, and spiritual needs. Ideally, our self-care should mirror the care we provide to others. Having knowledge about self-care is important; putting what we know into action can be challenging.

Counseling professionals are compassionate people who are good at taking care of others, but we may fail to treat ourselves with the same level of care. We must remind ourselves that it is not possible to provide nourishment to others if we are not nourishing ourselves. Similar to the flight attendant's instructions to put on your oxygen mask before helping others, if we don't heed this requirement, we will run out of "oxygen" and not be able to help anyone else.

When I (Michelle) was teaching an introductory counseling course several years ago, I assigned a self-care project to underscore the importance of practicing good self-care from the very beginning of counselor training. I hoped my students would formulate individual self-care goals that they were invested in pursuing and that they would be inspired to continue after the semester ended. I believed I was teaching my first-year graduate students something valuable, but they taught me something unexpected and fascinating: this "self-care project" was more stressful for many of my students than any of their other assignments! A number of them struggled with identifying or formulating an achievable self-care goal, and the scope of their ideas varied widely. Some plans seemed too ambitious; one student aspired to challenge himself to climb a mountain during the semester. Others seemed stunningly lacking in ambition; one student wanted to exercise *one* minute a day! What I recall most about that assignment is that something intended to be enjoyable proved to be burdensome for a number of students. Based on this experience and others, including my own resistance to certain forms of self-care, I wondered, "Why is it so hard for us as helpers to take care of our 'selves' when we are so passionate about helping others to take better care of themselves?" In working on *Counselor Self-Care*, the four of us have spent much time reflecting on this question. Our hope is that you will engage in introspection regarding your own self-care successes and struggles as you read this book.

Relevant literature is cited throughout the book, but you may notice that the text is not particularly citation heavy (as you might expect in a textbook). This is by design. As noted in the Preface, rather than providing an exhaustive review of the scholarly literature and research on topics related to self-care, we take a more personal approach to support you in your own self-care journey. No one model will work for all counselors, so we showcase a collection of experiences and highlight literature that can help you develop a model and plan for self-care that works best for you. We discuss self-care for helping professionals from many different perspectives in the hope of inspiring you to improve your commitment to and practice of self-care. Each chapter is filled with firsthand accounts of the many ways counselors and counselor trainees successfully (and sometimes not so successfully) take care of themselves.

Take a few minutes right now to think about the things in your life that threaten your wellness and your effectiveness as a counselor or a graduate student. Identify what you need in this moment to feel healthy, both personally and professionally. As you read, be mindful of how the stories in each chapter influence your feelings, your thoughts, and your behaviors related to self-care.

This chapter is devoted to some key topics at the heart of counselor self-care, such as the importance of adopting a wellness perspective and its influence on maintaining therapeutic presence; wellness and self-care as buffers against empathy fatigue; and the pursuit of happiness as a foundation of self-care. This discussion provides the foundation for the chapters that follow.

First, however, we turn our attention to the fundamental principle that self-care is not a frivolous indulgence. It is, in fact, our ethical duty to take care of ourselves so that we will be well equipped to put the metaphorical oxygen mask on our clients and students who need our assistance and who are depending on us to be well for them.

Self-Care as an Ethical Mandate

Self-care is the collection of positive actions that promote wellness and effective coping. Stated broadly, "self-care includes routine positive practices and mindful attention to one's physical, emotional, relational, and spiritual selves in the context of one's personal and professional lives" (Wise & Barnett, 2016, p. 210). Self-care is not a luxury; it is an ethical mandate. If we neglect caring for ourselves on a regular basis, our professional work suffers, so self-care is a basic tenet of ethical practice (Barnett, Baker, Elman, & Schoener, 2007). If we are drained and depleted, we will not have much to give to those who need our time and our presence. Wise and Barnett (2016) emphasize that we must be willing to take steps to protect our effective functioning if we are to provide our clients with the competent services they deserve. Wise, Hersch, and Gibson (2011, 2012) describe a developmental perspective on ethics and self-care for psychologists and examine the stress–distress continuum.

Amanda Connell, a counseling intern, took to heart the advice she received in graduate school about viewing self-care as an ethical mandate. Although Amanda has multiple demands on her personal and professional life, she is finding a way to *make time* to care for herself.

A Lifelong Struggle for Self-Care

Amanda Connell

Despite my clear understanding of the importance of self-care, achieving my goals in this area remains a lifelong struggle. My life circumstances and schedule create conflict in achieving the level of self-care that I would prefer to experience. The majority of my time is spent being a caregiver for my daughter, who is severely disabled. I also work for two agencies, and I just passed the law and ethics exams for MFT and LPC licensure. My newest venture is part-time teaching of a practicum in human services class at a university, which I find challenging and greatly enjoy.

Although finding sufficient time is difficult, I have worked self-care into my life. My absolute favorite form of self-care is taking vacations. I generally take two vacations each year, and occasionally I add a third vacation when I find myself particularly in need. Long ago I figured out that my true nature is an introvert. What that means for me is that I need time alone to "recharge my batteries." A large part of my life is spent in serving others, so when I take vacations, I go alone. It is the best and most freeing feeling to have a whole week to do what I want when I want to do it. When I return from my trips, I am a more effective mother, counselor, and teacher. Without these vacations, I would be encountering burnout.

A newer self-care strategy for me is saying "no" more frequently. Also, I ask myself if the new commitments are sustainable. I have been blessed in my life with offers for many wonderful professional opportunities. It has been challenging for me to turn down these opportunities because I really want to do these things and would thoroughly enjoy them. The problem is that there are only so many hours in a day, and when I stretch myself too thin, my health and overall well-being suffer. My schedule is demanding, but it works for me because I have found and pursued my passions in life. All that I do is meaningful and fulfilling for me, and as a chronic overachiever, saying "no" takes work. I noticed that I had been making commitments in the mornings when I feel energetic. My strategy today is to delay commitment decisions (even smaller social commitments) until the evening hours when I am most tired. It is easier to say "no" when my energy is already at a low point in the day.

Another extremely helpful aspect of self-care has been engaging in my own therapy and actively working toward self-actualization. Words I live by are "just because I can do something does not mean I should do it." I have learned to be emotionally kind to myself, and I strive to live a life of congruence and self-awareness. Many of the methods I suggest to my clients are incorporated in my own life, such as replacing negative self-talk with positive affirmations, regularly engaging in meditation and relaxation exercises, giving myself gentle reminders to return to my self-care plan as needed, and being vigilant about eliminating self-judgment as it arises. Laughter, joy, appreciation, and an innate trust that life will work out are all daily ingredients of my self-care plan.

Being a caregiver often includes a fair amount of sleep deprivation and interrupted sleep. Therefore, a major aspect of my self-care is to schedule and take naps regularly, which helps tremendously. A further area of self-care I enjoy is having a wonderful support system that includes family, friends, colleagues, and mentors. The people in these groups enrich my life and soul in countless ways, and I am grateful.

Engaging in regular self-care is enormously beneficial for me personally, and it is also a vital component of my effectiveness as a counselor and an instructor. Vacations, meditation, and sleep contribute mightily to my mental acuity, ability to connect with clients in the here and now, patience, and intuitive abilities. My support system helps me to be a more balanced professional. Consulting frequently with colleagues and mentors leads to new ideas and interventions and reduces feelings of isolation that sometimes occur for therapists in private practice. Saying "no" and limiting commitments allows me to have the energy to be fully present for my clients and students. Furthermore, my personal therapy contributes to my professional effectiveness by illuminating countertransference issues and concurrently expanding my therapeutic characteristics such as empathy, self-awareness, and genuineness. Developing and maintaining a solid self-care plan brings myriad benefits. I believe it plays an integral role in every facet of being an effective helper.

• • •

Each of these contributed stories is unique, and we encourage you to take this opportunity to peek through the key hole into the self-care experiences of other professionals. Amanda's narrative exemplifies the approach our contributors have chosen in describing their experiences and the key messages they hoped to convey. We anticipate that you may experience a range of thoughts and emotions as you read about our contributors' personal experiences. If you are a counselor educator, you may feel some discomfort reading students' stories; their stories may cause you to wonder whether you ever contributed to the poor self-care of your students. If you are a clinician, you may identify with another clinician's struggles and be willing to include some of his or her self-care strategies in your life. If you are a student, clinician, or faculty member of color and have been subjected to racial microaggressions or other blatant forms of oppression, some stories may resonate with your experience and embolden you to advocate for yourself. It is unlikely that you will connect personally with every piece, but we hope you read with an open mind, an open heart, and empathy.

Wellness and Self-Care

Wellness is an individual's holistic approach to health over the life span, and *self-care* is a counselor's specific attempts to improve his or her own health to better meet the many challenges of being an effective clinician and maintaining clinical effectiveness over time. If we are not engaged in self-care practices, eventually we will not have the energy or endurance required to be present with our clients. To acquire and maintain stamina, we need to incorporate a wellness perspective in our daily living. Although rewarding, following this path is often challenging. Wellness encompasses more than the absence of illness. It is the result of a conscious commitment to care for ourselves on all human dimensions. This is not a one-time decision. Rather, it is a process of making a series of decisions that lead to zest, peace, vitality, and happiness in our whole being. According to Hales (2017):

> Wellness can be defined as purposeful, enjoyable living or, more specifically, a deliberate lifestyle choice characterized by personal responsibility and optimal enhancement of physical, mental, and spiritual health. (p. 2)

Embracing wellness involves identifying our meaningful personal goals, discovering any barriers that might get in the way of reaching our goals, creating an action plan, and then committing to implementing our plan in everyday life. Achieving wellness requires effort, and the results are often slow.

An overarching goal of the counseling profession is to assist people in achieving and maintaining a state of wellness. Achieving this goal requires taking action to prevent illness and to create a more balanced and fulfilled life. Perhaps it is no wonder that self-care and wellness are integrally related. Pat Thomas, now age 73, teaches counseling at the University of Holy Cross in New Orleans. Over her 42-year journey as a counselor and counselor educator, she has embraced the concepts of wellness and holism in her own self-care and made it a priority to encourage her students to pursue a path of self-care. Her reflections highlight the concept of life as a banquet.

Pat's Wellness Reflections

● ●

Patricia A. Thomas

Life is a banquet and most of you fools are starving to death.
—Auntie Mame

I use this quote from Auntie Mame as a motto when I talk about wellness. I ask myself and others: are we willing to "settle" for just not being hungry (physically, emotionally, and so forth), for not feeling ill, or do we want to partake in the banquet that life has to offer?

While working as a school counselor in the early 1980s, I decided to pursue my PhD, and the search for an area of interest for my dissertation was part of this process. Coming at me from several different directions (workshops, books, and journal articles) were concepts related to what is now commonly referred to as "wellness." Thus began my journey in the area of wellness. Here it is 2017, and I am still as proud and enthused to be in this profession as I ever have been. I entered the helping professions in 1975 and have served as a counselor in a large public school system for 25 years; counseled families at risk of becoming homeless; counseled students, faculty, and parents after Hurricane Katrina; and taught in counseling programs at several universities. Trying to take care of myself has been a challenge in all of these situations. I believe we need to find things that become part of our lives for the long haul and also add new experiences as times, our bodies, and energy levels change. I would like to share with you some ways I have tried to maintain my self-care over the years as well as some more recent endeavors I have undertaken.

People and music have always grounded me and helped me keep things in perspective. For more than 25 years I have built into my life's routine several activities that help me maintain my wellness. One is having weekly coffee or dinner with friends who are important in my life. Taking time to share the week's events and provide support to each other has been invaluable. I combine being with important people and my love of music by going out at least once a week to do Cajun dancing. This French tradition (called a "fais do-do") provides an opportunity to go to a venue where a live band plays dance music and a group of "regulars" (many of whom are now friends) meet to dance and share the week's activities. In addition, although I haven't done it as much recently, for years I played guitar and ukulele and sang at a local coffee house. This gave me an opportunity to express my creative side. More recently, I have been participating in weekly yoga and Pilates classes and other strength and flexibility exercises.

An important part of my professional life for the last 15 years that has greatly contributed to my wellness has been international travel. I am fortunate to be a faculty member for several international institutes, and we bring students and practicing counselors to Italy and Ireland to compare how mental health services are approached in those countries and how they compare to service delivery in the United States. Meeting new people and experiencing cultures different from the one I live in daily not only expand my worldview but challenge me to assess how I look at the different dimensions of my life.

Over my long journey as a counselor and counselor educator, I have embraced the concepts of wellness and holism in my self-care and reinforced these concepts with my students. The wellness approach reassures and reminds me that when I am struggling in some area of my life, my struggle in that area does not define me. I can shift my focus to an area of strength, remind myself of my strength, and harness it to work through my struggles. I often assign myself "homework" to help me focus on becoming more aware and grow toward greater wellness.

* * *

Pat Thomas encourages us to strive for wellness rather than settling for a condition of "not being ill." After all, if we are not taking care of ourselves and are not well, it will be difficult to be therapeutically present in our work with others. It serves us well to look for areas of strength in our lives and to do what we can to build on these positive resources. As you reflect on the state of your own wellness, what grade would you give yourself?

Questions for Reflection

1. What are some of your greatest strengths?
2. To what extent do you use your strengths to shore up areas with which you struggle?
3. How might you incorporate homework assignments in your self-care plan that would draw on your strengths as you address any perceived or actual limitations or challenges?

Therapeutic Presence and Wellness

Psychiatrist Tom Jackson sees many patients each day who are depressed and anxious. His story describes avenues he pursues to remain vital and present with patients. On his days off, he is rejuvenated by long walks in nature in the mountain community where he lives. This communion with nature provides respite and helps him remain present for 10 hours of seeing patients each workday. Tom also practices yoga daily and engages in mindfulness meditation. He is committed to a healthy, low-carbohydrate diet, which results in a general sense of wellness. Tom's commitment to maintaining his overall wellness enables him to enjoy his work and to feel a sense of satisfaction in helping others.

Therapeutic Presence in a Psychiatrist's Work

● ●

Thomas Jackson

I have been a psychiatrist for 40 years, and I still love my work. How is this possible? Burnout rates in my profession are estimated to be 27 to 57% at any given time, and suicide rates are 2 to 3 times higher than those of the general population. Here I share some reflections on how I have kept my spark.

My profession has changed a great deal since I first graduated. In my early years, in addition to prescribing medication, I was able to "do some therapy" with individuals and facilitated a variety of groups. How things have changed since I began my psychiatric career! Other than initial diagnostic evaluations, the 15-minute medication check is the rule. In fact, I typically see more than 30 patients a day, with insurance reimbursement rates largely dictating this kind of schedule. Occupational hazards include continuous exposure to individuals who are anxious, depressed, suicidal, psychotic, and personality-disordered along with the hassles of managed care and laborious electronic medical records. It is no wonder so many psychiatrists end up feeling emotionally exhausted, personally disconnected, and simply overwhelmed. Despite these challenging realities, I really enjoy my work, and I am able to claim high success rates. A fair question to ask is, "How do I do this?"

Needless to say, having a lot of experience and a deep knowledge about medication is necessary, but this alone is not sufficient to ensure success with patients. My success rate seems to suggest that "something else" is going on, which I believe has to do with "presence." It is presence that opens the door to a therapeutic relationship. If I can be fully present, give patients my undivided attention, listen closely, and then respond to their greatest concerns, we have an opportunity to connect on a deep and potentially healing level, for both of us. It creates the space in which therapeutic "magic" can happen. Even in these very short encounters, patients often leave my office feeling that they have been heard and are cared about, and feeling somewhat more hopeful about their future. When this happens, I may be inspired and strengthened for the ongoing challenges of the day ahead. But I have no illusions that I can provide even a small fraction of the psychotherapy that many of my patients need, so I am grateful for the team of therapists in my practice who are often a critical component of my patients' treatment.

Remaining present for 10 hours of seeing patients is easier said than done and bears some further discussion. To begin with, I don't work 5 days a week, which is really important for my own mental health. I travel to the city and focus all of my energy on my patients for 3 days. I then have 4 days for self-care, returning to my home in a mountain forest where nature helps to wash away the burdens of work and where the "love of my life" awaits me. I am indeed fortunate to have a great relationship with my wife who makes sure that I take regular vacations and nurtures me.

Overall physical health is an important component of the ability to maintain presence, and I do my best to stay current on the latest research regarding ways to achieve optimal health. I recognize the importance of exercise, and I am rejuvenated by my long walks in nature. Daily yoga helps me to alleviate the normal aches and pains of aging, which, if ignored, can become a major distraction. A healthy, low-carbohydrate diet provides me with ample energy and a general sense of wellness. Mindfulness meditation helps to provide a sense of peacefulness, and sometimes between patients I'll take as little as 30 seconds to simply focus on my breath to clear my mind and feel more balanced.

My final key to remaining present with my patients is a sense of purpose in both my personal life and my work. Although I do not hold any specific religious beliefs, I consider myself to be a spiritual person. Despite lack of scientific proof of a higher power, it is something I choose to believe in because it feels good and gives me a sense of purpose. Every day, before I begin seeing patients, I set my mental tone for the day with a prayer that, with small variations, goes something like this:

> May I be guided in the decisions I make and the words I speak. May I provide the right medication in each case, and may I help each patient find the most harmonious pathway for his or her personal growth and happiness. And may I be filled and inspired by Divine love, and may it flow through me and touch the hearts of those that I serve.

• • •

Although Tom Jackson does not adhere to a religion, he certainly implements his spiritual beliefs by putting them into action in his work with patients. Taking care of himself is the key that enables him to be therapeutically present for his patients. He wants to do far more than simply prescribe medication and strives to form a working alliance with his patients, even though he has limited time with each of them. He believes that therapeutic presence is vital in helping patients stabilize and improve.

In my (Jude's) own research, I study therapeutic presence. I address how to define therapeutic presence for students and early professionals, ways to identify therapeutic presence when supervising counselors-in-training, and ways counselor educators can help their students develop therapeutic presence (Austin, 2016). In *A Practical Guide for Cultivating Therapeutic Presence,* Shari Geller's (2017) ideas align with the notion that the magic of therapy happens when the counselor is therapeutically present. This requires tuning in to clients physically, emotionally, cognitively, and spiritually. Through my own scholarly pursuits, I have discovered that therapeutic presence can be cultivated and expressed through intentional actions by the therapist. It is a developmental process that begins when students enter a counseling program and unfolds as they evolve in their careers. My research findings align with my own anecdotal observations as a counselor educator. Learning to be therapeutically present in session, as opposed to focusing too heavily on the technical aspects of counseling, can be a less anxiety-provoking way to learn how to be with clients early in a counselor's development. Managing this stress during early encounters with clients may improve the self-efficacy and self-care of counselors-in-training. To read more about being therapeutically present with your clients, we recommend *Therapeutic Presence: A Mindful Approach to Effective Therapy* (Geller & Greenberg, 2012) in addition to Geller's 2017 book.

Caring for Self and Others

Some believe that self-love and self-care are signs of selfishness. For us, it is not a matter of self-care *versus* caring for others. We can be invested in both. We may feel invested in promoting a good life for others and be instrumental in improving conditions in our communities. But to be genuinely involved in social action and bettering society, we need to begin with ourselves. If we engage in self-care, we stand a better chance of demonstrating concern for others and for taking better care of our clients (Barnett, 2017). Our degree of wellness is a critical variable in being able to care for others. Taking time to reflect on the quality of our lives is a good beginning for making changes in our behavior that will lead to increased wellness.

Skovholt and Trotter-Mathison (2016) address the concept of *empathy balance*, which involves being able to enter the client's world without getting lost in that world. If we demonstrate too little empathy, clients may experience an absence of caring, yet too much empathy can result in practitioners getting lost in the stories of their clients. Balancing caring for others with caring for self is an important goal (we return to this topic in Chapter 7).

Improving Your Self-Care Practices

Marja Humphrey teaches in the counseling and human development program at Johns Hopkins University, and she offers some essential ideas for counselors striving to achieve wellness and improve self-care practices. She reminds us how important it is to put ourselves on our schedule and to make sure we protect this time by establishing clear boundaries. She offers five suggestions to counselors who want to improve their self-care practices. Which of these particularly appeals to you?

Principles for Counselor Self-Care

Marja Humphrey

As a counselor educator, one question I am asked each semester, regardless of the course or current topic of discussion, is how I manage self-care. Many people who serve others struggle with self-care. We teach it but do not always implement our own suggestions. Yet we know neglecting self-care is an ethical issue because it directly affects our work with our students and clients. Here I offer five practical suggestions from my own lived experience for counselors seeking to engage in better self-care.

1. *Establish healthy boundaries.* Self-love often begins with having and maintaining healthy boundaries. Many self-improvement, business, or life coaching gurus would say you have to know your WHY. Why do I say "yes" when I say "yes"? Why do I say "no" when I say "no"? Saying "yes" to one thing means we are, sometimes by default, saying "no" to something else. A "no" to one thing allows us to say "yes" to something else. Decide on the criteria you will use to make decisions, and do not waver from it. You will be glad you did. Healthy boundaries show we honor our priorities, respect ourselves, value our own and others' time, and appreciate the opportunity to fully engage with others.

2. *Make an appointment with yourself.* Those who care for others often feel selfish when they do something that serves only them, but this is necessary. I have not always been the best at self-care, particularly when juggling multiple roles. As a professional woman, wife, mother, and daughter, it is easy to say time does not exist for self-care. Success has come to me when I schedule time for myself just like every other appointment. Practically, what does this look like? I unplug at least once every month for a few hours. It is on our family Google calendar. My cell phone is off (or on vibrate tucked away in a spa locker). This time doesn't always occur at the spa. It might be at home, simply getting up early in the morning for quiet time with a cup of coffee or tea. Reading and praying, writing in my journal, or being kind to my body with yoga are all practices that help me recharge and ready myself for the day. Build a self-care routine that sparks joy in you. Schedule and protect this time for yourself. You will be more fruitful in every area of your life as a result of it.

3. *Lay down your burdens.* Self-care as a professional also means learning how to healthily distance yourself from your work. Years ago, a few months after earning my master's degree, I worked at a psychiatric facility. Each day I listened to clients who were suicidal or homicidal, and after about eight months I couldn't take the sadness anymore. The hopelessness was too much to bear. I left work a little early, went home, and just cried. I had failed to realize how listening to these stories every day for months had transformed each story into a burden I was carrying. That night I took some time to process my emotions. The next morning I got up and went to work, having released all that I had taken on. You will find your own way to maintain this balance, but it is the process of doing it that is important. Self-care requires that we allow ourselves to feel all of our feelings and process the meaning behind those feelings without judgment. Instead of pushing those feelings away and simply moving on to whatever was next, self-care demanded that I pause and feel the impact of the work I was doing. It also meant I had to purge myself of the heaviness I felt so I could continue to work effectively.

4. *Reenergize.* Self-care prevents burnout. To reenergize, take time to remember why you chose and have continued in this profession. Reflect on your most challenging moments, your greatest victories,

and what you have learned along the way. I hope this will bring you back to the big picture so you don't remain bogged down in the everyday details of hard work. Yet reality is that life happens, and that's when our self-care breaks down. If you feel stuck in the routines of life, reenergize yourself by doing something different, something new, taking a risk, or going all in.

5. *Get feedback.* Self-care means I invite others into my process of achieving my best. I care for myself professionally by asking colleagues to provide honest feedback about my performance. When something isn't working well in my classroom or I feel stuck with a client, I consult with a colleague for suggestions and strategies to improve my work. We can receive feedback directly though consultation and supervision. Continuing education and involvement in professional organizations provide an indirect means of feedback. Feedback is necessary for growth.

My hope is that I have shared personal, practical, and professional suggestions that will have a positive impact on you in your self-care journey. Be kind to yourself.

• • •

We can all profit from scheduling time for ourselves, just like every other appointment. This very practical suggestion can reenergize us and prevent burnout. If you keep a planner or a calendar, block out some time for yourself over the next few weeks. Taking into account your lifestyle and realistic constraints (work, family obligations, school), set aside shorter or longer blocks of time each week for yourself. Whether you can comfortably commit to 30 minutes, 2 hours, or a full day, reflect on how you might like to spend this time. Even if you don't commit to a particular activity but prefer to use this time in a spontaneous fashion, give yourself permission to keep your appointment with yourself.

Empathy Fatigue and Counselor Impairment

In *Empathy Fatigue,* Mark Stebnicki (2008) writes about the stress generated by listening to the multiple stories of trauma that clients bring to therapy. These stories are saturated with themes of grief, loss, anxiety, depression, and traumatic stress. When these stories mirror counselors' personal struggles too closely, *empathy fatigue* may result, which shares some similarities with other fatigue syndromes such as compassion fatigue, secondary traumatic stress, vicarious traumatization, and burnout. Stebnicki believes that being mindful of our empathy fatigue buttons is critical for maintaining our physical, emotional, and spiritual well-being.

As counseling professionals, if we do not take steps to remedy burnout or make changes in how we deal with stress, the eventual result is likely to be impairment.

Impairment is the presence of a chronic illness or severe psychological depletion that can prevent a professional from being able to deliver effective services. Impaired counselors are unable to effectively cope with stressful events and are unable to adequately carry out their professional duties. Impaired therapists are dysfunctional to the point of actually hurting others, as well as themselves. Their impairment usually affects every aspect of their personal and professional life (Kottler, 2017). Recognizing that you are on a path toward impairment demands a high level of honesty. It is critical that you learn to monitor subtle indications and then be willing to take action to remedy a situation that will inevitably result in burnout. Counselors whose inner conflicts are consistently activated by listening to stories of their clients may respond by numbing themselves and distancing themselves, which clients may interpret as a personal rejection.

Mark Stebnicki, a professor in the Department of Addictions and Rehabilitation at East Carolina University, has examined the path to empathy fatigue in great detail. Here he points out how counselors are at risk for being affected by the same chronic, persistent, or transient physical, emotional, and psychological symptoms as their clients if they do not monitor how they are being affected by their work.

Managing Our Empathy Fatigue

Mark A. Stebnicki

In traditional Native American philosophy, it is believed that each time you heal someone you give away a piece of yourself. The journey to become a medicine man or woman requires an understanding that the healer at some point in time may become a wounded healer. This experience occurs naturally when you enter into your client's sacred space. I refer to this phenomenon as "empathy fatigue." It results from a state of psychological, emotional, mental, physical, spiritual, and occupational exhaustion that occurs as counselors' own wounds are continually revisited by their clients' life stories of chronic illness, disability, trauma, grief, and loss (Stebnicki, 2008, 2016). It is of paramount importance that professional counselors recognize this negative shift within themselves and that counselor educators and clinical supervisors who train them recognize this negative shift within the professional counselor's mind, body, and spirit.

I first coined the term *empathy fatigue* and wrote many published works after I served on the crisis response team during the Westside Middle

School shootings in Jonesboro, Arkansas. On March 24, 1998, an 11- and a 13-year-old shooter took the lives of four students, one teacher, and injured more than 15 others. The identity of the student(s) who pulled the school's fire alarm is still unknown, but the alarm sent hundreds of middle schoolers outside onto the playground where the two shooters opened fire from the woods. This was an inconceivable and heinous act of mass murder and permanent disability. In situations such as this, counselors who provide solace to students often experience empathy fatigue.

Many counselors spend a tremendous amount of time and energy serving in compassionate and empathic ways, searching for the meaning of their clients' mind, body, and spirit that has been lost to trauma, addictions, chronic life-threatening illnesses, disability, or other major life stressors. As a consequence, professional counselors are at risk for being affected by the same chronic, persistent, or transient physical, emotional, and psychological symptoms their clients experience.

Being mindful of our empathy fatigue buttons is critical for maintaining our emotional, physical, and spiritual well-being. This is critical for counselors today because I believe we are in the midst of a paradigm shift in the counseling and psychology professions. In the United States, this shift may have begun with the horrific terrorist attacks on September 11, 2001. Increasingly, counseling services are being provided to individuals and groups exposed to human-made and natural disasters: service members and veterans exposed to combat operations, civil unrest in the United States, civilian trauma acquired by refugees, immigrants, and asylum seekers from war-torn countries, and others who have sustained catastrophic life-threatening illnesses and disabilities. Indeed, the 21st century has become the era of disaster preparedness, disaster mental health response, and treating complex traumas in the aftermath of extraordinarily stressful and traumatic events (Stebnicki, 2016, 2017).

As we prepare for the next disaster, we soon forget the cataclysmic event that took place on December 26, 2004, when a tsunami and earthquake registering 9.0 off the west coast of northern Sumatra injured or killed hundreds of thousands of people. To date, thousands are presumed dead because they have not been found in countries that were affected by the tsunami such as Sri Lanka, India, Indonesia, Malaysia, and Thailand. The desolation left in the aftermath of these and other critical events creates a sort of historical trauma among world cultures and demands our attention.

Maintaining personal and professional wellness and managing empathy fatigue in one's career goes beyond acquiring continuing education credits at conferences and workshops. Some counselors will require a transformative personal experience to continue in their chosen profession. Multiple authors, practitioners, and professional counseling associations recognize that counselor impairment and fatigue syndromes are serious hazards and thus are issues of critical importance to all of us.

Taking personal responsibility for managing your empathy fatigue is key to cultivating resilience within the counseling profession. I have personally challenged myself with various personal growth experiences such as becoming a Reiki master and taking beginning- and intermediate-level shaman training, which has been a gratifying cultural immersion activity for me. I also take advantage of outdoor activities in the mountains and beaches in my state. I value close relationships with friends, colleagues, and family members. I have played acoustic guitar most of my life, and this has become a creative outlet for me. I continue to learn that maintaining awareness of our empathy fatigue buttons contributes to cultivating optimal levels of self-care.

• • •

Unquestionably, identifying what triggers our empathy fatigue is a key step in managing this condition. It can be extremely useful for us to find some kind of creative outlet that will reenergize us and enhance our wellness. Whether or not you consider yourself to be a creative person, finding a meaningful outlet to express yourself and to attend to your personal needs is of the utmost importance. Those who fail to do so may have an experience similar to that of doctoral student Sonia Ramrakhiani, who had difficulty separating herself from the problem-saturated stories told by her clients in the office. Working such a demanding job and doing such intensive clinical work without adequately attending to her personal needs took a significant toll on her well-being and affected her ability to be effective in her professional role. Recognizing how her work was affecting her life was a first step in overcoming her empathy fatigue.

Overcoming Empathy Fatigue

Sonia H. Ramrakhiani

I experienced empathy fatigue while working in a residential setting with adolescent girls engaging in self-injurious behaviors. Most of my clients struggled with borderline personality disorder or bipolar disorder. Each of my clients told a unique story of trauma, abuse, and neglect. Initially, I was able to sit empathetically with my clients as they shared their stories. Over time, sitting with these stories became harder, and I began to struggle with leaving these stories at work.

I noticed the signs of empathy fatigue when working with a 15-year-old client who struggled with abandonment and self-injurious behaviors. Our work in session was tumultuous; I felt pushed and pulled constantly. There were moment-to-moment shifts in session in which she adored me and then cursed me. At the end of our sessions, I felt as if I had gone through a spin cycle. My feelings and experiences while working with this client also influenced my work with other clients in this residential setting. I went through bouts of frustration and confusion. The frustration of feeling as though we took one step forward together only to take two steps back wore me down. Also, as a clinician who was accustomed to the clients' emotional shifts, struggling with this client and then every client confused me.

When it came to this particular client, I found myself completely lacking empathy. I felt like a robot, moving mechanically from one session to the next, without time to sit with any real emotions. I began to notice the same lack of empathy and mechanistic responses with all of my clients. I skipped lunch almost on a daily basis and worked on the weekends. I avoided spending time with my friends and family. The ultimate wake-up call was getting into a car accident when trying to make it on time for a group therapy session. Immediately after the accident I thought, "Who will run my group? Who will see my clients today?" Recognizing how at that moment I placed more value on my clients' safety and well-being than my own shocked me into awareness of my fatigue.

I decided I needed to work toward finding a healthy balance between my work life and my personal life. I began with acceptance; I stopped pretending that I was "fine" and accepted the toll my clinical work had taken on me. I also accepted my own limitations. Once I was able to accept what I was going through, I was able to seek help. I sought out a counselor and started processing some of my personal and professional struggles. I examined my interpersonal relationships and recognized the parallels between my personal and professional relationships. I began working toward fostering strong and emotionally supportive relationships outside of work. I noticed an immediate difference in my therapeutic relationships.

Overcoming empathy fatigue was one of the most difficult experiences I have faced in my career. I was able to take care of myself by accepting my thoughts, feelings, and actions as harmful to my health as a counselor. I then humbled myself and asked for help. Working on myself in therapy encouraged me to make changes that enriched both professional and personal parts of my life. Without taking these steps to care for myself, I believe I would have burned out and would not be an effective professional.

* * *

Questions for Reflection

1. If you had a full schedule of clients to see, what could you do to be present with each client? What can you do in between clients or during your time off to rejuvenate yourself so you can be more present in your work?

2. Have you ever experienced a fatigue syndrome such as empathy fatigue or compassion fatigue? If so, what was that experience like for you? How did you address your condition?
3. Working in intense environments and serving seriously troubled clients or engaging in disaster mental health work can indeed be stressful. If you work in such settings, what protective measures can you take to ensure that you avoid burnout and empathy fatigue?

Happiness: A Foundation of Self-Care

Empathy fatigue is not a terminal disease! Recognizing how we have lost a sense of ourselves can serve as a wake-up call toward making some basic changes in the way we are living. Reflecting on what we can do each day to increase our level of personal happiness is key to managing empathy fatigue and achieving wellness. One antidote to living a stressful life is to strive for happiness each day and to show gratitude for what we do have. Happiness is not measured by collecting material wealth but by living with purpose. Happiness is the product of a series of choices we make every day rather than a state we choose once and for all. If we are to spread joy, happiness, and peace to others, we need to find inner joy and inner peace. If we are to help others live a happier existence, we must first be alive and vital ourselves. If we are to instill hope in others, we must have hope and optimism in our own lives. If we are chronically unhappy, we cannot instill happiness in the lives of those we counsel. If we give and give, but are not open to asking for help ourselves and are not willing to receive what others want to give us, it is unlikely that we will retain our spark of vitality and creativity.

According to Killen and Macaskill (2015), subjective well-being, which is often equated with happiness, consists of having frequent positive emotions, infrequent negative emotions, and the presence of life satisfaction. They note that *gratitude* has been reported to "be the most beneficial character strength, and is consistently and robustly associated with life satisfaction and wellbeing" (p. 949). Gratitude can be used to counteract stress and may contribute to the development of personal resources such as being resilient; it is important to acknowledge the power of gratitude as a self-care strategy. One way to enhance our well-being, for instance, may be to maintain a gratitude journal in which we enumerate the blessings we enjoy in our lives and describe why we are grateful for even the simplest of things. Gratitude can help to reframe negative memories and decrease their adverse impact (Watkins, Grimm, & Kolts, 2004). Experiencing positive emotions such as gratitude is believed by some to increase the flexibility of coping strategies and to build social bonds during periods that are less stressful, which bolster our coping resources (Killen & Macaskill, 2015). Whether we keep track of what we are grateful for in a journal, write gratitude letters to those we appreciate, or find other ways to express our gratitude to others, we are attending to our own well-being and enhancing the quality of our lives.

Reflecting on gratitude can be a route to loving ourselves, which is a key ingredient to being able to care for and to love others. If we develop patterns of being kind to ourselves, we increase the chances of being kind to others. Schueller and Parks (2014) suggest that a key to experiencing happiness is to be kind to others. They add that "increasing the amount of social contact a person has and improving the quality of one's interpersonal relationships are both strong pathways to promoting happiness" (p. 149). Passmore and Oades (2015) claim that psychological research overwhelmingly supports random acts of kindness as being beneficial to the individual giver both mentally and physically. Kindness is a virtue that is foundational to wellness.

Upon reaching age 107, Joe Binder revealed the secret to his happy life and his longevity on the *CBS Evening News* (April 19, 2017). He tells us to be kind to people and not to hold a grudge, but to forgive those who injure us. In addition to practicing kindness and forgiveness, he exercises almost daily, and fun is part of his life. He dances with his girlfriend, Annette, who is half his age, and he still finds happiness in playing his musical instruments.

Kottler (2014) states that happiness is as much a state of mind as it is a result of life circumstances. Having a positive, optimistic attitude predisposes us to a range of benefits that accumulating possessions, striving for great wealth, and seeking status do not provide. We agree with Kottler's notion that "once you have enough to live on comfortably, having more things or making more money does not significantly improve anything—except the levels of stress associated with holding onto what you've amassed" (p. 41). If you want to live a happy life, Kottler suggests that you do the following:

- Focus on positive aspects of life.
- Maintain an optimistic perspective.
- Live in the present.
- Spend quality time with those you love.
- Forgive those who hurt you.
- Figure out what you love, and then do this as often as possible.

We do not achieve happiness without effort; it is the result of our choices and the actions we take. The Dalai Lama, the spiritual leader of the Tibetan people, has said that the purpose of life is to be happy, which is achieved by our intentions and actions. Petra Schoning, a licensed marriage and family therapist and board-certified master personal and executive coach, writes about happiness and the joy of being alive. She affirms the notion that personal levels of happiness can be improved (see Chapters 5 and 8 for more on happiness).

Happiness: The Joy of Being Alive

Petra Schoning

I always ask my clients in the beginning of our work together what they are hoping to achieve. The most frequent response I receive is, "I want to be happier." And even when the stated goal has been more specific, in the end, what my clients most often seem to be hoping for is an increase in personal fulfillment and overall levels of happiness. Research in positive psychology shows that personal levels of happiness can be improved.

I take my role as a therapist and coach very seriously and do my best to "walk my talk" in terms of my personal growth and self-care. Hearing clients repeatedly express this goal of greater happiness, I realized I needed to take a closer look at my own happiness level and what I am doing to increase it. People often think happiness "just happens" and that it will happen in the future when they have achieved certain goals or reached certain milestones in their life. However, this simply isn't true. So what are the determining factors? Although individual biology and life circumstances make up the largest part of our happiness level, a significant portion of our happiness can shift up or down based on what we do and what we think (Lyubomirsky, 2013). When I first started working on improving my happiness, I was a bit dismayed to find that I was only at about the 70th percentile on standardized happiness test measures. I expected a much higher score considering how long I had been a therapist/coach and all the growth work I had already done. Much to my surprise I discovered that I had a lot to learn about achieving greater happiness, and I made a decision to embark on my own "happiness project." My journey to ever-increasing happiness had begun!

Today, I am proud to say I am at the 93rd percentile in measured happiness! Over the years I have set many happiness goals, a few of which include eating well, managing my time with discretion, exercising regularly, scheduling time for fun, getting out into nature as often as I can, and practicing excellent sleep habits. Although my happiness goals have required endurance and a lot of hard work, my increase in happiness could hardly be more gratifying. Attaining happiness is currently something I engage in on a daily basis (with specific goals, score sheets, ongoing education on the topic, and daily reminders). And now, even on my worst days when I may be grappling with concerns such as health, relationships, or finances, I am still relatively happy.

When challenging personal concerns arise that demand my full attention, I am unlikely to experience joy. Although I struggle at times, I am able to maintain the perspective that I am thrilled simply to be alive. I can not only handle whatever challenge I am dealing with but also use these challenges as an opportunity for growth and greater happiness in the long run.

In my worldview, happiness is of prime importance in my self-care practice. I think each of us has the right to find greater joy in life and to avoid people or situations that consistently interfere with attaining it. On a fundamental level, I am convinced that achieving greater happiness requires taking on the responsibility of consciously making the choices that are right for me. Some happiness goals I engage in that require ongoing conscious decisions include greatly limiting my exposure to news, honoring my nature as an introvert and not committing to do things that are "not me," and having the courage to confront issues in my relationship with my husband when necessary.

I have found that when I decide to invest time and effort into increasing my happiness, not only do I benefit, but others with whom I have contact benefit too. I am convinced that happiness is infectious, and everyone around me, whether it be my clients, friends, or loved ones, share in the bounty. When I am kinder and more patient with people in my life, I tend to be kinder and more patient with myself. I use my time more wisely, and I find more time to do what I love, which for me includes hiking, camping, doing something new at least once a month, and participating in my Toastmasters Club. My ongoing "happiness project" is an investment I never regret!

* * *

Be Kind to Yourself

Now is a good time to assess how kind you are to yourself and what you can do to increase your kindness and patience with yourself. Take time to reflect on basic ideas that can enhance your well-being and happiness. Treat yourself with kindness and compassion, and reflect on the choices you can make to keep stress and disenchantment at bay. This can be accomplished by engaging in simple acts of kindness and doing your best to bring moments of happiness to others—not only to clients but also to people you encounter in the course of a day. Kindness and self-compassion are addressed in detail in Chapter 7.

Questions for Reflection

1. Random acts of kindness are believed to be beneficial to the individual giver both mentally and physically. Reflect on your acts of kindness and the impact they have had on you.
2. How would you assess your own personal happiness? What factors contribute to or detract from your happiness? If you are not satisfied with your current level of happiness, what can you do to increase it?
3. What is your reaction to the idea that happiness requires effort and that it is the result of our choices and actions?

Concluding Thoughts

By introducing the topic of self-care and encouraging you to create and implement a self-care plan, we hope that you will feel empowered to make positive changes in your life that will enhance your wellness and increase your happiness. As you reflect on the themes we highlight, remember that wellness entails more than the absence of illness. A philosophy of life based on a wellness perspective involves identifying your personal goals and creating a plan to attain them. Achieving wellness requires consistent work on your part, yet this can be a most rewarding path. As emphasized in this chapter, self-care is an ethical obligation for us in the counseling profession because it protects us from burnout, empathy fatigue, impairment, and other conditions that can detract from our effectiveness as helpers. Although it may be difficult to find the time for self-care, especially during busy times, you may discover that you need to make the time for self-care to be able to live and work effectively.

Chapter 2

Seasons of a Career

Self-care involves unique challenges at each developmental stage in a career. How you meet these tasks during graduate school has implications for how well you will be able to address them throughout your career. Wise and Barnett (2016) offer specific recommendations for positive self-care patterns during the various stages of professional development: graduate school, early career, mid-career, and late career. All four of us are in different career stages, and we describe the challenges we face in our present stage and how we do our best to thrive personally and professionally. Other individuals also willingly share the challenges of their particular season of career development in this chapter.

Graduate School

Self-care is an issue most graduate students in counseling and related helping professions hear about frequently throughout their training, and with good reason—it is absolutely essential. In fact, these basic lessons in self-care are analogous to a parent's sound advice to a child to "eat your vegetables" or "look in both directions before crossing the street." Just as parents hope to instill in their children healthy habits and give them the tools to succeed as adults, counselor educators are ethically obligated to impart to their trainees the critical importance of self-care in sustaining their effectiveness and vitality as helpers. If graduate training is akin to childhood, then your career trajectory can be imagined as a developmental process in which you build on the foundation formed in graduate school to develop into an autonomous, competent, and ethical professional. Of course, once launched into the professional world of counseling, our professors and supervisors (our professional "parents") are no longer nearby to remind us of the importance of self-care. We must now do that on our own; and just as many of us sometimes neglect to "eat our vegetables," we sometimes fall short of maintaining good self-care practices in the various seasons of our career as helpers.

If you are in graduate school, we hope your program emphasizes the value of self-care and facilitates your development of an action plan that will enhance what you are learning, both personally and professionally. As a graduate student, you can take an active role in reflecting on how you can incorporate self-care principles and practices in your life, even if your program does not provide this encouragement. Adopting a proactive and preventive approach to self-care will help you retain the stamina to meet the demands of your graduate studies. In their study of self-care practices and stress levels among psychology graduate students, Myers, Sweeney, Popick, Wesley, Bordfeld, and Fingerhut (2012) report that students experience stress due to the multiple demands of graduate programs, including coursework, clinical training, research, and financial considerations. Stress is associated with institutional demands, competition, performance anxiety, and lack of experience. Graduate students are expected to navigate these stressors and their new roles, and at the same time develop the knowledge and skills required to provide effective clinical services. Student anxiety during graduate school and early career days is common across all countries and cultures (Orlinsky & Ronnestad, 2005). Myers and colleagues (2012) believe that an important first step in improving self-care is for graduate students to engage in discussions related to coping with stress and anxiety. Their study supports including "self-care as a training competency to decrease the negative impact of stress on both academic and clinical training" (p. 63).

Our students often tell us that they are "stressed out" and that the demands of their classes are overwhelming and anxiety producing as the semester progresses. Statements such as the following are not uncommon:

- "I am worried about my performance as a graduate student. I feel the burden of having to get straight A's and to prove that I have strong clinical skills. That alone makes me anxious. Plus, I have to work a full-time job to pay the bills. I don't have time to do anything for fun anymore. I can't wait for graduate school to be finished so I have my life back!"

- "It drives me crazy not knowing if I will secure an internship for next semester. I keep sending out my CV to different agencies, but never seem to hear back from them. I know that there are limited spots available and that I am competing with students not only in my program but from other graduate programs in the area as well. Sometimes I wonder if I chose the right path. I want to help others, but I never thought it would be this difficult to get an internship and to complete my training!"

- "I often feel conflicted when my friends call me to go out with them on the weekend. I just don't have the time to hang out with them because I have papers to write, presentations to prepare for, and a lot of reading to catch up on. Most of them are not in graduate school and cannot relate to the pressure I feel, which makes me feel lonely, like we are drifting apart and have little in common. Oddly enough, I end up feeling sorry for myself and spending my weekend nights just binge-watching TV, so I probably could have gone out with my friends if I were more efficient with my time."

- "I started graduate school after my son and daughter were both in elementary school. I was excited to finally have some "me time" and to pursue my dream of becoming a counselor. But while I love being back in school, I sometimes feel out of place being a bit older than the younger graduate students. Also, I feel overwhelmed with the amount of work that's involved in juggling all of my roles. When one of my kids gets sick or needs extra attention with homework, my school work is relegated to the back burner. My kids come first, obviously, but it still stresses me out when I am stretched so thin that I cannot submit my best work."

- "What stresses me out more than anything is the thought that my countertransference might get triggered by clients when I start my practicum. I have been learning about countertransference in my classes, and I recognize that I have unfinished business that could easily surface if clients present with certain behaviors that remind me of my dysfunctional parents. I would feel terrible if I caused my clients any harm because of my countertransference reactions. I have thought about starting my own counseling to get a handle on these issues."

- "I grew up in poverty and am the first person in my family to attend graduate school. I feel indebted to my mother for helping me to believe in myself and, specifically, believe that I can make a difference in this world. After the 2016 presidential election, I am all the more determined to be a force for good and fairness in this world. My diversity and social justice class in grad school has only strengthened my resolve to be a social justice advocate for my clients. My current struggle is feeling overwhelmed at times by the amount of work that needs to be done to fight injustice. There are only 24 hours in the day, yet no matter how many hours I invest in my work, I feel like I am only making a dent. When I am not working, I find it hard to relax because I feel guilty about all of the work that I could be doing."

If you can relate to any of these stories or feel stressed out for other reasons, we think it is especially crucial that you not put caring for yourself on the back burner. If you do, you are likely to experience burnout as a student.

Michelle Muratori's Graduate School Experiences: Taming My Inner Critic

I (Michelle) recall the period of time between my master's and doctoral program when I was working in the field as an in-home family therapist for a social service agency and teaching psychology courses at a local community college. At the time, I was in a serious relationship and felt pulled in many directions all at once. Like many women who have to balance multiple roles, I felt pressure to perform each of these roles "perfectly"; however, there was a price to pay. My exhaustion caught up with me just as I received the news that I had been accepted into a doctoral program in counseling and human development (now counselor education) at the University of Iowa. I was faced with a unique challenge: I felt blessed to be given a wonderful educational opportunity that I had been hoping for, yet I was well aware of the demands that would be placed on me at a time in my life when I felt like I needed a break. If I were to take on this new challenge, I knew I had to find a way to replenish myself *while* I was working on my PhD, not wait until afterward. I simply could not postpone self-care for 4 or 5 years while I worked tirelessly on my doctoral degree. At the same time, I didn't want to postpone working toward my doctorate. I had to devise a strategy for moving forward with my educational goals while managing other aspects of my life, and achieving (or at least *striving for*) balance.

How did I approach this challenge? Having battled perfectionism my entire life, I was cognizant that I needed to place some boundaries on my perfectionism so I would not be derailed by it. I made a concerted effort to give myself permission to make mistakes or, perhaps more important, to not be so harsh on myself when I did inevitably fall short of my standards. For instance, I once completely forgot about an important meeting. Rather than hiding my head in shame, I decided to apologize to the facilitators of the meeting, but not punish myself by endlessly ruminating on my error (and believe me when I say that I am a very talented ruminator!). Although my doctoral work was extremely time consuming, I *made* time to connect with others and to develop friendships with my new peers, which gave me energy. Admittedly, there were some rather intense periods during my PhD program when achieving "balance" seemed like an impossible goal, but overall I am pleased that I was able to keep my perfectionism under control, which made my life much more bearable and prevented me from feeling immobilized at school. I had to challenge my own rigid thinking, which helped me to make the shift from a maladaptive perfectionist to an adaptive perfectionist! Over time, I reclaimed my energy and excitement for learning, and I am relieved that I was able to avoid succumbing to burnout.

Perfectionism: A Blessing or a Curse?

If you identify with Michelle's story and are a perfectionist or have perfectionist tendencies, you may need to reflect on ways to manage your internal critic so it doesn't disrupt your life and prevent you from reaching your personal and professional goals. Students and practitioners often worry about underperformance and strive to perform at the 100% level all of the time. Expecting and demanding 100% performance leads to long-term occupational exhaustion and caring burnout, as well as to a loss in creativity (Skovholt & Trotter-Mathison, 2016). Perfectionism is associated with behaviors such as striving for flawlessness, setting excessive performance standards, making painfully critical self-evaluations, and experiencing anxiety over failure (Johnson & Smith, 2016). Although perfectionist self-demands can drive behavior, such demands also may sabotage our success. Moate, Gnilka, West, and Bruns (2016) found that perfectionism is associated with stress and burnout among counselor educators. Graduate students who are aspiring to careers as counselors or counselor educators should be aware that perfectionism is not something that simply diminishes after graduate school ends. As helping professionals, we have the task of assessing how perfectionist strivings can have both positive and negative effects on our professional work in all the seasons of our careers. Moate and colleagues differentiate between adaptive and maladaptive perfectionism. *Adaptive perfectionists* hold high standards for themselves, yet they tend not to be overly self-critical when they fall short of achieving these high standards. *Maladaptive perfectionists* also hold high personal standards, yet they experience intense levels of self-criticalness when they do not meet their standards. In their study, Moate and colleagues found that "counselor educators with maladaptive perfectionism may experience high levels of stress and burnout in their demanding careers, which can result in difficulty in maintaining a sense of wellness" (p. 169).

Perfectionist strivings can persist throughout our educational and professional careers and start long before we ever set foot in graduate school. It is probably unrealistic to try to rid ourselves of our perfectionist tendencies, but it is realistic to assume that we can control our perfectionism rather than having it control us. Instead of being immobilized by maladaptive perfectionism and a barrage of self-criticism, we can strive to do our best to accomplish our goals and, at the same time, accept less than perfect performances. As you read the personal accounts throughout this book, reflect on lessons you can apply to yourself to help you realistically assess and manage internal perfectionist strivings. The key is to appreciate and enjoy your work, which is difficult to do if you are excessively self-critical.

Jerry Corey's Graduate School Experiences

I (Jerry) began my doctoral program in counseling in the early 1960s, at the same time as I began my career as a high school teacher. Although I enjoyed the counseling courses in my doctoral program, I loathed statistics and feared I would not be able to pass the required courses. My adviser and primary professor was instrumental in putting my fears in perspective. Whenever I felt like dropping out of the program because of my math anxiety, she assured me that my goals were attainable if I was willing to work hard and persist. It is easy to feel engulfed by fear and to stop too soon; it's important to remember that fears can be turned into challenges that can be stepping stones to success. I learned that by acknowledging my fears they became manageable, that asking for help is critical, and that self-discipline does pay off. My primary professor served as a mentor to me, and her support was key to my being able to sustain my motivation throughout the doctoral program. Eventually, with the help of a tutor, I passed statistics, but just *barely*. This extremely stressful experience taught me that I needed to acquire the discipline to apply myself to learning difficult subjects. All the encouragement from others would have been for naught had I failed to put in the time and effort necessary to learn. This lesson has been etched in my mind. My hope is that you will remain open to asking for the help you need, not only in graduate school but throughout your professional journey.

Questions for Reflection

1. What major barriers to self-care have you encountered as a graduate student? How can you address these barriers? If you cannot eliminate a barrier from your life, how can you work around or minimize it so you can attend to your self-care needs?
2. Achieving balance often seems like an impossible goal to those pursuing graduate degrees while managing other time-consuming tasks (holding part-time or full-time jobs, parenting). How would you assess your success in achieving balance in life as a graduate student?
3. Would you describe yourself as a perfectionist? If so, in what ways does your perfectionism affect your experience as a graduate student?
4. If you are interested in challenging your perfectionist strivings, what specific steps can you take to put perfectionism in perspective?
5. As a graduate student, how do you deal with setbacks? Do your fears and self-doubts inspire you to try harder to achieve success, or do they discourage you from trying?

Early Career

Transitions in life can be stressful, even when they bring about positive change. One such transition is leaving the safety net of a graduate program and launching your career as a helping professional. Most graduate students look forward to completing their training and being relieved of the stressors that come with being in school. Entering this next season of their life and career can indeed be very exciting; however, it is a period when many changes occur and major life decisions are made. Wise and Barnett (2016) suggest that students recognize typical developmental tasks of their early career such as forming and maintaining friendships, starting a family, purchasing a home, and getting established in a new career, all of which are sources of stress that can add to the professional challenges at this time of life. To navigate the stress of this transition period, Wise and Barnett highlight the importance of staying in contact with recent graduate students and becoming members of professional communities and networks. During this time, finding at least one mentor can be extremely helpful. Mentors offer a lot to those in graduate school and to those embarking on their careers as well. Studies of early career psychologists add credence to the idea that mentorship is a powerful means of enhancing one's professional competence (Mullenbach & Skovholt, 2016; Silva, Newman, Guiney, Valley-Gray, & Barrett, 2016; Skovholt & Trotter-Mathison, 2016; Troisi, Leder, Steigler-Balfour, Fleck, & Good, 2015). It is a good idea to pursue ongoing supportive relationships with colleagues and peer groups and to make use of professional networks as sources of support and consultation (see Chapter 7 for more on mentoring). Having and making full use of self-care action plans are essential in successfully dealing with the personal and professional tasks associated with getting established in a career. Nancy Chae's first year as a school counselor was exciting, but it proved to be challenging as well as rewarding. Because she gave so much of herself to her job, Nancy became depleted. It took her some time to recognize the signs of burnout and the need for self-care.

Challenges in an Early Career: Overcoming Burnout as a School Counselor

Nancy Chae

With a bright-eyed and bushy-tailed spirit, I began my first day as an elementary/middle school counselor in a charter school in Baltimore City. I was a recent graduate and the only school counselor for more than 300 students. I immediately put my graduate coursework and training to work: I created a needs assessment for teachers and staff and introduced myself to teachers, students, and families. I then began planning a calendar of classroom guidance lessons.

Then the feeling of intimidation set in: I had little understanding of the school's needs beyond data found online, and as a late hire, I had limited time to familiarize myself with and prepare for a new school and a new career. I was overwhelmed at first but motivated to learn about my position and find my place there. In addition to the expected school counselor responsibilities, I soon piled on several other kinds of duties that often kept me in the building until 10 p.m. I dove into my work headfirst, spending 60 or more hours in the school building each week. My administrator must have taken notice of my eagerness and my simultaneous inability to say "no" because I received more work.

My physical, emotional, and spiritual energy became depleted. I felt ashamed that it took a year for me to realize the need for self-care. This experience forced me to humbly admit to my burnout. Self-care was the last thing on my mind, and I even convinced myself that I was no longer an effective school counselor. I lost my focus, passion, and confidence.

After engaging in much self-reflection, I realized that self-care had to be a deliberate and purposeful act. During the summer before my second year, I analyzed my own personal and professional strengths and weaknesses. I created surveys for coworkers to share their perspectives of the counseling program, and I also made consistent efforts to communicate and meet with my mentors and peers as a reminder of why I pursued this important profession. Using this feedback, I made specific goals to plan for and move forward with the second year.

Because of the constantly giving nature of the counseling profession, we forget to give to ourselves; we cannot effectively care for others without caring for ourselves first. To protect my physical, emotional, and spiritual well-being, I found solace in restful and enjoyable activities unrelated to work, such as taking ballet classes again, returning to church services, Pinterest-ing (if I may make that a verb!) new recipes, reading inspirational books, and spending time with family and friends. Moreover, as a counselor, I had always listened to others, but I was very guarded about expressing my own feelings. I had to recognize and expose my vulnerabilities, and I became more open and honest about my feelings with my close support network. I soon found emotional and spiritual relief by coming to terms with my weaknesses, and I felt my genuine sense of self again.

When I returned for the second year, I had a clearer vision for the school counseling program. I recognized my allies and used those relationships to forge partnerships to benefit the school community. Moreover, I delegated or even declined tasks (skills that I previously had struggled with) that were inappropriate counselor duties so that I could redirect my energy to develop a productive program. At the end of the day, I attempted to set boundaries by separating work from home. I rarely brought work home, and I made an effort to enjoy cooking again and watching my favorite television shows. Although there were still challenges, the second year was more refreshing and focused than the first year, and I felt successful in implementing the goals and initiatives of my comprehensive school counseling program. Ultimately, at the end of the school year, I made the bittersweet decision to pursue a counseling position at a high school, where I have been for the last 4 years.

Without the initial challenges, I would not be the counselor that I am today. I took a hard and honest look at myself and reevaluated the direction of my choices and their impact on my wellness and wholeness.

Self-care is necessary for all counselors, but it must be deliberate, focused, and habitual for the sake of our health and to preserve the integrity of the counseling profession. Our students and clients need us, and we need to be well and confident to be there for them.

• • •

Jude Austin's Early Career Experiences: "Come Hell or High Water"

During my (Jude's) doctoral program, which was traumatic for me, my self-care suffered. I was willing to sacrifice my wellness in the short term if it meant that I could write the article or book chapter, present at the conference, edit the textbook, shoot the video, do the keynote speech, or attend the seminar that would help me to launch my career as a counselor educator. Admittedly, my lack of self-care as a doctoral student was a survival tactic more than personal neglect. As I share my experience as an early professional, you will learn about the threats to my self-care, how I navigated those threats, and my advice for other early professionals.

First of all, it is important to mention that I attempted to be nonjudgmental about my lack of self-care during my doctoral program. I knew I was going to graduate come hell or high water. I decided to call that chapter of my life "the struggle"; and I struggled immensely with these challenges (see Chapter 3 for more on this). It was in the last semester of my doctoral program that I finally was able to get some space between my program and me. This space gave me room to reflect on my experience and to consider what type of counselor education program and environment would fit me as a professional.

I was unwilling to sacrifice my self-care going forward. I wanted to turn the page on "the struggle" chapter, so I intentionally applied for jobs in geographical areas where my wife and I looked forward to living. I meticulously researched programs, their environments, and the ethnic makeup of the faculty, staff, and student body at each program, the universities, and the surrounding communities. I called everyone I knew who lived in those areas, I called alumni of universities where I planned to apply, and I made countless lists weighing the pros and cons of each potential opportunity. I wanted to set myself up to be not only successful but healthy.

During the job interview process I was keenly observant of faculty relationships, students' opinions about their programs, and their relationships with faculty. In most places, I found time to walk or drive around the area to get a feel for the environment. I asked questions geared toward wellness activities within the department. I also asked faculty members how they took care of themselves. I got some offers, as well as some crushing rejections. I ultimately ended up choosing a program that, to me, is as nurturing as it is demanding.

As a doctoral student, and now as an early professional, the core element of my self-care is my self-efficacy—my belief in my abilities—which helps me give myself permission to carve out time for self-care. When my self-efficacy is high, I am able to commit to a running and exercise plan, plant and tend to a small garden, spend time with friends and family, watch and enjoy movies and television shows, travel, and learn new things such as golf, cooking, and French. I feel more creative and hopeful. Writing and research ideas come more easily to me, and I feel that I am more therapeutically present in counseling sessions and classes.

When my self-efficacy is low, it feels like time is moving faster than normal. I find myself making a to-do list only to have it haunt me throughout the day. As I struggle to check items off my list, it becomes a constant reminder of my perceived inadequacy. My connection to my family and friends becomes strained, and I get short or snippy at home. When I should be enjoying time with my family, I am worrying excessively about my projects. I feel creatively stifled; I spend all day writing something, only to get a page or two finished. And I notice my patience is wearing thin in my interactions with both my graduate students and my clients.

My first year as a faculty member has threatened my self-efficacy. The experience of transitioning from doctoral student to faculty member is disorienting. I liken this to my experience of transitioning from college soccer to professional soccer. Everything moves at a different pace. Faculty and department meetings are intimidating; big decisions seem to be made at lightning speed. Matters related to the budget, admissions, student concerns, and recruitment are being voted on that were proposed before I arrived.

An unexpected threat to my self-efficacy and self-care was feeling that I did not belong. My faculty colleagues do a wonderful job of welcoming me and helping me feel I am a vital member of the group. But from time to time I struggle with a need to prove to myself that I was not hired because I am Black. In those moments of low self-efficacy, I think, "I have to show everyone that I deserve to be here." I find myself taking on more than I should, or writing and doing research to prove myself. To improve my self-efficacy, I reached out to other African American male faculty members and asked about their experience. Many of them had the same experience and gave me advice on how to handle these feelings. Some of this advice was to frankly discuss these feelings with my faculty colleagues. My connection to these African American male faculty members is now a big part of my self-care efforts. Sharing my experience and getting to hear their experiences help me to feel less pressure to prove that I belong.

Another significant and somewhat expected threat to my self-care was building a research pipeline. One of the most gratifying things about my position is the freedom I have to research what I value. However, with that freedom comes anxiety. I sometimes still feel that I need the permission of my dissertation chair to conduct research. During my first semester as a faculty member, I enjoyed the residual feelings of satisfaction and accomplishment from finishing my dissertation. By the second month, however, those feelings began to wear off, and the responsibility of building a body of work that would secure tenure came crashing down. I sprinted to start projects. I created an electronic folder for projects started, projects done, manuscripts submitted for publication, and manuscripts accepted for publication. As the semester progressed, I hit a wall. I looked at a barren "projects done" folder, then at an overflowing "projects started" folder, and I felt my self-efficacy plummet. I experienced feelings of inadequacy. I was exhausted from working many hours without making progress, or from ruminating about these projects even when I was not at work. I considered opening "the struggle" chapter again, sacrificing my wellness for achievement.

To improve my self-efficacy and self-care, I took some time and allowed the anxiety, pressure, and feelings of being overwhelmed to wash over me. I did not try to change anything or make it better. I remember sitting in my office and reevaluating my relationship with being tenured. In that moment, I decided that if I could not get tenure without sacrificing my wellness, then I did not want tenure at my current university. I have owned my struggle to get where I am now, having the privilege of career options, and I am intentionally deciding to be well, come hell or high water.

My advice for early professionals is to (1) take control of your self-care; (2) remain nonjudgmental throughout your self-care process and acknowledge that some life chapters may be harder than others; and (3) reevaluate your goals to be sure you are doing things for *your* right reason, whatever that might be.

In Chapter 4, I discuss my personal and professional stressors in this early phase of my career such as being a newlywed, moving to a new area, developing a research agenda, and finding a balance between my personal and professional life.

Julius Austin's Early Career Experiences: "A Challenging Transition"

The last year of my (Julius's) doctoral program was 2015, which was met with elation, frustration, excitement, and stress. I started data collection for my dissertation research in August of 2015, married my partner in October of 2015, was hired by Nicholls State University in November of 2015, successfully defended my dissertation and learned that my wife and I were expecting our first child in April of 2016, and graduated and purchased our first home in May of 2016. Until this last year, I was not fully aware that even positive life changes are associated with some degree of stress. With all these major life changes, I did not find time for self-care, and I disregarded my mental and physical health.

I remember waking up, face on the keyboard, and feeling shame for resting. I remember receiving emails from my wedding planner, the supervisor of my graduate assistantship, my realtor, and my dissertation chair within the same hour. I noticed several red flags that my self-care was in jeopardy: (1) I procrastinated on my dissertation edits, (2) I was late to meetings and returning emails/calls, (3) I disguised yawns in supervision sessions, and (4) I became increasingly irritable with those closest to me. I knew I had hit rock bottom in terms of neglecting self-care when I saw the look of frustration on my wife's face as she caught me having a Skype meeting in our hotel office at 8:00 a.m.—on our honeymoon! I realized that I needed to reorganize my priorities.

Transitioning to my clinical position at the Nicholls State University Counseling Center brought new challenges. The very first day at the university, I met with what seemed like the whole human resources department and slowly encountered a barrage of questions and statements about insurance, salary, course schedules, clinic procedure, clinical systems training, time sheets, faculty/staff parking spots and I.D. cards, campus maps, and retirement. I remember arriving at the point of information overload and making the decision to grab as many handouts as possible so I could slowly read over them at home that night.

The day after arriving on campus, I began accruing clinical hours for licensure. As I grew comfortable in my new role, I maintained a caseload of 30 to 40 clients and completed the final edits to my dissertation. The single most important action I took to grow comfortable on campus was contacting and agreeing to meet with 50 faculty/staff members at the university. I emailed two or three faculty members in each department on campus, explained that I was a new faculty member, and asked to hear about their experience on campus. I found that meeting with individuals in their office, where they felt comfortable, allowed for genuine discourse. After becoming familiar with my environment, I attended to personally caring for myself.

To maintain my self-care, I prioritized my time and committed to three fundamental areas of self-care: fitness, family, and reading for pleasure. To stay fit, I purchased an inexpensive treadmill and modified it by adding an adjustable laptop stand that enabled me to walk several miles while at my desk editing my dissertation and completing case notes. This makeshift treadmill desk allowed for systematic breaks from working, greater productivity, and less shame surrounding work stoppages. My commute to work involves an 80-minute roundtrip each day. On my commute home, I use a hands-free device and call each person in my immediate family. This provides time for me to decompress and detach myself from the clinical setting, as well as continue the strong bonds that my family has with each other. My brother Jude lives in Virginia, and my sister (Jasmine Austin) is a doctoral student at the University of Oklahoma. I cherish the time spent learning about their daily experiences. After contacting immediate family members, I check in with close friends and extended family members, and then my friends within the counseling community. I spend the morning commutes listening to audiobooks. My brother and I choose one audiobook to read together that we read at our own pace. I choose to listen to audiobooks that allow me to escape and to experience adventure and mystery.

As I reflect on my transition into my role as a faculty/staff member, taking a position in my home state allows my wife and me the benefit of seeing our parents every weekend, and my son benefits from having a close relationship with his grandparents such as I had with mine. Being home includes enjoying traditional Louisiana style home-cooked meals, reconnecting with my grandparents, and forming bonds with the Louisiana counseling community. More important, being home reconnects me with a part of my identity that had been neglected during my educational travels. This reconnection and integration process is a strong component of my self-care.

Reflections on Our Future Careers: "Learning From Our Elders"

We (Jude and Julius) are twins and recently turned 30 years old; there is a 50-year difference between Jerry and us. One thing we have learned from talking with our coauthors is that retirement is something earned, not given. In our conversations about self-care with Michelle and Jerry, as well as with other contributors to this book, we have come to view self-care as something that needs to be cultivated throughout our careers. We have learned that frantic, unintentional attempts to take care of ourselves when we experience challenging times is not the most effective self-care strategy. Building consistent and personal self-care strategies over time provides more benefits. With this approach to self-care, we can build a foundation of strategies and a mind-set that supports our resilience when we find ourselves in difficult times throughout our careers.

As we attend conferences and seek advice from colleagues regarding ways to be healthy throughout our careers, we have learned that a common thread is taking no phase of our career for granted. Many of our more experienced colleagues advise us against pushing toward the next phases of our career without truly appreciating our current phase. We have both felt a pull in this early phase of our career development to rush to get publications, certifications, licenses, and tenure. We both have noticed that we don't take as much time as we may need to fully appreciate our achievements. Being able to look back on a meaningful career, knowing that every phase was fully experienced and appreciated, is how our senior colleagues said they are able to welcome retirement.

Jerry Corey's Early Career Experiences

My (Jerry's) late 20s and most of my 30s was an extremely challenging time for me, both personally and professionally. A significant transition in my life occurred when I was 24 and met Marianne Schneider, a foreign exchange student from Germany. We were married in Germany 3 years later. Another significant turning point in my personal life was the loss of my 70-year-old father when I was 30 years old. I was fond of my father and think of him to this day. A few months prior to his death, I became a new father to our daughter Heidi. A couple of years later I became a father again with the birth of our daughter Cindy.

Having been married for only a few years and becoming a father to two daughters was a personal challenge for which I was not prepared. I struggled through the process of learning how to be a husband and a father. These were difficult roles for me to learn, partly because I immersed myself in my work, somewhat to the neglect of my family. I was overly concerned with charting my path as an early career professional, and I devoted an abundance of time to teaching, which was extremely fulfilling. I did not always do a good job of balancing my work life with my family life during these early years of our marriage. Despite my devotion to my work, we did manage to make time for family vacations, visited Germany for several weeks every summer, frequently headed out to the beach and the mountains, and went on outings with friends and other family members. We also made weekend visits to my mother's house, which enabled Marianne and me to have times together as a couple while our daughters spent special times with their grandmother. Taking this time as a family, and also as a couple, was certainly a central part of our self-care and was important in helping us to stay productive in our professional lives.

I found that developing an interest in exercising was a great help to me in meeting the demands of my personal and professional life. However, it took some time for me to see the value of incorporating self-care practices into my daily life. It was not until my mid-20s that I decided that I needed to make time for exercising and taking care of myself in other ways. Although no health crisis nudged me into beginning to exercise, I eventually realized that I was somewhat lethargic and needed to move to increase my energy level. When I began my career in high school teaching in 1961, I decided to bicycle from my apartment to school each day. I enjoyed this and began to feel more invigorated. Cycling, which I began early in my career, continues to be a vital part of my self-care program to this day.

From the perspective of career satisfaction, I greatly enjoyed teaching on both the high school and community college level for 6 years. However, I was open to seizing new opportunities to branch out and take on new professional roles. Shortly after I received my doctorate at the age of 30, I began a new position as assistant professor in the Teacher Education Department and as a counselor in the University Counseling Center at California State Polytechnic University in Pomona. My professional tasks as a counselor included doing both individual and group counseling and outreach work on the campus. In addition to my work as a counselor, I taught courses in both psychology and education. During this time, I wrote my first book, not realizing that this would become a major professional commitment that has followed me through to late in my career. Focusing on my goal of completing my first book supplied the motivation I needed to continue when I felt discouraged. I wanted to share my thoughts about creating ways to personalize learning in the classroom. Even though I was motivated to write and blocked off time to reflect and write, writing was not a smooth process. Indeed, I often struggled with getting words on paper and often doubted that I had anything worthwhile to say.

Along with being involved in writing, teaching, supervising student teachers, practicing individual counseling, and conducting personal growth groups, I was working toward becoming a licensed psychologist during my early years in the profession. When I began working as a counselor at the university counseling center, I was seeing many students for individual counseling and facilitating a number of groups for college students. It was difficult for me to get a sense of my effectiveness as a counselor. My self-confidence began to erode and led me to wonder whether I would ever become a skilled therapist. To make matters worse, I did not get much recognition or encouragement from some of my supervisors during my training. One colleague suggested that I might be better off as a teacher and that I should give up on my aspirations of becoming a counseling psychologist. Hearing this feedback was discouraging, but I decided to open myself to new experiences as a counselor and give myself some time to see if I could successfully meet these challenges. Making a decision to stay with the anxiety associated with being a novice counselor did pay off, even though I wondered if I had the ability to be effective in this professional role.

A lesson I learned from being a counselor in a university counseling center was the importance of persisting, even with the absence of external validation. It helped to tell myself that I probably would not be as effective as I expected to be when I first began this work. Although it is difficult to persist when reinforcement from significant others is not forthcoming, I gradually began to learn to look to myself for the kind of approval I had sought from others.

I encourage you not to give up when you experience self-doubts, but instead to challenge whatever might be holding you back. Sometimes you will be excited about your future as a counseling professional, and at other times you may be discouraged and wonder if it is all worth the effort. If you are willing to continue exploring your personal life, you will be better equipped to assist others as they struggle with their life concerns.

Questions for Reflection

1. If you are currently in an early stage of your career, how well are you meeting developmental tasks often associated with this period (forming and maintaining friendships, starting a family, and getting established in a new career)? If you are struggling with any of these tasks, what are the barriers? What would help you to better meet these developmental tasks?
2. When you have too many demands on your plate all at once, how do you prioritize what needs to be done first? Where does self-care fall on your priority list? If it is not as high on your list as you would like it to be, what are you willing to do to change that?
3. Can you think of any creative ways to incorporate self-care into your schedule when your time is very limited?
4. If you are an early career professional, have you questioned your competence and suitability for this line of work? What did you do (or can you do) to challenge self-doubt?
5. If you are in the early phase of your career, what kind of future professional life would you like to have?

Mid-Career

Over time, as clinicians and counselor educators gain more experience in their professional roles and focus on building their careers, it is likely that they will be expected to take on greater professional responsibilities, which are inherently stressful. For instance, clinicians may be promoted to positions that require them to supervise others and manage budgets while those pursuing positions in higher education may have to weather the challenges associated with going up for tenure. At the same time, they may be experiencing developmental stressors in their personal lives such as dealing with aging parents or children leaving the nest to go away to college or to enter the workforce. For mid-career mental health practitioners, Wise and Barnett (2016) emphasize becoming aware of developmental stressors, finding ways to maintain competence, and assuming an active role in engaging in lifelong learning. This is a time for practitioners to become aware of common risks for burnout and to monitor how well they are managing stress, both personally and professionally. It is important to adopt an active role in collaborating with colleagues and to avoid professional isolation. Becoming part of a network of colleagues can help us maintain our vitality and increase our competence (Johnson, Barnett, Elman, Forrest, & Kaslow, 2012).

Michelle Muratori's Mid-Career Experiences

Sometimes it is hard for me (Michelle) to believe how quickly time has passed and to admit to myself that I am at the midpoint in my career. A number of years ago, upon earning my doctorate in counselor education, much of my energy seemed to be channeled into getting established professionally. I was able to tame my perfectionism well enough to get out of my own way (with the support of a good therapist), and my productivity increased. My greatest weakness was the difficulty I had drawing boundaries with the amount of work I heaped on my plate. Shortly after finding my grounding in my new professional role as a counselor and researcher at the Johns Hopkins Center for Talented Youth (CTY), I decided to supplement my "day job" with adjunct teaching in Johns Hopkins University's master's in counseling program. I also took on freelance writing projects when time permitted . . . and quite honestly, even when time didn't permit! I somehow squeezed time into my schedule (often on weekends) to work on these projects, which left me little downtime for self-care. I loved everything I was doing and considered myself so fortunate to have these opportunities, which made it difficult to set limits on the number of projects I accepted. I think I was afraid that the opportunities would stop being offered if I turned them down. One of my challenges at that time was to make time for myself. I must admit that when it came to self-care, I was not doing such a spectacular job.

Several years have passed since I came to Johns Hopkins University, and I still juggle many of the same types of professional activities that I took on when I started. Although that may seem like I am stagnant (or perhaps that is my fear of how it might be perceived), I have enjoyed the variety of tasks related to both my full-time and part-time jobs. Combining these professional activities—providing services to students and their parents, teaching, conducting research, and writing—keep me interested and energized in my work. The projects and tasks that I work on consistently bring meaning to my life. Although I would like to be able to say that I have learned how to say "no" to some projects and opportunities, I am still working on that. I will give myself *some* credit though. I have occasionally turned down opportunities (invitations to write book chapters or to submit proposals to conferences), which is indeed progress!

As much as I enjoy the work I do, keeping up such a demanding schedule has been difficult, especially when personal crises have occurred. In 2016, I received the horrible news that my father had suffered a heart attack while I was attending a conference in Orlando, Florida. I left the conference and flew to California to see my father in the hospital. Although he had survived the heart attack, the doctors discovered that he had terminal cancer. My father was released from the hospital and received hospice services at home, where he died within weeks. It was so painful to watch him suffer, but I am eternally grateful that I could be there to support him and my family during that time. My supervisor at work and the department lead in the counseling program were extremely supportive when I needed to take time off to be with my family. Although tragedies can strike during any stage of one's life and career, it does seem more probable that certain developmental stressors such as dealing with aging parents will occur during one's mid-career stage.

As I have gotten older, and particularly since losing my father, I have come to realize how critical it is to make self-care more of a priority. I know that I need to take time to smell the roses. I do make more time now for non-work-related activities, such as attending concerts and events (such as the Women's March in Washington, DC) with friends, meeting friends for lunch or dinner, getting more involved in social/political activism at the local level, walking and enjoying nature, shopping for bargains (I cannot resist!), and watching movies and certain TV shows, but I still have room for improvement.

Jerry Corey's Mid-Career Experiences

In 1972, at age 35, I (Jerry) accepted a new teaching position with the job of developing an undergraduate human services major at California State University at Fullerton, a program that I have continued to be actively involved with for 46 years. I have taught a variety of applied courses such as group counseling, theory and practice of counseling, professional ethics, and experiential self-exploration groups. The coursework involved an integration of both the cognitive and affective domains of human functioning, and experiential learning was emphasized, which appealed to me. Students majoring in human services found their classes both academically demanding and personally meaningful, and they appreciated the opportunity to acquire skills needed to counsel diverse client populations as well as the opportunity to explore their personal concerns. In short, they valued the emphasis on the development of *the person* of the helper that was an integral part of most of their courses. Their excitement over the program was a motivational force for me to continue putting in a supreme effort to assist students who were engaged in personal learning.

Being deeply involved in teaching in an undergraduate program and writing textbooks, in my mid-40s I began conducting workshops in various parts of the United States and also in Europe, often with Marianne Schneider Corey, my wife and colleague. We began presenting workshops as a team during this time, which was and continues to be a meaningful professional endeavor. I learned a great deal by working with Marianne; one lesson I have learned and had reinforced time and again is Marianne's way of making a connection with a client or an audience. She continues to demonstrate the importance of being fully present and being herself. At this time, Marianne was an excellent example of a person who demonstrated congruence between her personal self and her professional self, and she certainly influenced me in this regard. These workshops were exciting, demanding, and enjoyable. These opportunities often came about because of books I authored or coauthored, and they represented yet another way to teach both students and mental health professionals. The rewards associated with these professional roles gave me the incentive to pursue paths that were meaningful.

My mid-career stage of professional development was in stark contrast to my early years in school when I felt I had no voice. I had finally come to believe that I had a voice and that I could use it to make a difference. This has been my motivation for doing whatever I could to enable students to find their voice and to use it—and to do whatever it takes to stay on course in their personal and professional journey.

Throughout my 40s I faced many professional challenges, yet the demands of work inspired and energized me. Not only was I teaching full time in human services, but I also assumed the responsibility of program coordinator (the equivalent of a department chair) for about 9 years. During summers and semester breaks, I was busy writing and revising books on counseling theory, group work, personal growth, and ethics. I also conducted workshops in various states, facilitated therapeutic groups, and trained students and professionals in group counseling. It was necessary for me to balance a multiplicity of professional roles, formulate long-range and short-term goals, acquire time management skills, and learn how to create some personal life amid all the facets of my professional life. During this phase of my career I found that a main pathway to self-care was making time for family vacations, associating with friends and colleagues, hiking, and bicycle riding. I also participated in a number of therapeutic groups as a member, which were of great value to me both personally and professionally. Serving as both the coordinator of the human services program and teaching full time was meaningful, yet stressful at times. The stress of trying to juggle multiple roles and tasks was not without a price. I was not very good at delegating tasks to other faculty members, and when I did request help on a project, I continually checked up to see what progress was being made. I would sometimes complete a job I had delegated to another person because the task was not getting done fast enough for me! I rarely did one thing at a time, and multitasking had become my normal pattern. This attitude certainly contributed to my stress level. Slowly I learned that I could not assume full responsibility for a program, and eventually I became skilled at asking for help and giving others a chance to provide assistance. Learning that I could not do it all was a significant part of taking care of myself.

Eventually, I learned that I could not live in a stress-free environment and that either stress controls me or I control stress. I struggled with learning how to let go of a sense of being completely responsible for the smooth functioning of our program. I was typically attempting to do far too much in too short a period of time. I developed severe headaches and pain and muscular tension in my shoulders and neck as my body began telling me that I needed to slow down. Psychologically, I was symbolically carrying the burdens for the entire department on my shoulders. One of my colleagues told me she saw me as being "stressed out" for much of the semester and recommended a Rolfing practitioner who specialized in deep tissue work to release muscular tensions.

Rolfing, which is known as structural integration, aims at bringing the body into alignment. When I began these body work sessions, I realized that stress was getting the best of me and that my headaches and pain were signs that I was not taking care of myself. Living a stressful existence had become my way of life, and I was not paying attention to what my body was telling me. Often I would rush through freeway traffic to get to my body work appointment on time, which further increased my stress level. I began incorporating Rolfing sessions into my self-care program, and today I am still involved in various forms of body work on a regular basis. An important lesson for me was realizing that maintaining my health and wellness has much in common with maintaining a car's performance and longevity—it is dependent on regular maintenance. By taking care of my body and learning how to reduce the effects of stress, I am doing necessary maintenance to improve my own performance.

During my early 50s I made some key decisions pertaining to balancing my work life with my personal life. I continued monitoring the number of hours I worked each week and made some changes in my work life that reduced pressure in my personal life. During much of our married life, Marianne and I have made time for vacations, even short times away, but often linked our professional travels with vacations. We each value self-care and engage in our own regular program to keep physically and psychologically fit. For example, one summer we did a couple of 5-day training workshops in group counseling with counselors in Ireland within a 2-week period. We arranged our schedule so we had time both before and after the workshops to see the sights, enjoy the country, and spend time with friends in different countries. We also took the opportunity to spend some vacation time in Germany and Norway. When we travel to another state to attend or present at a professional conference, a self-care practice we engage in is allowing several days before we work to enjoy the natural beauty and sights of that state. Eventually, we became better at blocking out time exclusively for personal travel rather than sandwiching a vacation into a work situation.

During the decade of my 50s I was doing everything I wanted to do professionally. However, I continued to learn my limits and sought a balance between my personal life and my professional life. I was still attempting to do too many things at once. Many of my personal needs were met from my involvement with so many projects, yet I came to realize that I couldn't do everything that I loved doing. A hard lesson for me to learn was to pause before too readily accepting an invitation for another workshop, a speaking engagement, or launching a new book. Because I lived with an overcrowded schedule and accepted too many invitations, I needed to learn the value of carefully reflecting on the pros and cons of accepting invitations, no matter how enticing they appeared to be. I eventually recognized that everything I was doing took time and energy. I had the difficult task of learning to say "no" to some interesting projects. I frequently had to remind myself that I am one person with limited time, and I could not do everything I might have wanted to do. During one year in my late 50s I realized that we were away from home almost as much time as we stayed at home (we were away for 152 days, and many of those days were for professional activities). We evaluated whether we wanted to do so much traveling and looked at the cost-benefit ratio of doing so many workshops in various places. This kind of assessment is a vital part of self-care, and it helps us in determining what changes we may want to make. I find that many of my students and colleagues have difficulty balancing the costs and benefits of getting involved in projects. As I mentor students, I frequently talk with them about establishing priorities and learning practical strategies such as time management, and I encourage them to think about how their professional or academic life can affect their relationships, family, and personal self-care priorities.

Over the years I have learned how essential clarity of purpose, motivation, and self-discipline are for engaging in productive work. Realizing that I am the one who decided to commit to projects keeps me focused and energetic. If I were doing what someone else expected of me, I would long ago have lost my enthusiasm for these projects.

Questions for Reflection

1. If you are at this stage of your career, what have your greatest challenges been? How have you addressed these challenges, and what impact have they had on your well-being?
2. If you are a mid-career professional, how do you balance all of your work-related responsibilities with your personal life? Are you satisfied with the balance you have struck? If not, what changes could you realistically make to improve your work–life balance?
3. If you are currently a graduate student or an early career professional, what do you envision your work–life balance will be when you reach the mid-career stage of professional development? What practices would you like to include in your self-care regimen when you reach this stage of your career? Are these practices similar or different from the ones you are including in your self-care plan today?

Late Career

The word "retirement" is likely to elicit a range of reactions among those professionals who are approaching the late career stage. Some may be looking forward to having more time to engage in pleasurable activities that have been pushed to the back burner; others may fear a loss of identity and be concerned about finding meaning and redefining their purpose as retirement approaches. Some may be concerned about their finances and their ability to support themselves and their families after they no longer have a stable source of income, whereas others may be better situated financially. Many older individuals heading toward retirement worry about their declining health as they age, and counselors and helping professionals are not immune to these concerns. We all must deal with the changes that come with aging, including changes in our professional roles, our financial status, our health, and our day-to-day activities. Kottler and Carlson (2016) propose that aging is mostly a state of mind. Our beliefs about aging largely determine how we will respond to the challenges of later life. The more optimistic our views about aging, the better we can prepare for and adapt to these challenges. For an engaging discussion of the demands of coping with aging in a psychotherapist's life, we recommend *Therapy Over 50: Aging Issues in Psychotherapy and the Therapist's Life* (Kottler & Carlson, 2016).

Retirement is an opportunity to redesign your life and to tap unused potentials; it is not an end to all work. There are many choices open to us as we embark on the path toward retirement. We can get involved with the projects we might have put aside due to the demands of our job. We can discover that retirement is not an end, but rather a new beginning. Retirement is a major transition in life that brings a variety of choices and transitions. A major developmental task we face as we retire is deciding which path (or paths) we will take to continue to find meaning in life. Some older adults continue working because they enjoy working and because it contributes to a meaningful existence. For some who continue to work for personal and interpersonal reasons after the traditional retirement age, "continuing to work may contribute to [their] physical and psychological well-being" (Kampfe, 2015, p. 230). For late career professionals, Wise and Barnett (2016) give special attention to remaining current and competent and to making plans for the transition to retirement. They recommend finding ways for maintaining a sense of value and meaning by giving back to the profession through mentoring, teaching, and finding ways of serving.

Randy Alle-Corliss is a clinical social worker who recently retired and is in the late career stage. He managed a mental health facility, and he is keeping professionally active in his "advancing" age. Like many in the helping professions, Randy held a number of different positions, including doing clinical work for many years and eventually assuming the position of an administrator and supervisor. Since retiring from his agency, he is building a private practice in counseling and teaching theories of counseling each semester at a university.

Surviving and Thriving in Retirement

● ●

Randall Alle-Corliss

As a department administrator for the largest behavioral health clinic in the Fontana service area in California for 10 years with Kaiser Permanente, I managed a very large, diverse clinic that treated complex and crisis-oriented cases through a number of specialized outpatient programs for adolescents and adults, as well as many other programs. My daily routine involved working on a variety of tasks and dealing with a multitude of issues with patients, therapists, psychiatrists, psychiatric nurses, social workers, psychologists, case managers, and clerical staff, to mention a few. I also was responsible for preparing budgets and financial reports, dealing with patient complaints, responding to a multitude of emails, keeping up with electronic record keeping, addressing human resource issues, doing employee evaluations annually, and conducting staff meetings. This certainly involved serious prioritizing and decision making and required managing multiple sources of stress.

Additional administrative support was clearly needed, and I continued to ask for it. Typically, in spite of my requests, this support was not forthcoming. I was the only department administrator responsible for 50 to 60 employees who had the help of only one administrative assistant. Despite this shortage of help, I gave my best efforts at managing all of this for more than 10 years. I remained a strong advocate for the staff and worked diligently to create a strong team approach despite our limitations. I continually evaluated my own performance through the identification of my own strengths and limitations and worked toward making any improvements deemed necessary. One of my greatest strengths was my ability to support and acknowledge the staff for their hard work and positive impact on patient care.

It is an understatement to say that this position was very stressful and demanded an inordinate amount of time. Even though I was in a late phase of my career and had a variety of professional experiences, sometimes I felt overwhelmed, especially on days when unplanned or unanticipated events occurred. I found these self-care strategies to be valuable in keeping my sanity and reducing the effects of stress:

- Focusing on the people I worked with every day and reaching out to connect with and support them.
- Using mindfulness practices and skills every day. I listened to mindfulness tapes on my way to work and practiced those skills, especially being in the here and now as much as possible.
- Practicing meditation every morning before the day began. This consisted of meditation focusing on phrases that reinforced being in the here and now, taking one step at a time, appreciating myself, breathing naturally, and seeing and appreciating the beauty in life and the connection between all things.

- Taking regular short vacation days, one long weekend every month when my wife and I planned trips, getting out into nature, and visiting my adult children and brother.
- Enjoying my back yard where succulents, plants, trees, hummingbird feeders, fire pits, birds, and nature surround me.
- Relating to my Cocker Spaniel, Sunny, every day. The deep love and comfort I give and receive from him restores my soul and spirit.
- Consulting regularly with my beautiful wife of 35 years, Lupe Alle-Corliss, a licensed clinical social worker who also works as a department administrator at Kaiser Permanente. This made life more bearable in this stressful position. When I felt overwhelmed, I could always ventilate and she would help by challenging my perspective.
- Making use of appropriate humor. I had a goal to make the people I worked with laugh at least one time every meeting. I have a strong belief that laughter lightens the soul and gives a needed perspective.
- Rounding each day, which involved walking throughout the agency facility to see the staff in their offices and touch base with them.
- Finding a way to balance being compassionate with the staff and continuing to set firm expectations when necessary.

The demands of my position as a department administrator were many, which made it essential that I create self-care strategies to help me retain vitality as a person and as a professional. Caring for self was an absolute must if I were to care for others. I took the ethical mandate of self-care seriously; this enabled me to successfully cope with work stress and ensured that my passion for my work was not diminished. I recently retired from my full-time position at Kaiser Permanente and am currently building a private practice as a clinical social worker. Although I do miss the people with whom I worked, I must admit that I definitely do not miss the stress of my agency position.

* * *

Jerry Corey's Experiences During Later Career

I (Jerry) am convinced that if I neglected my self-care practices, I would not have the stamina I enjoy today and I would not be able to continue to engage in productive work that has carried me into my later career. I attribute my health and the quality of my life largely to self-care practices. For many years, I have been committed to making the time to exercise—walking, hiking, or bicycling every day, rain or shine! I keep a record of my work activities and exercise activities. Over the past 3 years my average work week was about 34 hours; my exercise came to about 16 hours as a weekly average. Monitoring my work and self-care activities in my schedule book is a good way for me to evaluate balance in my life in those areas. Maintaining fitness in all areas has become a priority for me. Some of my friends tell me that I have turned my exercise routine into a compulsion and that I am an addicted exerciser, yet physical activities keep me physically and psychologically fit and are enjoyable and rejuvenating. I typically devote most of the mornings to keeping physically active and am often not able to begin my workday until after lunch.

A crucial part of my self-care plan is being involved in acupuncture as a preventive measure. When I tell people that I go to acupuncture sessions, they sometimes ask what problems I have, not appreciating that acupuncture is a pathway to physical and psychological wellness. I also have physically challenged myself by incorporating Pilates into my self-care regimen, a practice I began when I was 75. My Pilates teachers challenge me physically in my weekly lessons, and they do not pay attention to my groaning or complaining when they ask me to do challenging exercises. More than once I loudly proclaimed during a Pilates private session, "I'm too old for this shit!" They treat me as though I were young, and they are instrumental in keeping me young in many respects. Although Pilates and stretching exercises are not easy, I am convinced that these practices are paying off for me in the long run.

Another vital aspect of self-care is incorporating fun into our daily life. I consider many of my work activities to be fun, especially teaching, but there are other avenues of fun open to me. Marianne and I are fortunate to live in an area where concerts and music festivals are available, and we take full advantage of this, often enjoying these events with friends. About 25 years ago, I bought a 1931 Model A Ford, and it is always fun to give our grandchildren and friends rides in this antique car.

Although I formally retired from the California State University system as a *full-time* professor at age 63 in the year 2000, every fall semester I teach courses in group counseling and ethics in counseling as an adjunct faculty member at California State University at Fullerton. During my 60s and 70s I have enjoyed teaching only part time and like the freedom this brings. In addition to teaching, I have continued to give workshops and presentations at professional conferences. With my writing schedule and the teaching I do throughout each year, I am still deeply involved in meaningful work. Currently, I have the opportunity to create my own schedule. My writing schedule now occupies a major portion of my professional time, and my colleagues and I have been involved in the revision of one or more textbooks each year. At age 80 I still greatly enjoy the various facets of my work life and do not envision total retirement in my picture. Interacting with colleagues on exciting projects is meaningful, and I continue to find joy in working with appreciative and eager students who keep me young in my "advancing" age.

Questions for Reflection

1. If the late career stage looms near in your future, what are you doing to prepare for retirement? How do you anticipate you will you cope with the changes that accompany this transition? What are your greatest concerns about this phase of life, and what are you most looking forward to doing?

2. If you are in an earlier stage of professional development, what reactions do you have to Jerry and Randy's experiences as late career professionals? What lessons can you draw from their stories that may pertain to your own life and to the way you plan to incorporate self-care into your lifestyle now and in the years to come?

3. Stress is an inevitable part of life, and positions that are very demanding are likely to create a lot of it! Randy provided a bullet list of self-care strategies that he has adopted to manage his stress. Jerry also described his self-care regimen. Create your own list and include a column that contains self-care strategies that you could implement now and ones that you think will be important to adopt in later stages of your life and career.

4. Some individuals wait until they retire to develop new hobbies, believing that they don't have the time or resources to pursue these interests while they are working a full-time job and balancing multiple roles. What are the potential problems that can result from approaching self-care with this mind-set? What can you do now to ensure that you will spend your retirement years engaged in activities and hobbies that bring meaning and enjoyment to your life?

Concluding Thoughts

Throughout the seasons of our careers as helping professionals, we are likely to face demands that have the potential to wear us down and detract from our effectiveness unless we are vigilant about implementing self-care. As noted early in the chapter, the manner in which we meet challenging tasks during graduate school may reflect how well we are likely to address the tasks that we encounter throughout our career. If you commit to a self-care program early in your professional development and career, it will be easier to continue to incorporate self-care in your life as you get older and prepare for retirement. Although some people enjoy a life of full retirement, many are creatively involved in doing meaningful professional work with more free time to be involved in other pursuits.

Chapter 3

Self-Care in Graduate School

This chapter highlights the experiences of individuals currently in graduate school and those who have recently graduated. We follow the experiences of Julius Austin and Jude Austin in their journey through master's and doctoral programs and examine what they learned along the way about self-care and becoming counseling professionals. Topics include committing to self-care, setting boundaries, coping with anxiety, motivations for becoming a counselor, self-worth, self-care during the dissertation process, and suggestions for getting the most from graduate school. Julius and Jude share their experiences as individuals, as twins, and as minority students in a graduate program in counseling. You will also read the stories of current and past graduate students who have wrestled with questions of their own regarding how to practice self-care in graduate school when time and resources are limited. If you are currently a master's or a doctoral student, we hope you will reflect on your unique experience in graduate school and recognize the need to develop your own individualized way to care for yourself.

Julius Austin's Experience in Graduate School

I (Julius) was in the last semester of my master's program at the University of Mary Hardin-Baylor when I experienced the consequences of not caring for myself. I earned internship clinical hours at two locations, my graduate program's community counseling center and a local inpatient facility. The inpatient facility staff consisted of four counselors, including my brother (Jude) and I, who shared a caseload of about 70 clients. Because Jude and I were graduate students, we maintained a reduced caseload of 10 to 12 clients each at first. As the semester progressed, some counselors left and were not replaced, leaving the two of us to split the caseload into 35 clients each. I remember thinking, "Great, we'll definitely earn the required clinical hours to graduate." However, managing growing caseloads at both internship sites soon became overwhelming.

Most days consisted of working in the inpatient facility or at the on-campus clinic, or both, and then attending class sometimes from 4 p.m. to 10 p.m. The combination of the courses I had to complete, the caseload of clients I continued to see in the campus clinic, the process of applying to doctoral programs, and the extremely heavy caseload of clients at the inpatient facility perpetuated several negative behaviors. I communicated with my family less often, and the pressure to please my program and site supervisors provoked a "suffer in silence" approach on my part. I began to slip into a sleep state while in supervision and during clinical staff meetings, and I neglected my body, sometimes being too exhausted to shower or shave. I neglected myself because completing my degree—achieving a goal that I bled and cried over—had become more important to me than my self-care.

During one supervision session, I fell asleep while my supervisor was commenting on a skill I had demonstrated in session. My supervisor spoke my name loud enough for me to hear her, and once she had my attention she asked, "OK, what's going on?" This supervisor had taught one of the first psychology courses I attended when I was 18 years old; she had known me for 7 years at this point, and her question came from a profoundly caring place. Though I did not feel judged by my supervisor, I could not keep the shame from washing over me. I told my supervisor about the clinical situation at my off-campus site and the consequences of being short staffed, and she took quick action. My campus supervisor communicated with my site supervisor and frankly demanded that the inpatient facility decrease the client caseload. My campus supervisor also gave me specific instructions to get some rest.

In retrospect, I believe I fell into what I refer to as the *internship trap*. I needed direct client contact hours to complete my graduate degree, and these hours seemed terrifyingly unpredictable because they depended on whether my clients attended their sessions. Graduate students continue to encounter this trap today. The trap takes the form of a question, "Do you sacrifice your self-care to acquire the necessary requirements to complete your graduate education?"

When a person accepts the responsibility of being a graduate student, he or she also agrees to the unavoidable stress and multiple demands of graduate training. These demands can include emotional exhaustion, stressful cohort or faculty dynamics, compassion or empathy fatigue, and vicarious traumatization, to name a few. These demands often make self-care seem like a luxury not meant for graduate students. Myers et al. (2012) explain that factors of self-care include "sleep, exercise, use of social support, emotion regulation strategies, and mindfulness practices" (p. 57). One of the most important deterrents to these self-care factors for graduate students is time (El-Ghoroury, Galper, Sawaqdeh, & Bufka, 2012). Carving out time to implement self-care practices is difficult for most graduate students given their hectic schedules.

Although the boundary line between faculty and student can cloud students' understanding of how faculty care for themselves, faculty modeling of self-care awareness is important. Relationships between graduate students and faculty, whether healthy or unhealthy, influence the development of our counselor identity as well as our ideas about caring for ourselves. Positive relationships with faculty members are important, as are supportive relationships with classmates and peers. During parts of my master's program I spent more time with members of my cohort than I did with family members. Because of this fact, it is important to develop a culture of self-care within graduate cohorts.

My master's and doctoral program cohorts had distinct cultures that contributed to our collective self-care. Having experienced the dynamics of two cohorts at different institutions, I have concluded that the following ingredients are needed to establish a culture of self-care among students in clinical training programs:

1. *Healthy faculty relationships.* Unhealthy faculty relationships tend to manifest themselves throughout the relational processes of the cohort. A doctoral-level graduate student should be mindful of healthy faculty relationships when choosing a dissertation committee. The same advice is relevant for master's students who are working on a thesis.
2. *Sense of control.* With the expectations, pressures, and stress of graduate studies, students understandably can feel that their lives are overwhelmingly out of control. Cohort members provide an outlet to process emotions, check in about

assignments, and draw on collective knowledge to support each other.

3. *Sense of humor.* Clinical work, research, and education are all important aspects of graduate school, but finding humor in our experience is also important. Identify times when you are taking yourself too seriously and laugh. My caution is to *laugh with,* and not *laugh at,* a cohort member.

4. *Leisure.* My doctoral program cohort had annual Halloween and Christmas potlucks. We all brought food and played board games or watched seasonal movies. These activities gave us the opportunity to spend time with each other outside of the educational setting and to process our graduate school experience. If your program does not sponsor such events, take the initiative to organize leisure activities that promote camaraderie among cohort members.

5. *Friendship.* It is unrealistic to expect that you will be close friends with *every* member of your cohort. It is important to recognize this and set boundaries with cohort members who jeopardize your self-care.

Looking back, I realize I had differing self-care needs within both cohorts. I needed the freedom to explore my identity in the doctoral program while still maintaining contact with my cohort at the master's level.

Nicholas Lazzareschi, a graduate student in counseling, highlights the notions of time and being intentional about finding a healthy work–life balance. Part of committing to a self-care practice is becoming aware of barriers to taking care of yourself.

Committed to Practicing Self-Care

● ●

Nicholas Lazzareschi

I was first introduced to the concept of self-care in my undergraduate career when I was undertaking a clinical internship at a nonprofit in Los Angeles. During group supervision, my supervisor and all the other clinicians expressed the importance of self-care for themselves as well as for their clients. They explained that if they did not take care of themselves, they could not fully commit to the work they needed to do with their clients. This explanation made perfect sense, but I thought to myself that self-care was for people who did not have finals to study for and papers to write. At that time, I was steeped in my undergraduate studies, worked as a research coordinator on campus, worked at a for-profit adolescent treatment center, and was a single father. In other words, I was convinced that self-care was a luxury afforded to clinicians who had a more comfortable schedule.

In California State University, Fullerton's graduate counseling program, self-care was a topic covered in every class by every professor. During my law and ethics class, I learned that self-care was an ethical mandate in our profession. I took note of all the suggestions by my professors and started my own self-care program once again. Backtracking a little, let me explain that I have suffered from substance abuse issues most of my life. Heroin and methamphetamine ran my life until May 13, 2011. When I was working at getting clean, I exercised a lot and that seemed to help with my addiction, my anger, and my overall demeanor. However, when my daughter was born several months later, and when her mother started using drugs again 6 months later, my time to exercise was cut short due to my newfound responsibilities to my daughter as well as to my academic career.

Recently, I resumed some self-care practices. I started eating right and exercising regularly. In the beginning, I simply cut out all fast food and started drinking only water, iced tea, and black coffee. Three days a week I did cardio on a treadmill for roughly 35 minutes and then worked out in my backyard. During the first week, I lost 8 pounds and noticed significant increases in energy, which was very encouraging. I was hooked, but this time it was a positive addiction! This led to a weekly meal preparation program in which I would make almost all meals for the week on Sunday. I increased my workouts to 4 to 6 days a week. Furthermore, unless I had a paper due Monday, I did not do any school work on the weekends. I was able to get 99% of the work I needed to get done during the week. This left the weekends for my daughter, my family, and me. In fact, I even had time to read a book for pleasure during the semester. This may not sound like a lot, but I had never been able to read personal books during an academic quarter or semester.

Over the course of 14 weeks, I dropped 28 pounds and noticed significant benefits in all aspects of my life. First, my self-esteem skyrocketed due to weight lost and muscle gained. I felt better physically and was able to endure the strenuous workload required of a first-semester graduate student. There is no doubt that these benefits enabled me to stay on top of the reading, papers, and finals. For the first time in my academic career, I had the energy to do all of the required readings. My relationship with my daughter also improved because of the increased energy. Today I am able to be more present and can keep up with an extremely active 5-year-old.

I experienced so many benefits early on that I started taking as many self-care suggestions as possible. I went back to my own personal therapy to address issues that I had struggled with since childhood, started journaling, and sought out activities I truly enjoyed but had to put aside due to my academic and parental responsibilities. Further, I have committed myself to being as open and honest as I possibly can in all classes, assignments, and papers. There is no doubt that I would not have the endurance to take more than a full load of graduate school courses if it were not for my newfound self-care program. The benefits I have received from it have encouraged me to incorporate more self-care in my life. Some of my future plans include taking hikes with my daughter, playing a longer game of tag in the park, and participating in more outdoor physical activities that will benefit both me and my daughter. Personally, I believe an individual self-care program should be a part of every graduate student's life.

• • •

Nicholas Lazzareschi's graduate program highlighted self-care in every class. This focus on self-care in counseling courses creates a culture of self-care awareness.

Graduate students need healthy boundaries in their peer, faculty, and client relationships. Aaron Hatcher, also a graduate student in counseling, touches on the importance of maintaining appropriate boundaries with clients, which is key to practicing good self-care.

Self-Care as a Trainee

Aaron Hatcher

As a marriage and family therapist trainee working at an inpatient drug rehabilitation facility, self-care is one of my primary concerns. Daily I am faced with high-stress and emotionally taxing situations that require my full and undivided attention. To fully focus on the task at hand, it is essential that I maintain appropriate boundaries with my clients and invest in activities that rejuvenate me and promote my internal well-being. By engaging in activities such as hiking, reading, meditation, and musical expression, I can more easily set aside the stressors of the day. Perhaps most important is the ability to create and maintain appropriate boundaries with clients, which allows me the opportunity to fully participate in other aspects of self-care.

Defining a clear boundary around my responsibilities as a therapist is fundamental to my self-care. It is not my burden to bear the hardships my clients have endured. My clients are going through heartbreaking difficulties that often affect me personally. For my own mental and emotional stability, my clients' issues must remain my clients' issues, and not become mine. I cannot be a conduit of personal change if I am weighed down by the problems my clients face. The heartbreak can seep into aspects of my self-care and diminish the restorative qualities of the activities I enjoy. Maintaining the boundary is difficult, but it is very important to do so because, if it is broken, my effectiveness as a therapist can erode and my ability to be present in other aspects of my life declines.

Along with setting personal boundaries outside of session, it is necessary for me to set boundaries in session. My enjoyment in working with and interacting with my clients can be a catalyst for becoming overly attached and involved in the outcome of my work. Many of my clients relapse or leave rehab without prior warning, which is the nature of working in the addiction field. This can take a toll on my well-being. Setting professional boundaries and informing my clients of my role as a therapist has been helpful for me in reducing the personal impact of a client's relapse. I limit how much I self-disclose or simply remind myself of my therapeutic role, and I provide psychoeducation to my clients about the process of therapy. I believe this helps clients form appropriate expectations about the boundaries and limitations of our relationship.

To provide appropriate care and be effective in my work as a therapist trainee, I need to remember the importance of boundaries as a necessity for self-care. Like many individuals drawn to this field, I have a strong desire to help others. To do this well, having strong boundaries that are clear to me, as well as to my clients, is essential. This aspect of self-care is intertwined with all the others, and it opens a path for me to experience and involve myself in more traditional forms of self-care.

* * *

Caring for yourself in graduate school includes establishing a healthy boundary between professional and personal demands (Bamonti et al., 2014). The demands of rigorous academics and clinical training contribute to blurring that boundary line. Clara Adkins and Rhea Cooper, both master's students in counseling, have identified some key messages for graduate students who struggle with professional and personal boundaries regarding anxiety and vulnerability.

Coping With Anxiety Over Doing Well in Graduate School

Clara Adkins

In graduate school, most days I experience a constant, never-ending list of responsibilities combined with a persistent feeling of anxiety. Theoretically, I know self-care is an essential aspect of succeeding as a graduate student, but I sometimes feel I take care of myself best when I get all of my work done; completing tasks significantly reduces my anxiety.

I start every semester with an abundance of energy. As my work increases, my connections with friends and family decrease. Along with anxiety, I begin to feel isolated and overwhelmed, then guilty for not managing my time well enough to connect with my loved ones, then finally eager to find a balance.

I have noticed that finding a balance is crucial to coping with these feelings. To balance my self-care with the demands of graduate school, I take time off from school and work to spend time with loved ones.

Physical activity also helps me cope with the anxiety of doing well in graduate school. When exercising, I try to maintain a nonjudgmental attitude toward myself, especially when I struggle to exercise three times a week. Collaborating with professors and peers outside of the classroom also helps me cope with the anxiety of succeeding in graduate school. I take advantage of my graduate program's opportunities to study abroad, go to conferences, produce my own research, and collaborate on projects related to my passions.

It is easy to become unbalanced and allow the scale to tilt toward sacrificing my health for doing well in graduate school. When I feel the scales tilt, I am confronted with stress and overwhelming anxiety. Learning how to balance graduate school with taking care of myself helps me get through my program with a more positive attitude and motivates me to continue succeeding in my career. I know that this balancing act is a continual learning process. Throughout my career, I will try to be patient with myself as I strive to achieve balance.

• • •

Motivators for Becoming a Counselor

Rhea Cooper

I was accepted into a master's program for counseling in the fall of 2015. I went into the program with a significant amount of unresolved grief over losing a close friend in a car accident as well as the death of my grandmother due to a brain tumor. Going through grief in my crucial adolescent years caused me to become bitter and detached from my emotions. I had grown accustomed to masking my emotional turmoil and had internalized a cognitive distortion that vulnerability was weakness. I was the person other people depended on for support and advice. Playing this role caused me to be uncomfortable receiving help from others.

Due to this background and my beliefs, I did not believe I needed or deserved self-care going into my counseling program. I felt I should be able to take on the weight of the world and continue to give until I had nothing left. I slowly and painfully began to understand that I could not pour from an empty cup. In my program I was pushed to face my feelings of loss and grief, and this process was anxiety producing. The more anxiety began to rule my everyday tasks in graduate school, the more I realized how necessary self-care was going to be to my success. To take care of myself, I leaned on my peers and my professors. I started speaking openly to my colleagues about my feelings about the deaths of my loved ones. Talking about my experiences helped me let go of the idea that I was "OK" and did not need others. Letting go of this idea increased my genuineness and helped me to connect with my feelings of loss, which in turn improved my connection with clients.

As I reflect on my experience of loss, I know that I am motivated to become a counselor because I want to find some sense of purpose from the trials that I had endured. By assisting other people through grief, I feel that I am honoring the memory of my loved ones.

Because of my relationship with grief and loss, I have to remind myself of the importance of self-care, especially when I experience countertransference toward my clients and their presenting issues. Hearing stories of loss can trigger my own battle with grief. Even though I am able to bracket those feelings during a session for the sake of my clients, I have come to realize the importance of revisiting those emotions when I am alone.

I reach out to supervisors and peers whenever I see my red flags of compassion fatigue. These red flags include feeling drained, having less frustration tolerance, and finding it difficult to empathize with others. During these times, I remind myself that my efforts are effective even though I cannot clearly see the difference I am making in my clients' lives. I find moments to take advantage of being alone to process my thoughts and feelings, even if it is only for a few minutes each day.

My experiences with loss and grief are intertwined with my motivations for becoming a counselor and my need for self-care as a counselor. I find myself in an ongoing battle working to achieve balance in this process of self-care. It is a crusade that I may never fully complete, but I strive to improve daily in taking care of myself through processing my feelings. I have come to understand that self-care is integral to surviving my counseling journey and having a healthy, balanced, and productive life.

• • •

The Anxiety of Performing Well

Clara Adkins mentioned two prominent issues that I (Julius) experienced as a new graduate student—anxiety to do well and being patient with myself. Anxiety and patience seemed to ebb and flow throughout the duration of my graduate career, but I became aware of their role in my life the semester before I saw my first client. While learning the voice dialogue technique (a Gestalt experiment that allows clients to speak to, and hear from, different parts of themselves) in my prepracticum course, my professor allowed me to process two distinct parts of myself. *Mr. Austin* is the part of me that is anxious and avoidant, particularly in situations of responsibility that demand spontaneity and decisive action. *Dr. Austin* is the type of counselor I want to be—confident, calm under pressure, theoretically sound, and independent.

These two distinct parts of me played a role in my graduate student identity in unique ways. Mr. Austin perpetuated the idea that I was a phony or a fraud, and I was in touch with this part of my identity the majority of my time as a graduate student. The time spent as Mr. Austin was riddled with instances of avoiding genuine sharing in mock therapy sessions with my peers out of fear of being vulnerable, expecting my clients to process emotions I could not imagine talking about with my therapist, and letting professionalism in the counseling room block the process of being therapeutically present. Dr. Austin was present as my inner voice, and he brought three distinct feelings to the surface: (1) being ashamed of myself when I could not grasp a counseling technique, (2) feeling inadequate when a client decided to stop coming to counseling, and (3) believing I was inferior because I could not live up to Dr. Austin's expectations.

To make contact with Mr. Austin and Dr. Austin, I identified when I first became aware of these two parts of myself. I realized that they had been there since I started my graduate career and had played a cyclical game, the self-torture game, that signaled that my mind and body were completely unbalanced. My body (Mr. Austin) was stiff in session, demonstrated minimal body language, did not laugh, and experienced restrictive breathing. My mind (Dr. Austin) lived in the future, constantly comparing my decisions and behavior in session to Dr. Austin's expectations.

The single most influential statement from Ty Leonard, my prepracticum professor in my master's program, was "make the inside outside." This mantra allowed me to be present and to use my body and mind as tools in session. For example, I realized that my breathing became restricted when clients were pressuring me to decide for them in session. The process of making the inside outside was realizing what my psychophysiological symptoms meant and processing this meaning in the here and now with clients. With my peers and in classes, the anxiety and pressure from Dr. Austin was present when I could not grasp a concept or a technique. To make the inside outside, I processed my emotions with professors and my peers. They normalized my experiences, which drastically redefined my anxious feelings.

Transitioning From the Master's to the Doctoral Level

Clara Adkins and Rhea Cooper identified some key messages for graduate students who struggle with the professional and personal boundary at the master's level. When transitioning from the master's level to the doctoral level, this struggle may be lessened by asking relevant questions before entering a doctoral program. I (Julius) experienced a stark difference between my master's and doctoral programs. My master's program faculty were supportive of each other and their students, maintained appropriate boundaries with students, showed a strong commitment to diversity within the faculty, actively presented and researched in the profession, and had experience educating a diverse array of students.

I experienced my doctoral program faculty as relationally distant, which affected my sense of self. I sometimes felt culturally isolated and confused about expectations. As I reflect on my transition into my doctoral program of choice, I now realize that asking faculty these questions would have better prepared me to take care of myself throughout my doctoral experience:

1. How many African American males have successfully completed this PhD program? Why did they succeed or fail?
2. What is the recruitment and retention policy for domestic minority students and faculty members?
3. What is your program's philosophy on training master's students during prepracticum and practicum courses?
4. What information can you give me on the doctoral cohort I will join? What is the age, ethnicity, gender, and clinical skill makeup of the individuals in the cohort?
5. What is your policy on gatekeeping? What would my rights and responsibilities be as a student? Do you have a student handbook that contains this information?
6. How would you describe the relationships between faculty and doctoral students, faculty and master's students, and doctoral students and master's students?
7. What type of clients will I work with in the clinic or in the community?
8. How ethnically diverse is the master's cohort? What is the program's method of attracting and retaining students of color?
9. Why should I choose this program over other programs that have accepted me?

My brother and I collaborated to create this list of questions, which are based on what we wished we had known when transitioning to our doctoral experience. These questions were created to reflect our combined experiences throughout our doctoral journey.

Jude and I were the first African American men to graduate with doctorates in counselor education and supervision in the history of our university. Especially by 2016, I was not expecting to be the "first African American to . . . ," but I soon realized some faculty members did not know how to relate to me. We were uncomfortable with each other, and I experienced microaggressions through statements such as "be aware of how masculine you are" or "we want to know what you think, speak up more." I would have preferred to be asked, "How do you define masculinity as an African American man?" or "What does silence mean to you and your culture?" I immediately felt comfortable with my dissertation chair, even before I identified her as my dissertation chair, because she took the time to understand and explore my cultural worldview. Our sister, Jasmine Austin, a doctoral student in a communication studies program at a different university, shared experiences similar to my own discomfort. Here she discusses the relationship between self-worth and self-care as a doctoral student.

Self-Worth and Self-Care

● ●

Jasmine T. Austin

Preparing for my very first doctoral class involved selecting the perfect professional outfit, gathering all textbooks, and detailing notes on the first reading assignment. I highlighted quotations and drew red arrows pointing to handwritten and highly insightful questions in my notes. I used brightly colored sticky notes separating pages to emphasize the importance of words and to emphasize important concepts in papers written by academically renowned authors. I prepared and rehearsed the perfect 30-second introduction including my name, city of birth, research interests, and plan to save the world. I was prepared for anything that could be thrown into my path. Everything was accounted for—except the possibility of a classroom environment in which my voice would be insignificant among those of my cohort and professors.

Shortly after beginning the program, my perception was that graduate school was less about what you know and more about who you know. One student relentlessly name dropped, another boosted the ego of the professor, and one professor verbally attacked student contributions. One professor told me "that is the dumbest thing I've heard all day," and my contributions were constantly minimized or completely disregarded by classmates. I slowly crept into a shell of vulnerable silence. One class period, I kept a running tally of how many contributions I made in class that received no acknowledgment or response (13), and I began contributing minimally after that. My self-worth was suffering and my motivation was dwindling. My notes became less detailed, and I abandoned using sticky notes. I began trying to just get through the class period. My family members received emotional phone calls from me immediately following this class, and I questioned the very purpose of my being a doctoral student.

Feeling lower self-worth in class had a ripple effect on my daily self-care routine. I went to sleep earlier and woke up later. I began skimming the reading assignments instead of reading the content thoroughly for deeper comprehension. I exercised less frequently and began eating less healthy food. Reflecting on that class period when I had made many unacknowledged attempts to contribute, I realized it was time to boost my self-worth in the doctoral program before it continued to negatively affect other aspects of my life.

I concluded that verbal in-class participation was no longer a healthy option for my mental well-being. I found myself focused on others' minimization of my input instead of the high-quality contributions of my classmates. Once I could see past the name dropping and brownnosing, I found solace in being a fly on the wall, keeping my insightful and witty contributions to myself—where they were appreciated. My self-care included reducing participation in class and increasing my attendance during office hours. I scheduled standing weekly meetings with all my professors. I completed assignments early and presented them to the professors in their office for specific feedback. The one-on-one critiques helped me gain a better understanding of the material and earn the highest grades in the class on most assignments. Eventually, professors began asking for my thoughts during class discussion. I joined a new gym and became more active.

I ended my first semester with a 4.0 GPA because I recognized the relationship between my self-worth and self-care. Once I recognized this link, I took intentional steps to increase my feelings of self-worth. As my self-worth increased in this class, I was better able to take care of myself throughout the semester.

• • •

The Doctoral Dissertation Experience

My (Julius's) experience with a faculty member of color had a profound impact on my self-worth in my doctoral training. I thought this person's own educational and professional experiences would provide me with a unique perspective on the cultural undertones and psychological endurance required to complete my doctoral program. Unfortunately, the lack of communication, mentorship, or even acknowledgment at times left me questioning my very worth. I perceived this faculty member as having power to influence my education and as an elder in my profession. In my culture, I value the acceptance and acknowledgment of my elders. I turn to them for wisdom and for guidance, so it was culturally appropriate to welcome this person onto my committee as a vital member in my dissertation experience.

A series of unanswered emails, missed meetings, and lack of feedback at crucial points in the dissertation research process began to affect the quality of my research results and spoil the final stages of my graduate education. Our relationship became increasingly strained. This individual was not present at my prospectus meeting and did not provide any feedback on my prospectus document but later pointed out a discrepancy between my research methods and results and what was agreed upon during the prospectus phase of my dissertation. I remember feeling powerless, and I felt blocked from achieving my dream. This experience sparked a series of questions: (1) What if my research was not good enough? (2) What if I was not good enough? (3) Do I have control over my own success?

After graduating and beginning my career, I had the opportunity to engage in a dialogue with this faculty member without having to temper my thoughts out of fear that this discussion could interfere with my educational goal. After hearing my thoughts about my experience, this faculty member offered a genuine and heartfelt apology. I took solace in that, and it added closure for me. The doctoral dissertation can indeed be an intense experience and a difficult phase of training for graduate students. In the following piece, Danielle Sirles and Gerald Pennie discuss maintaining self-care throughout the dissertation process.

Maintaining Self-Care Throughout the Dissertation Process

Danielle N. Sirles and Gerald Pennie

The dissertation process is one of the most exciting and rewarding experiences of the doctoral program. It also is one of the most exhausting and brutal tasks a student will ever undertake! As mental health practitioners and researchers, we stress the importance of self-care to our clients and students, but it was a bit trickier to practice what we preach throughout our own dissertation process. To maintain self-care throughout this process, we remained flexible, took nothing personally, constantly gauged what we needed, and discovered our limits.

Writing a dissertation requires more tenacity and flexibility than any other academic endeavor. From the need to constantly submit and revise a document that has been in the works for some time, to the endless scrutiny of our methodology and use of theory, flexibility was key to our success and self-care. Flexibility allowed us to accept the inherent imperfections in our research; it allowed us to work collaboratively with members of our research team and dissertation committee; and it allowed us to "roll with the punches" when we encountered unforeseen obstacles along the way.

Learning not to take anything personally was easier said than done. It is easy to feel the need to defend every word and choice as if our lives depended on it. However, doing this only resulted in feelings of frustration and resentment. We had to remember that our committee members were there to extract greatness from us and our projects. In doing this, they sometimes made recommendations and demands that felt like a personal attack. We fought the urge to take it personally! We pushed ourselves to remember that their feedback came from a caring place.

To take care of ourselves throughout the dissertation process, we also checked in with our own selves and gauged what we needed on a regular basis. We constantly asked ourselves if we were eating well-balanced meals, finding time to exercise, getting sufficient sleep, balancing productivity with engaging in fun activities, and asking for help when we needed it from colleagues, friends, and family. Asking for help when we needed it proved to be crucial for both of us, and we would often check in with each other and would rely on each other for emotional and academic support. Having each other held us accountable for our self-care. We found that having an accountability partner for self-care throughout the dissertation process is just as important as having a work accountability partner!

Gauging what we needed also meant learning our limits. Everyone's personal warning signs are different, but some red flags we encountered included having a hard time focusing on anything but our dissertation tasks, constantly battling fatigue, feeling irritable, isolating ourselves from loved ones, missing meals because we were "too busy," and having periods when we loathed our projects. One of the most stressful times during this journey for me (Gerald) came at the end. I was working to complete the recommended revisions when my committee asked me once again to justify the use of my methodology. This left me scrambling to strengthen the arguments in my dissertation at a point in time when I thought the worst was behind me. My (Danielle's) frustration almost derailed me when a committee member with a firm grasp of the data analysis techniques used in my study moved to another state to pursue different career interests, leaving me in need of guidance.

We both felt frustrated and even lost at times, but we knew we needed to take a step back in these moments and reassess how well we were implementing self-care. Taking care of ourselves during the most trying endeavor of our academic careers was really difficult at times. Remaining flexible, taking nothing personally, gauging what we needed, and learning our limits are strategies that helped us reach our goal. We constantly reminded each other that we were not alone in this process, and we encouraged each other to reach out for help when we needed it. Above all, we believed that this process is survivable!

* * *

Jude Austin's Growth and Change in Graduate School

As I (Jude) reflect on my self-care process during graduate school, many of the experiences shared throughout this chapter resonate with me. I spent most of my time as a graduate student adjusting to the unavoidable stress and multiple demands of my graduate program. My master's graduate experience taught me this: Becoming a counselor is hard, and committing to self-care during this process is even harder. The most challenging aspect of graduate school for me was gaining more awareness of who I was within the context of a therapeutic relationship and bringing myself into that relationship genuinely and fully. For example, in my master's practicum, some clients triggered my personal reactions, and I had to carefully monitor my countertransference. I remember checking my personal reactions at the door until my supervisor said, "If you check yourself at the door, what do you think your clients are doing?" So I began my process of bringing myself more fully into my sessions. That process was and still is exhausting. I have learned that one way for me to cope with this exhaustion is to do my processing and thinking about the therapeutic relationship out loud in a session.

A large part of my reluctance to bring myself more fully into a session was a fear of failure. Like Clara Adkins and most other students, I strove to succeed in graduate school. As I began to be more myself in my work with clients by processing and thinking out loud, I redefined success and was more patient with myself. Success in graduate school became more about pushing myself to be brave in session—just as brave as my clients had to be to walk into the counseling center. I became more patient with myself by owning the fact that I was a student and thus was not expected to know everything. I was involved in my supervision, which anchored me, and I felt less pressure to succeed and more freedom to connect with my clients. I was less concerned in session with saying the wrong thing and more concerned with saying the genuine thing. This invited my clients to be more genuine with me. Finding a way to anchor myself and not judge myself improved both my effectiveness as a counselor and my experience in my master's degree program.

I went on to my doctoral program with a great amount of self-efficacy and enthusiasm to grow and learn. As a doctoral student, I struggled and fought to maintain my identity. It was difficult for me to connect with some of my faculty, and it was difficult for some of them to connect with me. I also felt that I did not get the support I needed. I felt like I was defending my philosophies and ideas to individuals who did not know me and who did not understand my experience. I frequently walked away from faculty interactions with negative feelings about myself. When I met with my cohort members, who were part of the dominant culture, they described drastically different interactions with faculty. I felt helpless, which fostered a great deal of self-doubt. As Jasmine described earlier in this chapter, my self-worth was tied to my ability to maintain my self-care.

When I began to meet other counselor educators and when I reached out to other African American counselor educators, I finally was able to step back from my doctoral experience and reflect on it more objectively. These relationships helped put my doctoral experience in perspective. I recognized the need to set boundaries between my doctoral experience, my professional growth, and my self-worth. I learned to become less emotionally reactive during interactions with my faculty and more observant. This enabled me to navigate experiences without allowing them to diminish my self-worth, which improved my self-care and my effectiveness as a counselor, educator, supervisor, and researcher.

When I began to write my dissertation, these boundaries helped me work independently and cope with situations that others in my cohort did not encounter. I had difficulty scheduling meetings with faculty and received little or late feedback from committee members who seemed to provide timely feedback to other students. I felt my work was being judged by a different standard than that of my White peers, and I finally had this experience validated by peers and faculty who were willing to acknowledge that I was being treated differently. Although my experience with setting boundaries helped me work independently, I found the dissertation writing process to be the most isolating experience of my life. To balance that isolation, I joined a local gym that met many of my needs for organization, community, exercise, and distraction throughout that time. I was part of that community until I graduated, and I owe them a significant amount of gratitude for providing a place where I felt safe.

Working to secure a counselor educator faculty position while completing my doctoral program provided other obstacles to my self-care program. I did not want to be hired because I was African American, so I pushed myself to publish and work on projects. It was as if the word "no" did not exist in my vocabulary. The job application process is a full-time job in itself. I was inundated with job postings from websites and listservs. I took care of myself throughout this process by being organized. I created spreadsheets with details about each position: the job title, university and program mission, job description, location, starting salary, current faculty, and other pertinent information. I created a system that allowed me to track the stages of the application process, and I spoke to five individuals who I thought would write letters of recommendation for me. During this period, I experienced a tremendous amount of anxiety. Once the application deadlines were met, the process of waiting began. I went through every scenario in my head: What if I don't get an interview? What if I get every interview? What if I don't hear back from anyone?

I took care of myself throughout this waiting process by preparing for phone or video interviews. I prepared for the questions I expected to be asked and for the ones I wanted to ask. I broke the interview process into three categories: paper, phone/video, or on campus. This made the process of preparing my answers less overwhelming. I relied on my organizational skills and my ability to focus on the small details as opposed to the big picture throughout the preparation process. I knew that I should focus on each step individually lest I put too much importance on one piece and get in my own way during interviews. I believed that the paper application process was a way to introduce myself to the search committees and to raise their curiosity enough to invite me for a phone or video interview.

When I was invited to my first phone interview, I felt overwhelmed by the pressure to get a job. I thought about what a job would do for my wife and me and our future children. I believe I put too much pressure on myself to succeed. To take care of myself, I reached out to my mentors who put the phone interview into perspective. Many of my mentors shared that the phone interview is the search committee's chance to get to know you. As my mentor explained, "the only way you can fail is if you do not allow them the opportunity to get to know you." I decided to be as genuine as I could be instead of trying to figure out what the interviewers wanted to hear. My mentors also encouraged me to appreciate the job interview experience while I was going through it. I took some time to reflect on the work and sacrifices that made the opportunity to interview for a faculty position possible. I thought about ways I could communicate these experiences and my passion to the interviewers. This strategy helped me mentally and emotionally prepare to speak with people who might become my new colleagues.

After I completed my interviews, I waited to be invited for an on-campus interview. I took care of myself throughout this nerve-wracking waiting process by preparing. I again contacted mentors and asked them what I should prepare for during the on-campus interviews. Many of them suggested that I prepare a teaching or research presentation that illustrated my knowledge as well as a realistic demonstration of my teaching ability. They suggested that I familiarize myself with faculty via their program website. I asked faculty and doctoral students in my program if I could practice my presentation in their classes. Preparing and practicing eased my anxiety and helped improve my self-care.

I prepared for the interview process to begin as soon as face-to-face contact was made with anyone from the university. The itineraries during the on-campus interviews were filled with meetings, presentations, small and large group interviews, tours, demonstrations, lunches, and dinners. There was very little space to regroup, breathe, or allow myself to process my experience. I felt constantly evaluated and observed. Within my limited space, I implemented some strategies to recharge and present my best self: I drank plenty of water, got adequate sleep, and practiced deep and full breathing during the campus tour and between meetings. I communicated with my family via text when appropriate. During the on-campus interview process, I connected with many faculty members, students, and staff members. Throughout the process, I struggled to balance allowing myself to connect but keeping myself safe in case I did not get the job. I experienced this inner tension more fully when I received my first rejection after an on-campus interview. I remember feeling a sense that stars had aligned and that this university would be the perfect environment for me to start my career and for my wife and me to live. I loved the faculty and thought there was mutual excitement about me working alongside them.

When the interview concluded, I went home and again took care of myself by preparing. I spent a great deal of time making specific plans should I be offered the position. In the midst of preparation, I received a call informing me that they would not be extending an offer to me for that position. I was heartbroken, and I felt like a failure. I replayed the entire interview process in my head and tried to figure out what I could have done differently.

This was one of the lowest points for me in graduate school. I was in a doctoral program that threatened my belief in my abilities, my self-care, and my mental and emotional well-being. I was also completing my dissertation research and preparing to defend my dissertation. I was living alone. I went through an emotionally exhausting job search process, followed by a job interview process, yet I was not chosen for the position. To take care of myself, I gave myself a week to mourn the loss of that job. During that week I continued my exercise program, regularly contacted my family and friends, and tried not to run away from my emotions. I wondered if I had the energy to go through the interview process again only to be rejected.

Shortly after this rejection, I was invited to another on-campus interview with Old Dominion University's Counseling and Human Services Department. Although I was excited, I cared for myself by being present in the moment during the interview process. I avoided imagining what it would be like to work there, I did not think about where I would live, finding friends, or any other aspects regarding the future if the job were to be offered to me. I believe remaining present in the moment during this on-campus interview allowed me to be more genuine throughout the process. Shortly after my on-campus interview, I was offered the assistant professor position. During the negotiation process, I was mindful of all of the things I would need to support my self-care. Throughout the entire job search process I was still collecting and analyzing data for my dissertation study and contributing to textbooks and doing other scholarly work.

My experience in graduate school shaped the professional I am today. I learned what I want and do not want my students to experience in their graduate program. I learned what kind of faculty member I want to be and not be. I also learned what impact I want to have on my students as well as the kind of impact I want to avoid having. In retrospect, preparation, organization, humility, and perseverance were the keys to my self-care throughout the job search process. In addition, finding mentors who expressed their care for me helped me feel supported. Because of my graduate school experience, I now know what I need to do to maintain my self-care as a new professional.

Twins' Experiences of Self-Care in Graduate School

We (Julius and Jude) are identical twins. We were born into a relationship that provides us with a unique perspective on building therapeutic relationships in graduate school. Although we cannot read each other's mind, we do have a deep connection to each other's thoughts and feelings and how they influence our relationship. Throughout graduate school, we have learned to use this natural connection with clients and students. As we reflect on our experience in graduate school, we realize that our most unhealthy times were when general circumstances or specific instances impeded our ability to connect with each other and with those around us.

Our least healthy experiences together as graduate students occurred while attaining our doctoral degrees. It was during this time that we had to confront the idea that institutional racism existed in any, let alone in our own, counseling doctoral program. We imagine that the way we describe these experiences will be received differently by readers who have varying degrees of privilege or experiences in counselor education. We hope our experiences spark empathy, recognition, and awareness within readers who may not be cognizant of the difficulties some minority students face in graduate school today.

As we adjusted to being doctoral students and counselor educators-in-training, our program had to adjust to having African American males in their program. Shortly after beginning the graduate program, we learned we would be only the second and third African Americans to complete this graduate program in the university's history and the first African American males to graduate from a program that had been accredited since 1982. This created an atmosphere in which we felt a pull to lose our culture in order to have a safer experience in our doctoral program. We received feedback that seemed clumsy and more out of cultural ignorance than for the benefit of our growth. These circumstances caused us to feel confused, disconnected, undervalued, and both needed and unwanted at the same time. The threat to our self-care as doctoral students was having to constantly question our experiences, particularly because our cohorts from the dominant culture had completely different experiences. The drastic differences between our experiences and those of our cohorts resulted in our feeling alienated.

Our health was significantly affected by our feelings of alienation, being disconnected from our faculty and peers, confusion, and feeling discriminated against on different occasions. Some discriminatory actions were innocuous such as faculty changing their vocal tone and dialect when speaking to us compared to other students. Other actions were blatant, such as faculty refusing to sign paperwork or to schedule meetings that students of the dominant culture had less difficulty arranging. Questioning our reality eroded our self-esteem and our mental health.

We took care of each other by creating a space where we could reflect on and process our experiences together. We validated each other's experience, which eased our feelings of confusion. By clarifying the meaning of our experiences, we were able to develop a plan to confront our faculty and to find resources. Our self-care plan included:

1. Gaining a better understanding of our experiences.
2. Seeking out mentors who made us feel safe to share our experience with and get advice.
3. Creating opportunities to safely express our concerns to our faculty.
4. Working with faculty to create and implement culturally sensitive policies.

Unfortunately, we did not feel understood, and no policy changes occurred. We worked hard to support each other in this challenging environment. We stuck to steps one and two of our self-care plan throughout the remainder of our doctoral experience. We used each other as sounding boards and provided for each other what our faculty and peers could not provide for us.

Our most poignant takeaway from our graduate school experience is our belief that we can face any experience in our professional career if we continue to support each other. We are currently working at different universities and spend limited time together, which has not been easy for us. Attending graduate school together gave us a greater appreciation for how difficult this experience can be for students who are without a twin and face these challenges alone. Now, as counselor educators, we strive to provide a space where our students feel safe to express their thoughts and feelings without judgment, to feel connected with their peers and faculty, and to feel a sense of equality in our classrooms and programs.

Embracing Challenges and Getting the Most Out of Your Graduate Education

Graduate school years are a period of intense personal and professional growth. Whether you are a master's student grappling with self-doubts about your competence and suitability for clinical work or a doctoral student burdened with anxiety about the dissertation process or passing the PhD comprehensive exam, few would argue that graduate school can be stressful and difficult to navigate. For this reason alone, self-care is a must! One way to get the most out of your graduate school program and to buffer yourself from the negative effects of such intense training is to seek out mentorship. Some of the contributors' accounts directly or indirectly described how mentors helped them navigate their graduate education and improved their sense of self-efficacy and well-being. Here are a few messages to consider for deriving the maximum benefit from your graduate school education:

- Ask for help when you need it, and be assertive in asking for what you need in your education and supervision.
- Be willing to recognize your fears, doubts, and negative self-messages; and be willing to takes steps to deal with what might hold you back.
- Move outside your comfort zone and take risks, both personally and professionally.
- Ask yourself where you can best put your unique talents to work and where you can make the greatest contribution.
- Develop self-discipline, be willing to work hard, and don't give up when the road is rough. Don't let discouragement get the best of you.
- Realize that you will probably have to make financial sacrifices during graduate school and as a new professional.
- Be an active learner and come prepared to get the most from supervision.
- Be open with your supervisors about your mistakes and share with them what concerns you most about your work with clients.
- Strive to do your best, but avoid the trap of perfectionism. Don't equate making mistakes with being a failure.
- Join major professional associations and attend professional conferences if you can to enrich your learning and network with other counseling professionals.
- Write proposals to present with fellow students and faculty at conferences.
- Read professional journals, watch videos on counseling, and attend continuing education programs.
- Say "yes" to opportunities as often as you can, especially early in your education and career. Once you are established in your career, you can be more selective about the opportunities you choose to take.

Questions for Reflection

1. Reflect on your self-care needs during your time in graduate school (past or current) or in any other intense learning environment. What strategies were/are most helpful and least helpful in managing your stress?
2. What is your reaction to the statement that one way you can take care of yourself in graduate school is by making sure all your school responsibilities are completed?
3. How do you know when graduate school responsibilities are having a negative impact on your ability to care for yourself?

4. Most people do not have a twin sibling with whom to attend graduate school. In your own life, who do you rely on the most for emotional support during stressful times?

Concluding Thoughts

This chapter highlighted several aspects of self-care in graduate school, including motivators for becoming a counselor, self-worth and self-care, growth and change in graduate school, maintaining self-care through the dissertation process, and embracing challenges and getting the most out of your graduate education. These stories were meant to spark awareness and to be a catalyst for change in your life. It is our hope that you visualize yourself in the shoes of the contributors, and Jude and Julius Austin as well, and find commonalities in their attempts at caring for themselves in graduate school. Self-care during this rather intense period of time, whether it be a 2-year master's program or a 5-year doctoral program, is a process that will look different for each of you. It is important to understand your self-care needs and to cultivate an environment that meets those needs. Although it may be difficult to carve out time for self-care while also trying to meet educational and research deadlines, finding a balance between attending to your personal needs and navigating the rigors of graduate school may continue to influence your idea of self-care long after this experience comes to an end.

Chapter 4

Personal and Professional Stressors

Why do counselors struggle to take care of themselves? Why do we take better care of our clients than we do ourselves? Why do counselor educators sacrifice so much personally for tenure? Why do we overbook our schedules? Why do we accept having a caseload of way too many clients when we are stretched to capacity with far fewer of them? What drives the internal emotional and cognitive mechanisms that cause so many of us to maintain high achievement at the cost of our health? There is probably no single answer to many of these questions, and there appears to be no end to this line of questioning. Many contributors who have shared their experiences seem to have a similar self-care journey. This journey includes a pattern in which individuals experience a prolonged period of stress, slip into something akin to burnout, have an "aha moment" that shocks them into awareness, choose to make a change, and then try, with varying degrees of success, to follow a self-care plan. In this chapter, we address these questions and examine the impact that personal and professional stressors have on us. We cover topics such as losing our way as counselors, experiencing setbacks, the influence of personality traits and control issues on self-care, wellness and grief, and adjusting to positive personal changes.

Life and Stress: You Can't Have One Without the Other

Let's face it, life is inherently stressful, and one reason clients seek counseling is to unburden themselves of their stress and pain.

Whether hoping to come to terms with a dysfunctional or toxic relationship, grieving the loss of a loved one, working through a traumatic experience, or having to make a consequential life decision, people often reach out for professional support when struggling to cope with stressors—not when they have a good handle on their stress. Counselors are trained to listen empathically for hours to stories laden with pain and sadness. They hear stories revolving around emotionally difficult themes such as loss and despair, oppression and powerlessness, rejection, and outrage. To be fair, counselors also hear positive reports from clients who share their stories of success, personal growth, and healing. However, the process of achieving these great strides often involves a lot of hard work and the willingness to delve into painful psychological and emotional territory. Thus, by the very nature of their work, counselors are likely to get a potent dose of stress on a daily basis simply through listening to their clients' experiences.

In addition to listening to the stressful content of client disclosures, counselors are likely to encounter a range of other stressors that simply are part of the terrain of their jobs. These include dealing with high-risk clients; keeping up with paperwork; dealing with the demands and internal politics of agencies, school systems, or other institutions; facing financial pressures; dealing with insurance companies; encountering risks of ethics complaints; working in isolation; managing value conflicts with clients; and learning to leave work at the office, just to name a few. Certainly the work we do as counselors is not easy.

Faced with so many professional stressors, it would be ideal if counselors' personal lives were relatively stress free. Unfortunately, counselors and other mental health practitioners are not immune from the pressures and stresses that affect everyone else. Counselors may experience the death of loved ones, interpersonal conflicts with family members and others, divorce and custody battles, financial problems, physical and mental health issues, racism, sexism, other forms of discrimination, and struggles finding a healthy work–life balance.

Moreover, living in the age of globalization and social media, we cannot escape the constant bombardment of stressful news about local, national, and international events. Attached to our smartphones, it takes mere seconds to find out about crises occurring locally and throughout the nation and the world as they unfold in real time. It can be exhausting for counselors to have to process their own reactions to major stressful events occurring in the world, and then to spend so much time each week helping their clients process their reactions to the same events.

Losing Our Way and Finding Our Way Back

At times, we may find that we lose our way due to competing demands from our personal and our professional lives. Whether we are graduate students juggling demanding school, work, and personal/social schedules or seasoned professionals who have taken on more projects than we can reasonably handle, many of us neglect our self-care, arguably, when we need it most. But if we are lost, we do not have to remain lost. Leah Brew, a professor and chair of a counseling program, describes how she tries to engage in self-care, but fails at it continuously. With the multiple professional roles she wields, it is difficult for her to find a balance between her personal and her professional life. As you read Leah Brew's account, can you relate to parts of her story?

Self-Care: Lost and Found?

● ●

Leah Brew

I am an only child with an anxious, highly sensitive, and introverted temperament, who was raised by anxious, highly sensitive, and introverted parents, and unsurprisingly developed a self-diagnosed dismissive-avoidant attachment style. I spent most of my childhood at home alone, a latch-key kid with parents who believed that children were to be seen and not heard. I complied. I was expected to overachieve and to internalize all my feelings. I complied here too. Looking back, I can see myself as having lived in a little silo, with a flavor of loneliness and existential angst.

In my master's program I learned about myself. I discovered that my anxiety was partially related to my temperament. I also scored high on Introversion on the Myers-Briggs Type Indicator, which meant that I needed to be alone to recharge. I ascertained that the combined influences of my upbringing and temperament increased my anxiety and feelings of stress. In fact, chronic stress-related tension and migraine headaches started at the age of 8 and lasted until I studied biofeedback in my master's program, where I learned to self-regulate. This was my introduction to self-care. I learned to consciously spend time alone to rejuvenate. I found I needed regular exercise and time to meditate to clear my head. When I engaged in these self-care behaviors, my headaches became infrequent and were usually allergy-related if they did emerge.

During my doctoral program, I was able to better articulate my feelings of loneliness and learned about my attachment style. As a consequence of these discoveries, I longed for interpersonal connection and to have an earned-secure attachment style, which I believed was the remedy for my loneliness. In 2001 I moved from Texas to California for an assistant professor position, and I was poised to work on myself even more. I sought to create a better version of me by continuing my self-care and focusing on my personal growth.

By the time I met my husband 4 years later, I believed (and still do) that I had reached my goal of moving toward an earned-secure attachment style. I made that determination by assessing the health of my friendships and by how healthy I perceive my husband to be; my previous relationships had always been less healthy. I lost that sense of loneliness that had plagued me my entire life. By the time my husband and I married, my life felt rich and full, and I was skilled at self-care. One year after marrying, we had a daughter. My pregnancy and her early infancy were delightful. Six months later, everything came crashing down. I had just received tenure the year my daughter was born, and I was voted in as department chair. This was 2008, when the economy crashed. As part of learning this new job, I had to navigate severe budget cuts, lay off adjunct faculty, take away release time to increase teaching loads of our full-time faculty members, and enforce ridiculous furloughs that required we do 10% less work (which didn't happen) for 10% less pay (which did happen). With a baby, an increase in responsibilities, and the new financial environment, I abandoned my self-care regimen that year.

Since that time 8 years ago, I have learned my job well. The budget cuts have abated, but I have failed at balancing my primary roles as mother, wife, department chair, professor/instructor, and a counselor and a supervisor in a private practice. I rarely have any alone time, and most of my roles require intense interpersonal interaction. So I am often anxious.

I have given up trying to balance these roles. I have realized that balance is a fallacy impossible for many working mothers to achieve. Something has to be done poorly. I simply rotate my priorities to get through each day. I make exercise a priority, except at midterms and finals when my grading increases. My meditation is infrequent, but maybe two-thirds of each semester I get to practice yoga. I try to be present with my daughter and not look at my emails when we are spending "family time," but not during midterms and finals. My husband gets the short end of the stick with only a few date nights each month and a few hours on weekend nights to watch TV. However, I thoroughly enjoy how I spend my time with my family and at work. I suck at self-care though; I fail at it continuously. I strive for it but now look at it as an aspirational goal. At least I love my life, and I try to engage in self-care. Oh, how I try!

● ● ●

Experiencing Setbacks in Our Self-Care

The challenges that Leah Brew encountered as a department chair during an especially difficult economic period illustrate the unfortunate fact that life can throw us curve balls. Even when we make progress in prioritizing self-care in our daily lives, it is unrealistic to expect that we won't ever experience setbacks. Sometimes, through no fault of our own, we must adapt to changing circumstances and may find it more difficult to make time for self-care. Thus, for some of us, instead of expecting a linear progression in which we steadily improve our self-care practice over time, it may be more realistic to anticipate fluctuations in our self-care depending on what's happening in our lives. I (Michelle) certainly have experienced periods of time when my workload was so demanding that I had limited time to invest in self-care and my self-care suffered. On nights when I have come home from work late, for instance, instead of taking the time to prepare a healthy meal (which admittedly would have been better to eat earlier in the day, not at 11:30 p.m.!), I grab something out of the fridge that is convenient and perhaps not so healthy. I struggle with finding balance in my life and can easily become so absorbed in work that I neglect self-care. I am coming to accept that achieving balance is an elusive goal, at least it is for me. Sometimes I do a better job of giving myself sufficient time to relax, get some physical exercise, and eat more nutritious meals, but I have much room to improve. One thing is for certain: Balance, once achieved, does not seem likely to last indefinitely. Life is just too unpredictable and dynamic. The balance I have struck today may look different than the balance I strike tomorrow. To borrow Leah Brew's words, "rotating priorities" seems to aptly describe the way I approach my life.

Judy Van Der Wende, a psychologist in private practice, describes a pattern of getting lost in the demands of her work, and then finding her way to a more balanced life. She talks about challenges she faced during her mid-career phase and how she developed simple self-care strategies to find her way back.

Learning to Smell the Roses

Judy Van Der Wende

Being a full-time psychologist in private practice for the last 15 years has taught me the necessity of taking care of myself. I was quite surprised when I began practice and found that virtually all of the older, wiser practitioners I shared office space with had back problems. I noticed their tendency to sit all day, seeing client after client without a break, using time between clients for phone calls and paperwork instead of stretching and walking. I determined not to make this mistake.

Of course, I did exactly the same thing. We all do. Losing my way and finding it again has been part of my process of becoming a better psychotherapist. What I did not expect was to default to old, learned coping behaviors when faced with the stress of starting a private practice. I didn't expect to be so confused and worried about clients as a new therapist and not know what to do with these feelings. I didn't expect to automatically default to my old coping behaviors, such as depending on coffee instead of exercise. It was confusing to find that old strategies were now counterproductive.

The frustrating and maddening thing is knowing what to do differently—having a background of exercising and meditating—but getting stuck anyway due to the onslaught of current pressure. The life-saving change for me was attending a stellar continuing education class focused on the biology of sleep.

I not only learned about sleep, but I actively started making the lifestyle changes to improve my sleep. Every change reinforced the next, and the changes became delightful. It was fun to share this information with clients from a learned, felt perspective rather than advising them based on theory. What a great conversation starter this became, and what a terrific way to connect with clients!

Making changes to sleep led to short 10- to 15-minute walks twice a day (and more when possible), meditating twice a day (progressive relaxation plus visualization for another 15 minutes), and converting the backyard into an organic garden. A significant change was in learning to breathe with a technique that slows the fight-flight response. My husband and I also chose to stop drinking alcohol, soft drinks, and caffeine (I am not there yet with the caffeine!).

All of these changes have been significant, but they did not stop the underlying Type A beliefs that drive me, like so many others who achieve doctorates. I would work 12 hour days 7 days per week if left to my own devices; there is just that much to do. I am now working on the idea of being "good enough," simply doing my job, not feeling driven to do that job plus, plus, plus. Clearly this is an ongoing process. One of the joys of being a therapist is having the opportunity to teach others how to feel better. I have been able to learn what I teach and have incorporated these changes. I have found it particularly helpful to use some cognitive behavioral tools to change my limiting Type A beliefs. For instance, I evaluate the "should" and "oughts" that plague me at times and have taken steps to challenge problematic beliefs. Also very helpful has been learning better boundaries. I am more clear on separating "work" and "play" and sticking to the separation. It is hard to change, but feeling better is incredibly reinforcing.

I guess you can call this my "Learning to Smell the Roses Phase." I ask myself, what is the point of all the hard work if you can't enjoy it? Changing my own beliefs will take a lot more work, but my daily meditating, walking, and healthy eating have been so good I actually feel ready to smell those roses. The effect on clients is profound—having a therapist who walks her talk is deeply meaningful to many. I have learned to watch out for my old default coping behaviors, to take a breath and relax instead of pushing harder. And I sleep very well indeed!

• • •

Questions for Reflection

1. What are your warning signs that you are starting to lose your way in your self-care practice? When you notice these signals, how do you react?

2. If you have lost your way due to competing demands in your life and an overloaded schedule, what do you think would be most helpful in getting your self-care back on track? What one small step could you take today in the direction of finding your way back to self-care practices that you enjoy and that replenish you?

3. Do you believe achieving balance is a fallacy, as Leah Brew stated, or is it something you can achieve and sustain?

4. If you have a propensity to engage in Type A thinking and relentlessly push yourself to exceed your limits and neglect your self-care needs, what underlying beliefs or cognitive distortions drive this behavior?

5. How do you incorporate your failed attempts at achieving balance in your goals toward self-care?

Personality Traits and Personal Stressors

Personal stressors can manifest in myriad ways and vary in severity (or intensity) and duration. Some of this stress may result from our personality traits or our own unresolved internal struggles. We may wrestle with perfectionism, self-esteem issues, anxiety, or depression, for example, which can exacerbate our feelings of stress. Although we regularly assist our clients in examining how they get in their own way, we may neglect to take an inventory of the ways that we hinder ourselves. Addictions counselor and doctoral candidate Stephanie Robinson found that coming to terms with her intense need to engage in controlling behaviors was instrumental in helping her to improve her self-care practice. As you read Stephanie's account, consider the characteristics or traits that create stress in your life.

Coming to Terms With My Need for Control

Stephanie Robinson

My way of coping with life's stressors had always been to be in control. I was a "controller" from an early age. My mother regularly shares the story of my younger sister and I playing school—I was the teacher, my sister was the student. When my sister wanted to be the teacher and I wouldn't let her, she told my mother, who insisted I let her be the teacher—so I became the principal. I couldn't even play without being in control. I experienced this same need to control in many situations growing up and into early adulthood. I was not introduced to the concept of self-care until I entered my master's program at Loyola University New Orleans, and I soon realized that I desperately needed an outlet for my intense need to control. I began by examining my current self-care behaviors and found I was doing little to address this issue. I began to actively work on this "controlling" characteristic, and I continue to work on this aspect of my personality today.

I am a doctoral student now, and the focus of my dissertation and research is on the addiction counseling licensure process. I also work part time at a local university, and I have a small private practice specializing in work with individuals with addictive use disorders. Clients with addictive use disorders present their own set of challenges, and more often than not they have a comorbid diagnosis: generational systemic family issues, intense trauma, extreme boundary issues, and very often personality disorders. These mental health combinations can make for intense sessions. In addition, I am a mother to a 3-year-old girl and wife to a man who works equally as hard as I do. With the many hats I wear on a daily basis, how could I possibly have time for self-care, and how could I possibly not engage in more controlling behaviors?

After doing a lot of personal work and a lot of self-reflection on why I control, I have found a system of self-care that works for me and my busy life. The time I spend with my family provides the most relaxation, enjoyment, and decompression for me. My day starts with mommy-daughter alone time. Every morning, I drive my daughter to school, which is our alone time. We sing and talk about things 3-year-olds talk about, or sometimes we just sit quietly with each other. This morning alone time with my daughter provides me with the balance and gratitude I need to begin my day. Most evenings, she and I spend a few hours alone again before my husband gets home. We dance, we build with blocks, we read (usually the same story over and over again), or watch whatever movie she is into at that moment. Unless it's an emergency, I do not take phone calls and I do not do work. I try very hard not to think about my clients or my school work. When my husband gets home from work and our daughter is tucked into bed, he and I have our alone time. We eat dinner together almost every night. My weekends are typically reserved for my family as well. It could be the three of us going on a family outing or just my daughter and me going to gymnastics.

As planned out and controlled as this system for self-care sounds, it doesn't always go this smoothly. I experience setbacks, and sometimes there are emergencies. Sometimes my husband works late or has to go out of town. Sometimes my daughter cries the whole way to school and wants nothing to do with me in the evening. Sometimes . . . life is in control. It is during these times that my need to overly control resurfaces and I'm forced to sit with what make me uncomfortable—not being in control. My ongoing personal work and the boundaries I have set for my work–life balance have taught me an important lesson: Attempting to control what I cannot control is an effort in futility that will only ever result in frustration.

● ● ●

Stress in Our Personal Lives

In addition to personality traits and internal issues, stress may result from our connections with others. The roles we adopt in our personal lives, such as being partners/spouses, parents, sons and daughters, extended family members, friends, neighbors, and community members, also bring stress at times.

Many of our friends and colleagues in the counseling profession have shared the everyday challenges they face navigating their multiple family roles and responsibilities. One friend expressed concerns about affording the exorbitant cost of her daughter's college tuition at a private university while simultaneously worrying about the affordability of health care for her aging mother who is showing signs of dementia. Another colleague feels constantly stressed about her son's recently diagnosed learning disability and the negative impact it is having on his self-esteem and well-being, especially when certain classmates tease and bully him. Terminal illness and the death of loved ones often push us to our very limits, rendering self-care all the more a necessity. Norma Day-Vines, the program lead and professor of the counseling and human development program at Johns Hopkins University, poignantly describes the tragedy that struck her and her daughter's life and how she found self-care in a most unexpected way—caring for their new pet.

Wellness and Grief

Norma L. Day-Vines

From the time our daughter was about 5 years old, she begged my husband and me for a dog. She would write us letters, prepare and conduct PowerPoint presentations, and ask to visit the local animal shelter. With the demands of work and parenting, and no matter how convincingly she promised to walk and feed the dog, we knew having a dog was not practical for us. Were we to get a dog, we thought there was a strong possibility that our daughter might retreat from her earlier promise to care for her pet. Fast forward several years to 2012, when my husband was diagnosed with a very aggressive form of cancer. After 27 years of marriage, I realized that we would probably not grow old together as we had planned. I believed that couples were connected for richer or for poorer, better or worse, but in my wildest dreams I never imagined that sickness and health would be a marital challenge before the age of, say, 65 or 70. Following a protracted battle with the disease, my husband passed away. The grief was unimaginable.

When it became clear that my husband would not survive, I suggested that he give our daughter a memento to remember him. Honestly, I had a piece of jewelry in mind; however, his idea was a dog. I made good on his promise, and we bought her a chocolate Labrador Retriever puppy. Little did I know that the dog would facilitate my grief process.

Although the grieving process was difficult for both my daughter and me, the dog actually made life more manageable in some ways. Having a dog helped me grapple with my unimaginable grief. For the first year following our loss, I walked the dog every morning at 5:30 a.m. Exercise helps combat depression, boosts mood, reduces anxiety, improves sleep, and sharpens memory, and I believe the residual benefits of having a dog helped me manage life more effectively.

Prayer also has been an integral source of my well-being. My husband was a very spiritual man, very active in our church, served on the deacon's ministry, and took delight in serving the Lord. In the months prior to his death, at his insistence, I joined a women's group that helped me understand the importance of praising God through life's inevitable trials and tribulations. The women's ministry was an important source of restoration for me. In a word, the Bible served as the ultimate bibliotherapy.

I experience tremendous gratification from parenting. My daughter and I spend a lot of time together. We go to the gym regularly and enjoy movies. She is on an equestrian team, which takes up a fair amount of time. More recently, her coach offered her a job at the barn. She feeds the horses on the weekend. On Friday nights, I usually join her the hour before the barn closes and assist her with her chores. Working with animals has been an important source of consolation for her.

In my spare time I enjoy reading. Needless to say, I haven't had as much time to engage in leisure reading as I had previously, but reading is an important part of my self-care. I also enjoy traveling, and I pencil in time at least twice a year to visit the ocean, listen to the waves, and just exhale.

I love fresh flowers, and every week I buy flowers and arrange them decoratively in vases all over the house. In the spring and summer, I cut roses from my rose bushes. Flowers leave a lingering fragrance that lifts my spirits. In fact, in addition to their aesthetic qualities, I've read that flowers trigger happy emotions.

My daughter and I are comforted by our faith, the passage of time, each other, and many fond memories of my husband as we work to find our new normal. My self-care rituals keep me grounded and help me stay focused so that I can maintain a healthy work–life balance.

• • •

The untimely death of Norma Day-Vines's husband and the unfathomable grief that she and her daughter experienced are, as she acknowledged, stressors that could not have been anticipated a few years earlier. However, when faced with adversity, she was able to embrace self-care and move forward with support. Norma Day-Vines's story embodies resilience, strength, and grace under the most stressful of circumstances.

Questions for Reflection

1. When faced with personal crises such as the loss of a loved family member or friend or another tragedy, how do you tend to cope? What self-care strategies have you relied on in the past?
2. What resources do you have or need to acquire to strengthen resiliency in your life? From where do you draw strength during life's trials and tribulations?
3. Norma Day-Vines benefited from participating in a women's ministry as a source of self-care. How would you describe your support system? If you experienced a personal stressor that tested (or perhaps even exceeded) your ability to cope, who would you want to include in your support system?

Positive Life Changes and Stress

Positive changes and events in our personal lives also create stress and pressure. Personal growth entails risk-taking and embracing change, which may catapult us out of our comfort zone. As noted in Chapter 2, we (Julius and Jude) have recently transitioned into new professional roles while simultaneously meeting new positive milestones in our personal lives, and these changes have created their own stress for us.

Using Both Hands in Life

Since I (Julius) was a young child, my father has consistently repeated this phrase to me: "Use both hands boy." This phrase has held different meanings for me throughout my life. When I was in elementary school and doing chores around the house, the phrase meant "Pay close attention to what you are doing." Throughout high school and college, it meant "Be aware of your environment." In graduate school the phrase meant "Think before acting." When transitioning into my first year as a professional, the phrase meant "Be decisive." Currently, my father's phrase means "Be responsible for your relationships." Maintaining relationships with others produces the most stress for me in my life. When I place pressure on myself to maintain or define relationships, or when a shift in my environment forcibly alters relationships, I feel stressed.

In my personal life, earning a doctoral degree, marrying my partner, becoming a father, and owning a home have altered my relationship with my parents. My parents provided for and protected me since birth, and I seamlessly fit into that groove. In forming my own family and meeting other monumental developmental milestones, my parents' role has shifted more toward being supporters. I felt the shift especially when my partner and I bought our first home. My mother seemed nervous about us taking on the responsibility that comes with owning a home while trying to maintain our marriage and careers. My mother, more than my father, vacillated between wanting to protect me from making a poor decision based on lack of experience and supporting me through this developmental stage. As my partner and I successfully balanced our relationship, careers, and home, I could literally see the tension and worry leave my mother's face. It is important for me to recognize the sacrifices my parents made to provide the opportunities for me to achieve the things that they could not. As I grow older, I understand that the relationship they have with me is also going to be in flux, and I know that some confusion is a normal part of the process as our roles shift.

Shifts have occurred in my professional relationships as well, as I have advanced in my education and career. It is important for me now to cultivate a circle of individuals I can learn from, who will challenge me, and who will accept me as I develop professionally. I feel very open and receptive to this challenging stage in my life. However, as an undergraduate, I remember feeling overwhelmed by the number of people who were in my life. Later, in graduate school, my close relationships seemed forced due to the ready-made cohort of which I was a part. At each of these stages, the circumstances have influenced how I interacted and established relationships with others.

Avoiding Personal and Professional Stress Traps

Most of the stress I (Jude) experience, both personally and professionally, involves some form of effort on my part to please those around me. I know it is an impossible task, but it is part of my personality. There is a common saying in counseling, "You get the clients you need." Well, I believe this extends to all of life's experiences as a counselor. When I encountered clients and supervisees with high expectations of me, and when I landed my first job in an award-winning, high-achieving counseling program, this saying rang true for me. Being aware that this is my baggage within relationships gives me a fighting chance to access support through self-care. I face plenty of potential traps, both personally and professionally, regarding my need to please.

During my first year as a professional, I buried my grandpa. Then I became a doctor, husband, resident of Virginia, faculty member, professor, adviser, supervisor, uncle, and author. To me, these events speak to the integration of the personal and professional parts of my life. To use a Gestalt metaphor, they are like two dogs within me. Oftentimes, I feed one part more than the other, and they both end up suffering. I go into greater detail of how I manage my self-care in Chapter 7, but here is a brief account of how I have managed to avoid some of the personal and professional traps I face.

Trap 1: Codependence

My personal and professional parts are codependent on one another. For example, 4 years from now my work will be sitting in front of a tenure and promotion committee. My work and their decision will determine whether or not I keep my job. Professionally, I feel a sense of urgency regarding meeting the tenure requirements in my contract. I also feel a sense of responsibility to my department chair and colleagues to achieve tenure so we can continue our great work and serve our community. Personally, I feel that I am missing important quality time with my wife, siblings, parents, and nephew because I am focused on getting tenure. I also know that in a couple years, when my wife and I start having children, keeping my job will be extremely beneficial. In this trap, I am stuck answering the question, "Do I sacrifice quality time now for future security?" I don't have the right answer for this question, yet I try to find a balance and be transparent with my wife about my feelings regarding finding a balance. My wife is both understanding and supportive. In many ways, she knows what I need better that I do. She knows when and how to motivate and nurture me. When I have her support to work on a project for long hours when a deadline is approaching, I feel less anxious about disappointing her regarding our personal time. Our relationship is especially helpful when I am unsuccessful. For example, I recently sacrificed time with my family to submit an article for publication. That article was rejected, and I felt gut-punched because of the time I lost with family and the potential damage to my tenure process. Having my wife's understanding and support was an essential piece of my self-care process.

Trap 2: Cultural Responsibility

In my soul, I know that my struggles are a privilege. Many individuals sacrificed so much for me to have the opportunity to have these struggles. My grandpa was a civil rights activist who marched with Martin Luther King Jr., and he made many personal and professional choices that I am benefiting from today. I feel an obligation to him and to others to be successful. When I engage in self-care activities such as golfing, exercising, or watching movies, I feel guilty and my self-talk goes something like this: "You shouldn't be here when you have that chapter to write" or "Well, you can't complain if you fail" or "Are you really doing the best you can do?"

To help avoid this trap, I spend time talking to elders in my family. I ask them about their hopes for me and how I can make them proud. Their responses have less to do with success and more to do with my well-being. I know what they want for me is safety, happiness, health, purpose, courage, ambition, understanding, and connection. It seems to me that giving up when I face challenges would disappoint my ancestors. Knowing this makes it much harder to give up, and their caring provides solid anchor points upon which to build my self-care strategies.

The Impact of Cultural Stressors

One can certainly argue that cultural stress is personal stress. In fact, many reading this may feel that it doesn't get more personal than this. As practitioners and scholars in the field of counseling, we know very well that racism, xenophobia, homophobia, sexism, and other forms of oppression and discrimination have long contributed to the distress and suffering of countless individuals, including the clients we serve, and perhaps even ourselves. Angela Coker, a seasoned counselor educator, attests to the formidable challenges faculty members of color sometimes encounter, including microaggressions and discrimination, even within departments that train counselors. She describes a painful incident she faced as a counselor educator and the vital role self-care has played in maintaining her emotional and personal well-being.

Pretty on the Inside and Pretty on the Outside: Navigating Self-Care

* *

Angela D. Coker

Self-care is a friend I intend to keep. It requires monitoring our physical health as well as maintaining emotional balance and personal well-being. This message can be highlighted in the familiar saying, "It is important to be both pretty on the inside and pretty on the outside." This is a commonly held sentiment expressed in many communities, especially when discussing the physical or attitudinal attributes of others.

As an associate professor in counselor education, I have largely enjoyed my journey as a counselor educator, during both my pre- and posttenure stages. I have been fortunate to work with a host of good colleagues who have mentored me along the way. However, the vast majority of counselor education programs still lack diversity, and as a faculty member of color I have found myself the "only" in majority White academic spaces. Extensive research highlights the deleterious mental impact microaggressions and discrimination can have on faculty of color. Examples range from questioning one's intellectual credibility to blatant disrespect or even racial name-calling. Such experiences can be extremely isolating and tax one's emotional resources.

As I reflect on my own cultural location—a female who is African American and is an academic—I have been challenged many times to practice self-care as a means of maintaining "prettiness on the inside." I have personally experienced three stereotypes as a counselor educator at various times in my career. I have been perceived as a Superwoman, an individual possessing a willingness to take on multiple responsibilities while disregarding my own needs; as a Mammy-like figure, a woman who takes on a listening and caretaking role of others; and as an Angry Woman who is emotionally combative and overly reactive.

One painful incident occurred during a multicultural class I was teaching when I was made to appear as the big bad Black instructor who hurt the feelings of the White student. The class topic was racial discrimination and the subtle ways racism may affect human interactions. One White female student stated she was offended by the topic and began to cry. Her tears evoked sympathy from other White students and immediately caused a rift in the class between individuals who understood the underlying sociopolitical issues being addressed and others who were new to the conversation. This incident was taxing for me because managing conversations about race was already difficult, but it was 10 times more challenging to simultaneously self-monitor to keep members of the majority culture comfortable in the process. I was left feeling physically tired and emotionally drained. I felt my blood pressure elevate, and I was left in a state of emotional limbo. I questioned whether or not I should be upset, and I had to redirect my thinking about how to appropriately respond to my environment emotionally. Incidents like these have required a full arsenal of self-care techniques.

In addition to navigating racial stereotypes, I have had family responsibilities such as raising daughters, being a partner to my husband, and a daughter to my mother. I have had a lot of demands pulling on my time, energy, and resources. Like so many women professionals, I still complete the bulk of the domestic chores in my home, not because my partner is unwilling but because often I have felt socially obligated to manage household affairs.

It is hard for me to make time for myself. It is a continuous struggle that I must remind myself to pursue daily. Personal activities I engage in to practice self-care include meditation, international travel as time permits, time spent with nature (this has always grounded me spiritually), and listening to music. I also monitor my nutritional intake and exercise regularly. To manage some of the cultural stressors, I practice self-talk and remember that finding balance between my professional life and my personal life is key. I tell myself that being in academia is my profession but not my total existence. It is important that I do not seek my only validation from the academy; I find time to be with family and close friends because they all knew me before I became Dr. Coker. I also seek support from communities of color and other individuals who are allies, which has been a critical component in my self-care and coping repertoire (Coker & Bryant, 2016).

Being pretty on the inside and being pretty on the outside requires work regardless of who you are. However, it can be particularly challenging for faculty of color who must operate under the gaze of White colleagues who often have the power to determine tenure and promotion decisions. Ultimately the focus of self-care must be on helping everyone thrive, not just survive, while living and working in a diverse society.

● ● ●

Questions for Reflection

1. If you identify as being from a marginalized group, what stereotypes have you experienced? Have you been subjected to microaggressions or discrimination in your personal life or in your professional role? If so, what happened, and how did you react to the mistreatment? What did you do to take care of yourself?

2. If you are a member of the dominant culture, what steps can you take to ensure that you are "both pretty on the inside and pretty on the outside"?

3. Angela Coker describes how often she was the "only" faculty of color in majority White academic spaces. Have you had a similar experience? If so, how was that for you, and what did you find to be helpful in navigating the situation?

4. If you are a member of the dominant culture, how can you practice cultural sensitivity toward colleagues, faculty, or students who identify with marginalized groups?

5. As a student, how did you respond to learning about multiculturalism?

Coping With Calamity:
Dealing With the Aftermath of Disasters

As mental health professionals, we are faced with the challenge of making a difference in a world replete with complex problems—both natural and human-made. It can be stressful to provide services to individuals, couples, and families with complex needs, but providing assistance to communities in crisis, such as those affected by a massive earthquake, a powerful hurricane, a mass shooting, or a terrorist attack, are exponentially more intense and stressful. Disaster mental health has emerged as an essential specialty area within the helping professions and has generated a growing body of literature (Felix & Afifi, 2015; Jacobs, Gray, Erickson, Gonzalez, & Quevillon, 2016; Millegan, Delaney, & Klam, 2016; Stebnicki, 2017). Mental health workers who provide much needed psychological first aid to disaster survivors need to take protective measures to safeguard themselves from the hazards of vicarious traumatization, compassion fatigue, and other stressors. Self-care and attending to one's spirit are critical, as Fred Bemak, a professor of counseling and a champion of international social justice work, explains.

Maintaining Personal Spirit and Dignity in Postdisaster Situations

Fred Bemak

I have worked in many postdisaster situations, which indeed is highly stressful. Each and every time I see human beings facing more tragedy and misery than anyone should ever have to experience in a lifetime. Providing counseling in the midst of such deep suffering and anguish pushes counselors to extremes and requires extraordinary efforts to maintain balance, harmony, and the grounding necessary to be helpful to others in such calamitous circumstances.

When doing postdisaster work, it is essential to nurture and care for your spiritual health to lay the foundation for personal care. Someone recently asked me, "Don't you get burned out doing postdisaster work?" My response was to explain how I move into and through these situations with full and continual awareness of the deeper meaning of the experience and my purpose in being there. This mindfulness provides a strong base for staying grounded, energetic, and unwaveringly compassionate. Acknowledging that the disaster itself is a life's event, and that life's events happen, helps me realize what an honor it is to be in each and every moment in the midst of the disaster. This realization also enables me to employ my skills as a trained counselor and maintain the balance I have found as a human being, both of which position me to deeply connect and help disaster victims undergoing extreme pain and suffering. Keeping this existential perspective provides a solid anchor point for me and helps me sustain energy and vitality for 15-hour days filled with clients' tears, anger, pain, fear, and frustration.

My spiritual and existential awareness during a disaster provide a center that is much like the solidity I found when studying martial arts. There is a whirlwind of movement, activity, and physical engagement, yet the breathing and the mind remain calm, concentrated, peaceful, and pinpointed with complete focus and awareness on the moment at hand. This level of elevated concentration learned from martial arts translates well to postdisaster work, assisting in keeping my mind, body, and spirit at an almost altered state of consciousness. When working in a postdisaster situation, it is important to get into a "zone" of peacefulness, spirituality, and respect for human dignity, especially when surrounded by chaos, confusion, panic, and fear.

This spiritual foundation is the doorway to the other self-care that is so important during a postdisaster crisis situation. Even though there is always another client, another person in desperate need, and another crisis, counselors must have clear boundaries to sustain a balanced spirit and care for their own mind and body. Good nutrition is a must. I regularly "tear" myself away from the endless numbers of victims in dire need to find a quiet place to have food and water. Nourishment is important in replenishing oneself and staying in the "zone." Combined with good nutrition is finding moments of quiet. This is especially difficult in postdisaster circumstances when there is no private space, but only frenetic activity and an atmosphere riddled with sorrow and confusion. I oftentimes take a short walk, leaving the immediate work area, breathing deeply, and resettling myself in the spiritual zone. The harmony of spirit, mind, and body is an absolute must for counseling in postdisaster situations and cultivates the self-dignity and sustained compassion that is essential for meaningful counseling in dramatic crisis situations.

• • •

Questions for Reflection

1. Disasters occur without notice. If you were called to provide mental health services in your community after a disaster, what do you envision your greatest challenges would be? What might be triggered for you when you are surrounded by chaos, confusion, panic, and fear?
2. Fred Bemak notes that it is crucial to nurture one's spiritual health when doing postdisaster work to lay the foundation for personal care. How would you assess your spiritual health? How do you nourish your spirit during life's most challenging times?

The Hazards of Chronic Stress

As long as we are alive, we are likely to experience a certain degree of stress. It is part of the human experience and can enhance our lives by challenging us to find creative solutions to the problems of everyday living. However, when stress becomes a chronic condition, it can take a serious toll on our lives and compromise our health and well-being. In writing about the hazards of therapeutic practice, Kottler (2017) identifies sources of stress that can be grouped into four categories for practitioners. *Client-induced stress* involves clients who are intensely anxious and depressed, clients who display angry outbursts, and suicidal clients. *Work environment stress* takes a toll on counselors and involves nonsupportive colleagues, infighting among the staff, excessive paperwork, time pressures, and overbearing supervisors. *Event-related stressors* are unforeseen things that happen to us such as major health problems, major life transitions, legal actions, and family problems. *Self-induced stress* pertains to our inability to take care of ourselves, which can involve self-doubt, excessive need for approval, striving for perfection, and poor lifestyle choices. A pattern of distress emerges from each of these sources of stress that includes psychological, behavioral, and physical symptoms. Kottler emphasizes that not only do our minds and bodies suffer but our relationships often become strained as well. Stress related to both our personal and professional life can result in serious psychological, physical, and behavioral disorders.

A growing body of research reveals the negative toll exacted from mental health practitioners in symptoms such as moderate depression, mild anxiety, emotional exhaustion, and disturbed relationships. Physical maladies such as ulcers, hypertension, cardiovascular disease, cancer, endocrine and metabolic disease, skin rashes, migraine and tension headaches, and other conditions can result from chronic stress. These conditions vary from being minor nuisances to life-threatening. When left unaddressed, chronic stress can deplete us of energy and lead to burnout. It is essential to recognize the hazards of the helping professions if we hope to develop effective self-care strategies (Norcross & VandenBos, 2018). Mental health professionals who have numbed themselves to their own pain will not be able to deal with the pain of their clients. A key problem for many counselors is denial of any of these disabling symptoms. Kottler (2017) points out that we may notice when a colleague has lost energy and is displaying classic signs of burnout, but it is more difficult for many of us to recognize the signs and symptoms of burnout in ourselves. As counselors, we must be vigilant for the signs of burnout and must engage in self-care if we are to avoid becoming impaired practitioners.

Stress and the inevitable burnout that typically results from inadequately dealing with chronic stress is a major ethical issue facing counseling professionals. Fried and Fisher (2016) noted that clinicians and researchers have begun to call attention to the negative consequences of prolonged and extreme emotional stress among practitioners who work with vulnerable and at-risk populations. As you become aware of ineffective ways you cope with stress, replace them with constructive ways to control stress. You can learn to control stress rather than being controlled by it.

In sharp contrast to those who experience burnout in response to chronic stress, some helping professionals seem especially resilient and experience minimal negative effects. Mullenbach and Skovholt (2016) investigated resiliency in expert practitioners and identified these high-level stressors and self-care strategies of participants in their study:

- Issues and events that challenge competency are stressful.
- Encountering unmotivated or resistant clients is highly stressful.
- Peer relationships, both in the work environment and in the broader professional community, are beneficial to practitioners. Breaches in these peer relationships result in a high degree of stress.
- Personal life crises have a negative impact on professional roles. Direct acknowledgment and resolution of personal problems allows for congruence between the personal self and the professional self.
- The importance of maintaining a balance between their personal and professional lives is recognized.
- Establishing nurturing connections with family, friends, and other social groups is valued. Ongoing professional support was also emphasized.
- Self-exploration is valued, and the commitment of practitioners to understanding self was a key approach to self-care and had a positive impact on their sense of resiliency and wellness.
- Practitioners demonstrated a proactive style in confronting stressors associated with both their personal lives and their work.

This study underscored the demanding nature of the helping role and emphasized the value of self-care strategies as a way to ensure practitioner wellness and professional vitality. It offers us hope that there is much we can do to lessen the negative impact of stress in our lives.

Resilience is the capacity to bounce back from major stressful events with minimal negative effects. Resilience is not so much a personality trait as a process that occurs when we react successfully to stressful situations. We are not born resilient; rather, we develop this capacity to cope with stress throughout our lives. Those who are resilient are not immune to stress and temporary self-doubt, but they adapt quickly in stressful situations. Resilience can be thought of as a set of learned behaviors that are largely dependent on our beliefs about our ability to cope.

Questions for Reflection

1. Have you experienced any psychological or physical symptoms as a result of chronic stress? If so, what steps can you take to relieve these symptoms?
2. If you believe you are heading toward burnout, what can you do to reverse this negative trend? What are some self-care strategies that might help to reenergize you?
3. To what degree do you see yourself as a resilient person? How can you increase your resilience?

Concluding Thoughts

Based on the quantity and intensity of stressors that counselors regularly experience in the course of their careers, in their personal lives, and just as citizens in this very stressful and ever-changing world, it is no wonder that self-care is considered an ethical mandate. In this chapter, we have explored how counselors and counselor educators have been affected by and have navigated the personal and professional stressors they have experienced.

Mental health professionals who have numbed themselves to their own pain will not be able to deal with the pain of their clients. Professional work with people who are diagnosed with mental health conditions can be rewarding, but it often is highly stressful. Practitioners who suffer from burnout are likely to do more harm than good for their clients. Counselors who are psychologically and physically exhausted rarely provide effective assistance to their clients. There are no simple answers to the question of how to maintain our vitality; each of us must find our own answers for self-care. It is unrealistic to think that you can have a stress-free personal or professional life, but stress can be managed. By recognizing the signs of stress and monitoring how you think, feel, and behave in stressful situations, you can increase your resilience. In the next chapter, we explore a wide variety of strategies for managing stress.

Chapter 5

Managing Stress in a Stressful World

In this chapter, we explore various methods of stress management in depth to help you identify specific outlets for coping with stress. The routes to stress management include meditation, mindfulness, relaxation, yoga, Pilates, tai chi, experiencing nature, sound nutrition, exercise, recreation, service to others, personal therapy, and cultivating the practice of self-reflection. In addition, some attention is given to cognitive behavior therapy, which has a great deal to offer counselors in constructively dealing with the impact of stress. By modifying certain beliefs, counselors can put a different perspective on stress. This is a holistic approach to self-care that encompasses the physical, emotional, mental, social, and spiritual aspects of caring for yourself. Key messages on incorporating self-care and keeping stress under control are presented through the voices of graduate students and professionals. Learning to balance work with recreation and to effectively manage personal and professional tasks are two essential elements for managing stress.

Dattilio (2015) warns that mental health professionals tend to neglect their own mental health despite their devotion to promoting the mental health of others. "Unfortunately, mental health professionals have traditionally underestimated the importance of lifestyle functions and stressors that affect their work, almost to the point that it is hypocritical to what they preach to their clients" (p. 393). It is important for mental health practitioners to create a balance between caring for others and caring for themselves. Dattilio recommends that professionals establish realistic and achievable goals for themselves and monitor their progress toward these goals. He points to developing strategies for coping with the demands and stress of professional work and highlights the role of diet, rest, relaxation, and exercise in taking care of oneself. It is important to develop a compassionate attitude toward ourselves as we strive to meet our goals. We hope you will assess your lifestyle behavior and determine what changes you want to make as you read these strategies for stress reduction. A self-assessment of your self-care practices is provided at the end of the chapter to help you consolidate your thoughts and lead you to taking action.

Walsh (2011) provided a comprehensive review of therapeutic lifestyle changes (TLCs) that promote wellness for clients, and these self-care strategies are an extremely useful wellness approach for counselors as well. Ample research and clinical evidence supports the value of these therapeutic lifestyle changes: exercise, nutrition and diet, time in nature, relationships, recreation, relaxation, stress management, religious or spiritual involvement, and service to others. Walsh contends that TLCs are sometimes as effective as psychotherapy or pharmacotherapy, and they offer significant therapeutic advantages such as enhancing health and well-being. Walsh's model specifically incorporates elements of mindfulness, spirituality, and positive psychology as ways to promote physical and psychological health.

Combating Stress in a Stressful World

There is no doubt that we live in a stress-filled world. Trying to change the world is a daunting task, and meaningful systemic change is a painstaking process that requires time, effort, energy, patience, and persistence. We can, and arguably should, take an active role in trying to make a difference in our communities and in the larger society via social or political activism, advocacy, and other volunteer work. All of these actions can increase our stress, however, so it is to our advantage to learn constructive ways to control the stress that comes our way and to help our clients do the same. Stated bluntly, either we manage the impact of stress, or stress controls us.

Stress affects each of us in different ways, and how stress affects us has a lot to do with our perception of reality and our interpretation of events. We can learn more constructive ways of coping effectively with the stress associated with being a counselor in everyday living. Pay attention to what your body, mind, and spirit need in order to reduce stress. This might include a combination of physical activity, good nutrition, adequate rest and relaxation, contact with friends and loved ones, and some form of mindfulness practice.

A good way to begin learning more about stress management techniques is by reading one of the many fine books on this subject. Jon Kabat-Zinn has achieved a reputation for teaching mindfulness meditation to medical patients to relieve chronic pain and stress, and we recommend two of his classic works: *Full Catastrophe Living* (1990) and *Wherever You Go, There You Are: Mindfulness Meditation in Everyday Life* (1994).

Mindfulness

A key form of self-care involves developing a mindfulness approach to daily life. The goal of mindfulness is to keep us in the here and now, focusing on *what is* rather than on *what if*. Mindfulness practice is similar to meditation. Mindfulness practice clears the mind and calms the body, which enables us to focus on here-and-now awareness in a nonjudgmental way. In mindfulness practice, individuals train themselves to intentionally focus on their present experience with an attitude of curiosity and compassion. Through mindfulness practice we can learn to focus on one thing at a time and to bring our attention back to the present moment when distractions arise. With practice we can intentionally focus on our present experience rather than dwelling on the past or being preoccupied with the future. The practice requires an ongoing commitment to cultivate its principles in each moment; it is something that is *caught* more than *taught*. When we are able to practice the skills of mindfulness, our thinking is clearer and we are better able to increase our awareness of the world around us. Mindfulness is not limited to periods of formal practice; rather, it is meant to become a way of life.

It is easy in today's world to get swept up by distractions. Helping professionals are not immune to temptations such as spending time on social media or splitting our focus between the cyberworld and the real world. Although I (Michelle) rarely spend much time on social media, I have explored it enough to understand why so many people are drawn to it. Whether staying in touch with family members and friends, engaging in lively debates about political or social issues, or understanding the perspectives of people living in one's own community or even halfway around the world, social media can be a wonderful tool. I often wonder, though, whether excessive use might influence our attention span and our ability to sustain a prolonged focus on a task (such as a conversation with a person or writing a paper or a report we are assigned). A number of researchers have been intrigued by similar questions. Prabu (2015) examined the effects of cell phone distraction while studying; Gupta and Irwin (2016) explored the role of Facebook as a distracter from the primary learning task in classrooms; and Hollis (2016) studied mind wandering and social media distractions in online learning. It is likely that researchers will continue to expand this line of inquiry because social media is such a widespread phenomenon, and one that is here to stay.

How often do you find yourself paying only partial attention to the person with whom you are talking (a family member, a friend, an acquaintance, or the grocery store cashier) because your focus is drawn to your smartphone? Whether social media has exacerbated this lack of focus or not, we often engage in multitasking, and in doing so we miss much of what life has to offer in the present moment. Many of us justify doing several things at once because we have so much to do. In your day-to-day life, how often do you fall into this pattern of being easily distracted and doing several things at once? Developing a mindfulness approach to living and focusing on our present experience can help us manage stress in everyday life. It is a path toward putting life into perspective. An excellent resource to learn more about applying mindfulness to daily life is *The Mindfulness Solution: Everyday Practices for Everyday Problems* (Siegel, 2010).

Meditation

Meditation is a process of directing our attention to a single focus as a way of centering. Meditation may include repetition of a word, a sound, a phrase, or a prayer. This practice sharpens our concentration and our thinking patterns with the goal of eliminating mental distractions and relaxing the body. Essentially, meditation is simply being still, paying attention to our thoughts, and trying to clear and settle our mind. It is a tool to focus on the present moment rather than on what has been and what we will be doing later today, tomorrow, or next week. The goal of meditation is to increase awareness, become centered, and achieve an internal focus. Contemplative skills such as meditation and yoga are now practiced by millions of people in the United States and hundreds of millions worldwide (Walsh, 2014). People value meditation because it helps to cleanse their mind of distractions, which helps them to perceive reality more clearly. Mark Young, a professor of counselor education at the University of Central Florida, describes how meditation has become a valuable self-care practice for him.

Meditation as a Route to Self-Care

Mark E. Young

I have been a meditator for 45 years. In my work as a practicing counselor, I have found it to be the most accessible and effective method for dealing with the stress of therapeutic work. It is accessible because I can practice it unobtrusively between clients or on my lunch break, providing me with a private oasis in the turmoil of my professional work. Meditation is a proven method for decreasing stress. My colleagues and I conducted a randomized treatment in which counselor trainees received either meditation training (Jyoti Meditation) or a wellness curriculum. When student counselors meditated 30 minutes per week or more, we found that they showed significant stress reduction and increased empathy compared to those participating in wellness training (Gutierrez, Conley, & Young, 2016). In other words, we found that meditation must be practiced regularly to have an effect. If you only attend a meditation class, you won't get the benefit. Meditation needs no technology or props, has no side effects, and costs nothing. Do you have time to meditate? Yes you do, if you place value on meditation.

One of the first things I noticed about my own stress was that physical relaxation was not enough. I might have had a massage, exercised, and spent time in the hot tub, but when I started thinking about my troubles, all that relaxation evaporated because I had no control over my negative spiraling thoughts. When I meditate, I focus away from those thoughts and gently coax my mind to leave me alone for a while. Mental relaxation leads to physical relaxation, but it doesn't work the other way around. Most important, meditation makes me happy. I experience joy and peace not only when I am meditating but for hours afterward. This is the real reason I meditate every day. Without that bliss, life becomes tiresome and troublesome.

Meditation has given me a different perspective on life. When I meditate, I don't make mountains out of molehills. Meditation gives us the ability to avoid getting caught up in the drama of mishaps that may occur along the way. Finally, meditation makes me a better counselor. Murray Bowen used to say that the therapist should be a "nonanxious presence." I often thought about myself as a rock against which clients' troubles, like waves, could strike but not move me. I meditate to be that steady presence not just for myself but for those I can help. Meditation won't eliminate the thorns of the outer environment, but it can give us some heavy boots. If we operate in a stressful world by being cool on the inside, that peace will radiate to others. To learn more about the kind of meditation I practice, read Rajinder Singh's (2007) *Inner and Outer Peace Through Meditation*.

• • •

Each of us can benefit from finding some way to center ourselves and to promote reflection. We can modify this recommendation to fit our situation, and we are likely to discover that devoting even a short time to centering is worth the effort. Another approach to meditation and mindfulness is described by Aparna Ramaswamy, a counselor educator and performing artist who leads meditation classes in the master of counseling program at Johns Hopkins University. Expressive art forms such as dance can become meditative experiences that integrate mind, body, and soul.

Meditation and Mindfulness in Counseling

Aparna Ramaswamy

I understand meditation as a process that gives me an awareness and fosters the integration of my mind and body. Moving meditation through classical Indian dance has been particularly helpful for me in this process of mind–body awareness and integration. Classical Indian dance found me when I was 5 years old, growing up in southern India. I was a reluctant student, but I persisted. Dance and music were an essential part of my childhood and adolescence, just as sports and academics added other dimensions. Growing up in a society with porous boundaries between conventional academics, traditional artistic education, and spiritual infusion, life was a balance of arts, studies, religiosity, and communal interactions. This intricate yet simple model of living is challenging to embody in present-day Washington, DC metro living!

The interwoven practice of stimulating both body and mind autonomously co-creates inner balance and harmony. When I dance to music, it is not about my technical artistry but about dancing's meditative experience. I step into a dance form, and as synchrony develops I feel a oneness within me, and the distinction between my body and my mind dissolves. Even the spectator is moved by the witnessed and participatory oneness of my dancing. Similarly, when I sing or listen to beautiful music, I experience an immersive appreciation of the melody and rhythm and feel at one with the music. Meditation in music and movement creates balance within me, giving rise to a sense of harmony with all that exists on the outside.

I practice meditation as a deliberate routine that involves a yoga concept of breath regulation called *pranayama*. I find it simple and effective in calming my wandering mind. As I lead meditation classes, I learn more about it. Teaching meditation and mindfulness in counseling classes at Johns Hopkins University has brought to my awareness that meditation refers to the process of cultivating oneness, whereas mindfulness is awareness of the phenomenological experience.

As mindful counselors-in-training, my students discovered experientially that a prerequisite for mindfulness is a counselor's disciplined practice of any preferred form of meditation. Irrespective of the modality used, students disclosed that they overcame their initial resistance to meditating as the semester progressed, and they were surprised at the ease with which they could meditate (many held a bias that their mind could not possibly stop racing!). The resulting calm they felt soon after meditating convinced them of its effectiveness, and most revealing was how it transformed their disposition toward family, friends, and counseling clients. Students shared that they were able to suspend self-doubt and negative thinking about their own inadequacies as counselors-in-training. Student meditators began to feel a distance from environmental triggers: Behaviors that earlier had aggravated them did not elicit the same response. They noticed they were less preoccupied with perfection, less reactive to external situations, more empathic toward others, and, above all, others noticed a change in their disposition and presence during interactions.

My students and I were curious to know if neuroscience could corroborate our subjective meditative experiences. We experienced meditation as calming, and neuroscience evidence confirmed that meditative breathing calms the parasympathetic nervous system, increases dopamine, and prolongs the experience of happiness, understanding, equanimity, and tranquility (Luke, 2016). Neuroscience studies have shown that the corpus callosum, which bridges the right and left lobes of the brain, is more active in musicians and creative artists, thereby creating inner balance and harmony. Meditation seems to create balance within the brain, stabilizes neurotransmitter activity, lays new neural pathways for processing information, and creates feelings of inner calm and wellness. Neuroscience corroborates the subjective experiences of meditation and mindfulness.

As a counselor, I am grateful that meditation continues to transform my therapeutic presence in a counseling setting. As challenging as life is, I strive to maintain balance in my life through various meditative practices: dancing, music, seated meditation, walking in tune with nature by the Potomac, laughing in togetherness with others, and engaging in teaching/learning collaboration with my students. Meditation involves a balance of togetherness—a oneness that rejuvenates and inspires me.

● ● ●

These powerful testaments to the mental and physical benefits of mindfulness and meditation are echoed by others in the clinical and research communities who appreciate the benefits of these practices and see great promise in incorporating elements of mindfulness into therapeutic practice. Jo Marchant (2017) earned a PhD in genetics and medical microbiology and has contributed to a growing body of scholarly literature. Marchant posed the question, "So can stress-busting mindfulness stop us from becoming ill in the first place?" Although the research in this area is preliminary, Marchant indicates that there is "some tantalizing evidence to support the idea" (p. 31). For example, in one study, participants who practiced mindfulness had fewer colds, and when they did become ill, they recovered more quickly and experienced less severe symptoms. Moreover, recent research has found that mindfulness training reduces markers of inflammation in the blood and increases activity of telomerase, an enzyme that slows cell aging. Marchant states that some small studies have demonstrated brief effects on pain and mood from meditating for "as little as 5 to 10 minutes per day for 3 or 4 days. The effects of lengthier mindfulness courses seem to be more significant and longer lasting" (p. 31). It seems advisable to view mindfulness as a lifestyle change rather than a miracle cure: "The more you do, the greater the impact, and the benefits last as long as you keep practicing" (p. 31).

The idea that the benefits of mindfulness meditation last as long as you keep practicing aligns with my (Jude) and my colleagues' approach to mindfulness during clinical meetings. I volunteer at a local clinic one day a week, and every Wednesday we come together to discuss our cases. During the first 15 minutes of these meetings, we take turns leading the group through a mindfulness activity. We encourage creativity, so we have participated in mindful walking or eating, therapeutic drumming, and guided imagery. At first I struggled to stay in the present moment and let go of thinking. My mindfulness experience in those early days consisted of starting the activity, focusing on a project, feeling guilty for thinking about work, trying to clear my mind, being unable to clear my mind, stressing over my attempts to clear my mind, then the activity would end. When processing our experience of these activities, a colleague suggested that I try not to judge myself throughout the process. Paradoxically she suggested that I intentionally focus on my to-do list and everything I needed to do. She coached me to focus on my breath and allow myself to see my list. I pictured my list on the whiteboard in my office and how I would check the first thing off my list. I prioritized my objectives and developed strategies. I occasionally placed my focus on my breath, then I went back to my list. Soon I began to experience less anxiety about the work I needed to do. Instead, I increasingly felt more grounded and became eager to tackle the items on my list. My list seemed more manageable, and I felt more secure in my abilities to accomplish my tasks. I have continued to practice mindfulness with my colleagues, and now I rarely envision my white board. I think about my family, my inner feelings, dreams, goals, and meaningful experiences. For me, mindfulness and meditation does not produce a quiet mental space but more of a loud open space wherein I prepare myself for life.

Tai Chi

The ancient Chinese practice of tai chi is designed to exercise the body, mind, and spirit; gently work muscles; enhance concentration; and reduce the effects of stress on the body (Hales, 2017). Tai chi is often characterized by a gentle, flowing movement of the body combined with deep, rhythmic breathing. Many studios offer this most ancient of arts in its classical form, and today many more classes are being offered that emphasize tai chi's health benefits. To achieve maximum benefits from tai chi requires regular practice. Among the benefits to those who practice tai chi are decreased anxiety and depression, increased stress management, improved aerobic capacity, increased energy and stamina, and improved muscle strength. As a form of exercise, it is extremely low impact and puts very little stress on major joints of the body, making it suitable for all ages and levels of fitness.

As the four of us were writing this book, we set aside some time to meet to exchange ideas at the American Counseling Association's convention in San Francisco. Next to the conference site was a park where we walked and talked. Each morning small groups of people could be seen practicing tai chi. We were impressed with the grace and calming effects of this practice and easily understood how tai chi can calm the body, mind, and spirit and buffer the impact of a hectic and stressful pace.

Yoga and Pilates

Yoga originated in India, and *yoga* means "union" in Sanskrit. Yoga is often described as the union of the body, mind, and spirit. It focuses on breathing, the body, and centering. People may practice yoga to reduce stress, maintain health and vitality, increase awareness, deepen spirituality, or improve flexibility. Yoga provides numerous health benefits in both preventing and treating physical illnesses, and it is an excellent buffer against the effects of stress. Yoga addresses posture, positive thoughts, and breathing and can unwind stress at the clinical and molecular levels (Seppa, 2015). Sandi Fulcher is an experienced yoga and Pilates instructor as well as a retired counselor, and she tells us how she discovered yoga and Pilates and how these practices can benefit counselors.

Yoga and Pilates as Pathways to Self-Care for Counselors

Sandi Fulcher

Counseling may seem like a benign profession from a self-care perspective; however, the common counseling posture of sitting for many hours, leaning forward with rounded shoulders and a forward neck and head position, coupled with frequent head nodding to nonverbally communicate acceptance and affirmation is not so benign. Continuously maintaining this posture can cause hip, neck, shoulder, and back issues and can easily put unhealthy pressure on our heart and lungs and organs of digestion, elimination, and reproduction, which, in turn, can cause many unwanted health problems. In addition to postural issues, counselors are empathetically absorbing the emotional experiences of clients.

Yoga provides both a mind and body release; it counteracts the physical postural issues by placing the body in many different positions that stretch and strengthen the body. Yoga also counteracts the emotional effects of empathetic listening because it must be practiced with a mind–body connection, which is very meditative. Yoga allows the body to both physically and emotionally release as we move through the different positions or postures, freeing the body from the harmful effects of a counselor's work.

I entered the counseling profession in my early 30s and practiced until retirement in my early 50s. I was very fortunate to have a fulfilling and varied career. In my undergraduate human services program and my master's program in counseling, I had many internships, classes, and supervision groups, which culminated in my becoming licensed as a marriage and family therapist. Needless to say, all of these experiences placed my body in the poor postural positions I have described. In addition, in my private practice in counseling and in my work in both hospitals and outpatient chemical dependency programs, I did a great deal of sitting for 20 years.

Upon retiring, I was in a lot of physical pain, especially in my back and neck. I began practicing yoga, and I found it to be soothing to both my body and mind. My body began to unwind, releasing the tension created over the years from sitting and absorbing so much of the emotional pain that my clients had expressed. My body began to realign and to straighten, my posture changed, and the pain dissipated. I am now approaching 70, and my body is healthier than ever. I stand tall with good postural alignment, with shoulders back and down and head and neck in the correct body alignment. I coupled my yoga practice with another mind–body exercise known as Pilates, which nicely complements yoga's benefits.

Pilates strengthens the physical core (or center of the body) through exercises that target the small muscles throughout the body, which creates pelvic, hip, and shoulder stabilization. Pilates assists people in becoming present with their body and discovering how to control and move their body correctly. Pilates brings the body into correct alignment, reducing the stresses caused by misalignment. This practice can correct muscle imbalances; improve posture, coordination, balance, strength, and flexibility; and increase breathing capacity.

I became committed to both yoga and Pilates upon recognizing the wonderful benefits each of these disciplines provide. I became certified to teach both practices, and I consider these two disciplines therapeutic and a continuation of my career as a counselor. I continue to help others, but now on a physical level rather than on a psychological level. In my current practice, I see many psychotherapists who have developed the same physical issues that I developed: back, neck, hip, and shoulder issues. Both yoga and Pilates help them reinstate proper alignment, gain body awareness, and begin the release of the postural issues caused by sitting still in their work for hours at a time.

* * *

Reflect on how your body reacts to sitting in classes, at the computer, or working with clients. Sandi Fulcher claims that yoga soothes both the body and the mind and that Pilates reduces stress caused by misalignment. Are either yoga or Pilates practices of interest to you?

Questions for Reflection

1. Do you practice mindfulness or meditation? If so, what impact has it had on your physical and mental well-being? How regularly do you engage in this practice? Is it something you would like to increase?
2. How could you incorporate mindfulness exercises into your therapeutic practice if you are currently working with clients? Which clients might benefit the most from these wellness strategies?
3. What are your thoughts about yoga, Pilates, and tai chi as ways to manage stress? If you have tried any of these, what was your experience?
4. If you, like many others, have limited time to engage in self-care, how can you modify your schedule to make time for mindfulness, meditation, yoga, Pilates, tai chi, or another activity that might help to reduce your stress?

Being in Nature

Nature provides numerous benefits as a path toward enhancing both physical and mental health. For thousands of years, wise people have recommended experiencing nature as a source of healing. Yogis go into the forest, Shamans enter the wilderness, and Christian Fathers retreat to the desert. Nature calms the body and mind, reduces stress, removes mental trivia, and calls to mind what matters most in life (Walsh, 2011). The Dalai Lama suggests that wellness and happiness are enhanced and supported when people spend at least 30 minutes a day in nature. We appreciate the Dalai Lama's outlook on life, his view of the meaningful life, and his thoughts on wellness and happiness. We recommend his book, *An Open Heart: Practicing Compassion in Everyday Life* (Dalai Lama, 2001), for further study.

I (Jerry) place a great deal of value on being in nature as a form of self-care. Physical exercise in the form of walking and hiking has long been a regular part of my self-care regimen. I find that I am able to clear my mind and rejuvenate my soul when I take a long walk on a familiar trail in the mountain community where I live most of the year. In fact, many of my ideas for books and the classes I have taught were conceived on a hiking trail! There is something about the fresh air and breathtaking scenery that frees my mind and allows me to think creatively. During my earlier years as a professor of human services, when I juggled a lot of responsibility in my career and was also active in writing textbooks, I often retreated to one particular spot overlooking a creek in the mountains. I would sit for hours with my yellow pad of paper (long before iPads were created) and write. Nature was, and still is, a major source of meaning and inspiration in my life. In fact, just this summer we spent time in Germany, and one of my favorite activities was walking alone along lovely forest paths and bike riding along a river. I realize that most of you do not live in a mountain community, yet I hope you do not foreclose on the idea of making time to be in nature. Most cities have parks with trees and ponds; this exposure to nature can refresh you.

Religious/Spiritual Involvement and Meaning in Life

Religious and spiritual involvement can be a vital component of self-care and can help you put life in perspective. Spirituality and religion exist in all cultures. If therapists include spirituality in therapy, they must be comfortable with spiritual concerns as a topic of discussion. It is important to be aware of and understand your own spiritual or religious attitudes, beliefs, values, and experiences if you hope to facilitate an exploration of these matters with clients.

Meditation, prayer, being in nature, mindfulness, connecting with others, enjoying the arts, and yoga are some ways spirituality can be a valuable resource. The key is to find out what works for the client (Johnson, 2013). For many clients, spirituality or religion are core aspects of their sense of self, worldview, and value system. Religious or spiritual concerns may be relevant to the reasons that some clients seek therapy; some clients may find that their sense of spirituality is a key component in understanding their problems and resolving life issues. Walsh (2011) identifies religious and spiritual involvement as a significant aspect of lifestyle that mental health practitioners would do well to consider, both for their own life and in their work with clients. He asserts that religious and spiritual concerns are vitally important to most people who come to therapy and that religious or spiritual practices are a major means of coping with stress. Walsh points out that religious and spiritual involvement is most likely to be beneficial in therapy when it centers on themes such as love, acceptance, and forgiveness.

Religions have sometimes been a force for dividing people into antagonistic camps and have resulted in great harm. Unfortunately, we see evidence of that today. The Dalai Lama (2001) believes that the ultimate goal of all religions is to produce better human beings who will demonstrate caring and acceptance of others. Despite our differences, we can strive to make this world a better place by treating one another with compassion and kindness. The Dalai Lama teaches that religious beliefs are but one level of spirituality, and he talks about core spiritual values that include qualities of goodness, love, compassion, tolerance, forgiveness, human warmth, caring, and kindness toward oneself. We would do well to reflect on these ideas to determine how we can incorporate these actions as a part of our care of self and care of others. In Chapter 8, some contributors demonstrate how their religious/spiritual involvement contributes to finding meaning in life and taking care of themselves.

Susannah Wood, an associate professor of counselor education at the University of Iowa, realized that the stress of her professional work was affecting her health and wellness. She turned to meditation, prayer, and reflecting on being grateful to increase her self-care.

Reflections on Self-Care

Susannah M. Wood

In retrospect, I have to say that the biggest obstacle for my self-care practice was *me*, and more specifically, my conflicting emotions of guilt and frustration. I know the power of self-care: it prevents burnout, it allows me to be a solid counselor educator, and it can prevent or ameliorate physical illness and mental drain. It connects me back to *me* in a time when it seems every minute is spoken for by a task or other people. My career necessitates working with others, and that can mean less time for simple self-reflection. Taking a chunk of my morning for prayer and meditation, or another few chunks of the week for yoga practice or a walk or a run, seemed . . . greedy. I was consistently bothered by my own self-talk: "I could be using this time to work on X and Y and Z"—because there's always something, right? In 2013 my body handed me the bill (with interest) for all that time I had put toward the end of the alphabet (putting X before A).

It came as a shock that I could no longer continue at the breakneck pace I had set without a heavy cost. I realized that self-care wasn't selfish, wasn't a sign of weakness, and wasn't interfering with my work. In fact, it was the other way around; *not* practicing mindfulness, meditation, and prayer and not going to yoga was interfering with my growth, my mental and physical health, and in the long run interfering with my joy and sense of meaning. Putting meditation on the back burner really left me wondering if what I was doing meant anything to anyone anyway. It has taken time, and I am not nearly in the place I would like to be with my self-care practice, but beginning my days with these activities has become a requirement, not an obligation or a luxury. It has become the first letter of my alphabet and something I know I can stand on.

Engaging in prayer, meditating, and keeping a gratitude journal mean different things to different people. For me, they do a few important things:

1. I recognize what I do have rather than dwelling on what isn't working, or what isn't fair, or what I can't change. Sometimes it takes a lot of time to recognize this. Emotions rise and fall in meditation. I may not be left feeling at peace with whatever struggle or uncertainty I am facing, but I do become aware of what I already have that can help me with what is going on around me.
2. Meditation and prayer put things in perspective. With the advent of apps, I can connect with meditators around the world who all have their own pain, their own struggles, and their own private joys. I realize I am not alone, and that it's not all about me. Although my situation is unique to me, the pain, fear, anger, regret, guilt, and sorrow is not, which helps me realize that I do have power and I can deal with my life. I also can choose to help others, even if it's just to listen, and that may be the most powerful thing I can do for another human being. Often it's not about fixing the problem or the pain, it's about sitting with a person who is sitting with his or her own pain.
3. Pursuing joy and contentment can be a full-time and full-life activity. It does not mean I can or should avoid pain. For me, meditation means sitting with my own self and whatever it brings that day. It also reminds me that I am my own biggest obstacle; I could very well be creating my own suffering . . . and even creating suffering for others.

I am not perfect with my self-care practice, but embracing and working with it is a good place to start. It's OK if you only meditate for 5 or 15 minutes a day. Whatever it takes, *do it,* and be OK with floundering around for a bit until the greed and the frustration and the guilt shake themselves off. I'd like to think I am a better counselor educator because of wrestling with these feelings when I sit in the morning and meditate. Although I am not perfect, maybe I am a little bit better.

• • •

Susannah Wood describes how she became her own greatest obstacle to self-care. What are some ways you do this in your own life? What do you think would help you to stop getting in your own way? Reflect on what spirituality means to you and how you could put your spiritual beliefs in action as you encounter people in both your personal life and your professional work.

Questions for Reflection

1. To what extent do you view nature as a source of healing? When you spend time in nature, what impact does it have on your sense of well-being?
2. What benefits do you derive from being in nature? How might being in nature be a resource for self-care?
3. What role, if any, does religion play in your self-care regimen? To what extent do you consider yourself a spiritual person? What are some ways to foster spirituality in your own life as a form of self-care?
4. To what degree do you derive meaning in your life from spirituality or involvement in faith-based activities?

The Role of Nutrition and Diet in Self-Care

Irregular and inconsistent eating patterns are a key nutritional problem for many of us. I (Michelle) admittedly have fallen into this trap. My eating patterns vary depending on what's on my agenda for a given day. When I teach late night classes, I often come home and eat something that is convenient to prepare rather than something that is healthy. On evenings when I am not teaching and don't feel as rushed, I tend to be more mindful about what I am putting into my body. I definitely am aware that I have room to make positive changes in this regard. I want to be healthy and develop better nutritional habits; putting what I know into practice is the real challenge.

Healthy nutritional habits do not have to take a great deal of time, especially when new patterns are developed and a varied diet becomes part of daily life. By learning how to eat wisely and well, how to manage our weight, and how to become physically fit, we can begin a lifelong process toward wellness. By establishing healthy eating habits, we increase our ability to maintain the vitality that is necessary for us to provide quality care to our clients.

There is considerable evidence pointing to the essential role nutrition plays in mental and physical health (Walsh, 2011). Nutrition experts advise us to eat a variety of foods that supply all the nutrients our bodies need, and there are many books on this topic. Although it is easy to feel overwhelmed by all of the information currently available about diet and nutrition, it is critical to become informed consumers when determining how we will nourish ourselves. Scherger (2016) asserts that achieving health has a lot to do with the choices we make: "Everyone's life is a journey and we make many choices along the way. Far better health and longevity with a greater health span are within our reach" (p. 3). We recommend Dr. Joseph Scherger's (2016) short and informative book, *Lean and Fit: A Doctor's Journey to Healthy Nutrition and Greater Wellness.*

Designing Your Exercise Program

One of the most important things we can do for ourselves to promote general wellness is to build physical activity and regular exercise into our daily lives. Regular exercise helps prevent disease, promotes health, and prolongs and enhances life. Students may say that they cannot afford lessons in yoga or Pilates, yet one form of exercise that most people can do on a regular basis is walking, which costs nothing. Brisk walking for about 30 minutes a day helps your heart, lungs, and circulatory system. Walking also helps to control body weight and invigorates your body and mind. A consistent walking program can relieve stress and is an excellent way to prevent a host of illnesses. I (Jerry) am committed to my exercise program. I walk every day, usually in the morning before I get involved in work projects. After walking for about an hour, I typically ride a bicycle for another hour. Some days I hike for 2 or 3 hours. Lately I have been devoting about 17 hours a week to various forms of physical exercise. Some would say I am an exercise addict, and I could not argue with this, but I see this as a positive addiction. Although it does take self-discipline, the rewards are worth the effort I devote to keeping fit through a consistent exercise program. I generally feel energized, have stamina, and am able to be alert largely due to moving.

Our (Jude's and Julius's) approach to designing an exercise program began with an honest conversation about the role exercise could play in our lives. One of our most important values is spending time with family, even if it is through phone calls or video chatting. We also value diligent work, and we try to put our best efforts into projects at all times. Our exercise program needed to align with these values. Exercising 6 hours a day would not fit our current lifestyle. We work hard to take a nonjudgmental approach about our program. We have a saying that helps us not be so hard on ourselves, "All we can do is all we can do." If walking a mile is all we can do now, then that is enough. Instead of constantly thinking we could be doing more, we try to enjoy the experience of exercising.

My (Jude's) plan involves training for half-marathons. My wife is an avid runner, but I am not. Having played soccer at a high level, I tend to equate running with pain and competition. It has taken me some time to think about running as a way to stay physically and mentally healthy. After an honest conversation with myself, I looked for a motivational structure to help me with my exercise plan. I started using a running app on my smartphone that allows me to track my workouts in real time and includes walking, running, cycling, and hiking. Every day around 5 p.m., the running app sends my wife and me a message informing us about our next run. I enjoy prepping for runs with my wife. We talk about our course in the city, the time, food we should eat before and afterward, and what we need to bring on the runs. I listen to audiobooks during my runs, and needing to hear what happens next motivates me to run a bit more. During the runs I try not to concern myself with my pace, breathing, or focus. When I can't run, I walk or play volleyball with a faculty colleague and research partner. This gives us time to connect and talk about our projects, students, and experiences. Connection and activities devoid of pressure are staples of my exercise plan. These two elements can be found in any environment where I can grow and be successful. I don't try to fit into an exercise mold; rather, I try to make exercise fit my needs and my lifestyle.

Most people are aware of the benefits of exercise, but many of us tell ourselves and others that we are simply too busy to take the time for physical exercise. Unlike Jerry, Jude, and Julius, who have incorporated physical activity into their daily/weekly lives, I (Michelle) struggle with this. At times, I do a relatively good job of taking walks as a form of exercise; however, when the weather gets colder, I often use that as an excuse to remain physically inactive.

An exercise program needs to be planned with care to minimize the risks and maximize the gains to your overall wellness. We suggest that you find something suitable for your age, physical condition, and life circumstances and that you want to make a regular part of your life. Some may prefer exercising in a group, others may exercise on a stationary bicycle while watching television or listening to music. Some like jogging, and others may participate in competitive sports. If you select a form of exercise that you enjoy, you are likely to engage in this practice on a regular basis. Many grassroots groups are getting together for free fitness activities. One community group that promotes self-care and strives to be inclusive is the November Project. To get started, follow this link: http://november-project.com/how-to-join/. Key components of the November Project are positivity and community. Check out the possibilities in your town or city.

There is no right path to exercising; each of us must design our own plan to keep us physically active and psychologically engaged. Not only does exercise do a good deal to keep us physically fit, it can also be a source of enjoyment and relaxation, as well as a way to cope with the stress of daily life.

Questions for Reflection

1. When you evaluate your diet and nutrition, how well do you fare? If you could give yourself a letter grade for your diet and nutrition, what grade would you earn?
2. How satisfied are you with your current nutritional practices? If you are unsatisfied, what changes do you need to make in your diet? How likely are you to implement these changes? How will making these nutritional changes improve your well-being?
3. How much physical exercise do you get each week? Is it sufficient? If you are not satisfied with your level of physical activity, what could you do to increase it? What gets in your way or prevents you from exercising?

Re-Creating Ourselves Through Recreation

Finding enjoyment through activities that are not related to our jobs is essential to our well-being and is an excellent way to reduce stress and prevent burnout. As much as you may feel invested in your work, you are likely to compromise your effectiveness as a helper if you rarely take breaks and fail to develop other interests. Even rewarding work takes energy, and most of us need a life besides work to derive satisfaction. Recreation involves creating new interests that become our path to vitality. A challenge many of us face is balancing work, family, and leisure pursuits. We need to remind ourselves to pause long enough to savor and enjoy experiences that nurture and rejuvenate us. With some imagination, we can identify activities that not only provide a time out from work but enhance our relationships with others. Consider the benefits of focusing on reenergizing yourself through recreational activities. Pursuing a new hobby or resuming interest in an old hobby can become a vital part of your stress management strategy.

Many years ago, I (Michelle) was an in-home family therapist and worked with a clinical supervisor who was an avid birder. He and his wife often took weekend trips to sites where they could spend time together outdoors and watch birds. He developed expertise about birds and was fascinated with them. This pastime was exactly what he needed to balance the intense demands and stress of serving a client population that struggled to meet the basic tasks of independent living and constantly were in jeopardy of having their children removed by Child Protective Services. These clients needed a great deal of support from mental health professionals and other community resources. I sometimes felt ill-equipped to help them in all of the ways that were needed, and I too needed to find an outlet for my stress. I did not become a birder, but I enjoyed going to dinner and a movie with my then partner John or connecting with friends. I continue to have a demanding schedule, but I do make time to attend concerts and go to the movies. I am inspired by art, music, theater, and dance (which I used to study many years ago). Reconnecting to art through theatrical and musical events would energize me, reduce my stress, and bring meaning to my life.

My (Jude) recreational needs have shifted as I transition from doctoral student to professor, and from bachelor to husband. As a doctoral student, my recreation included time alone. I felt as though I was always around others and busy teaching, supervising, and counseling. As an introvert, it was recharging to have time to watch television series, read books, and go for walks alone. As a faculty member, I find myself going out for dinner with colleagues, meeting for coffee with students, and walking around campus with advisees. As a husband, my recreation involves activities such as watching movies or enjoying food together, playing tennis, running, walking in parks, enjoying the state zoo and aquarium, and visiting with friends for game nights. Most recently, I have been learning to play golf. I hit the ball straight 2 out of every 10 swings, but I enjoy doing something I have never done before.

I (Julius) am still coming to terms with the changes in my recreational needs as I balance work and a budding new family. Before my son was born, my wife and I worked out together, saw movies in the middle of the week, or simply enjoyed each other's company at home. As a new parent and professional, family-friendly activities are my newest source of recreation. Attending kite festivals, movies in the park, dinosaur exhibits at a community center, or rolling around on the floor making funny faces at my son are all new forms of recreation. I am becoming more intentional about modifying my recreation to include much needed family time after a long workweek.

I (Jerry) value recreation and do make the time to participate in many activities. Walking along the shore at the beach, I am envious of young people on surf boards or parasailing out into the ocean. I appreciate the agility of those who gracefully skateboard on campus. Although I would love to participate in these daring forms of recreation, I realize my limits and let myself enjoy watching others. Marianne (and some of our friends) and I often enjoy concerts (both classical and jazz). I played tenor saxophone and clarinet in the college band, but frankly I never was a very accomplished musician. Now I love hearing the big bands, and I am especially fond of listening to an entire saxophone section perform their artistry with precision, grace, and harmony. If I were talented musically, I could dream of going "on the road again" and performing professionally like Willie Nelson.

Some combine their musical talent with counseling, and others use music as a path for self-care. Brandon Wildish achieved a master's degree in counseling but chose to transform his musical talent into his main career. His story illustrates how we can re-create ourselves through our self-care activities.

Music as a Path for Self-Care

Brandon Wildish

I hold a special place in my heart for the counseling profession, but my first love has always been music. I find it ironic that what I learned in my counseling program helped me discover the courage and clarity of thought to pursue music as my career. In many ways, I owe my success and confidence in the music business to my counseling degree. The countless hours of introspective work and self-evaluation required to be an effective counselor provided an opportunity for me to gain clarity and solidify my life goals.

While earning my master's degree, I supplemented my income as a musician. I did well booking gigs, but I never intended to make it a full-time profession. I was focused on becoming a licensed therapist and was immersed in my schooling and diligently working at my practicum site, accruing the necessary hours to graduate.

My practicum site was at a nonprofit organization that primarily focused on individual therapy for children and adolescents. I felt fortunate to be part of a team that was organized and successful in maintaining a steady stream of clients, but my workload was immense and sometimes burdensome. I felt bogged down with the amount of paperwork required for each client.

I attempted to give myself fully to each of my clients in our sessions and often took my work home with me. I found it difficult to create boundaries for my work life, and I frequently spent time reflecting on previous sessions, combing over potential meta-messages or personal foibles. It became clear that I struggled with leaving my work at the workplace.

Music became my saving grace in tackling fatigue. Rather than combat my blurred boundaries, I embraced them. My schooling had taught me that journaling was a useful tool for gaining clarity of thought, and I adapted this idea to music and began to write songs about my experiences in counseling. The process helped create a calm in me that I could not otherwise achieve.

Initially I found myself writing songs with a destination in mind, creating a fully defined marketable product. It soon became clear to me that I needed different rules if I were to use music as my tool for self-care. I abandoned my expectations and assumptions about song writing and allowed my most immediate thoughts and feelings to dictate my chord progressions and their degree of intensity. Sometimes I didn't feel the need to write any of my thoughts down. I simply allowed my feelings to be expressed through my guitar. My songs could last seconds or several minutes. From a conventional sense, the songs were muddled and seemingly elementary, and I found this incredibly liberating! I needed both the art of creating music and the freedom to not have my music mean anything to anyone else for it to effectively work as my form of self-care. I would leave my song-writing sessions refreshed and feeling accomplished despite their haphazard format.

My process of creating music has been a powerful tool for both self-efficacy and clarity of thought. The perspective I gained by conceptualizing my therapeutic work through music began to seep into my sessions, and I started to view the client–therapist relationship as a kind of song. A rhythm can be found in each therapy session. The client determines the tempo and style of "music" based on his or her choices of topics, body language, and emotional energy brought into the room. I would try to "jam" along with what the client was playing in session, and we would see if anything seemed to strike a chord. It's a bit abstract, but it worked for me and helped temper some of my anxiety and the pressure I created for myself around being a therapist.

Ultimately I decided to pursue music instead of therapy, but I have not completely ruled out counseling as a potential path to pursue. Should I return to counseling, it is certain that I will be bringing my music with me.

• • •

Playing music and listening to music can be wonderful form of recreation, a way of relaxing, an avocation, and an avenue for managing stress. Brandon found music to be a source for dealing with the demands of his work, a way to manage boundaries, and a key pathway to self-care, and he also found a way to serve others by being a professional musician.

Providing Service to Others as a Lifestyle Pattern

Service to others is one of the therapeutic lifestyle changes that can enhance the quality of our lives (Walsh, 2011). Perhaps you gravitated toward counseling in the first place because you derived satisfaction and fulfillment from helping people navigate their struggles. Your career may be characterized as providing service to others, and you might well be thinking, "I already spend my working (and waking) hours helping people. Why would I want to spend my limited free time doing more of that in the name of self-care?"As part of your self-care, we hope you will reflect on all of the service that you have provided to your clients and think about the difference you have made in their lives. We can become consumed with keeping up with the demands of our jobs and fail to take the time to engage in self-reflection about the positive changes that we may have played a role in facilitating.

You may need to place boundaries on how much you are "serving" others for the sake of preserving your own wellness, but some of you may become energized by the notion of seeking out opportunities to provide service to others in new ways. In recent years one of our colleagues, a counselor educator, has made multiple trips to a country devastated by a massive earthquake and plagued with many other problems to empower young girls there to persist in their education. Although these trips are nothing short of challenging in so many ways, she has expressed a passion for providing this service and now views it as part of her calling.

Changing the Way You Think as a Route to Managing Stress

Our beliefs largely determine how we interpret events. It is the meaning we give to these events rather than the events themselves that influences how stress affects us. Cognitive behavior therapy teaches us that our thinking greatly influences how we feel and how we act. Cognitive behavior therapists help people become aware of their cognitions—the dialogue that goes on within us—

and how their thinking affects how they feel and act. The cognitive approaches offer specific strategies to individuals for modifying self-defeating cognitions and for developing sound thinking that leads to less stressful living.

If you are a practicing clinician, you are most likely already familiar with the principles and techniques of cognitive behavioral therapy. Nevertheless, we are all prone at some time to engage in self-defeating thinking and ineffective self-talk. If we recognize the nature of our faulty beliefs and understand how they lead to problems, we can begin the process of defusing these self-defeating cognitions. Because we have the capacity to escalate the stress we experience, we also have the means to lessen it. Cognitive strategies can be employed to retain vitality on both personal and professional levels.

One useful approach to managing stress is by learning to identify and challenge, and ultimately change, our faulty beliefs. Exploring ways that our cognitions influence us is a useful route to achieving happiness. Human service providers often incorporate a wide range of dysfunctional beliefs that impair our capacity to function effectively when people seek our assistance. We may distort the processing of information, which can easily lead to faulty assumptions and misconceptions. As counseling practitioners, we can complicate our life by believing that we *must* be all-knowing and perfect. If we feel anxious about the job we are doing, it is time to examine our basic assumptions and beliefs to determine how they are influencing what we are doing and how we are feeling. As we become more aware of our faulty thinking, we are in a position to change these patterns (Ellis & Ellis, 2011). We can learn the difference between those aspects of reality that we can control and those that we cannot change, and we can choose how we interpret and react to our situation. The Serenity Prayer provides a useful lens to manage stressful situations by reflecting on what we can do to increase serenity in our lives.

> God, grant me the serenity to accept the things I cannot change, courage to change the things I can, and wisdom to know the difference.

Debbie Joffe Ellis, a leading proponent of rational emotive behavior therapy and a licensed psychologist, mental health counselor, and adjunct professor of psychology at Columbia University, explores common beliefs that create misery and suggests a pathway to changing self-destructive beliefs into constructive beliefs, which can increase our happiness.

Remembering We Are Human Too!

● ●

Debbie Joffe Ellis

Like many in our profession, I want to do the best work I possibly can in my practice with clients, teaching, and writing. I have experienced loss, grief, challenges, and disappointments in my life, and I have my sensitivities and vulnerabilities. It serves me marvelously to do my best to prevent burnout and unnecessary upset. For me, self-care includes being gentle and compassionate with myself and applying the tenets of rational emotive behavior therapy (REBT), which is my theory of choice.

My remarkable husband, Albert Ellis, created REBT and heralded the cognitive revolution in psychotherapy. We experienced immense joy in our lives together, yet we also endured brutal events in our work life during his final years and as his health declined. He was a solid and unwavering model for me of refusing to succumb to attitudes of despair and hopelessness, even during great trials and tribulations.

When it comes to my self-care, basic commonsense activities include healthy eating, exercising, getting sufficient rest, spiritual nourishment, enjoyment, and recreation. It includes preventing upset and making an effort to create and maintain a healthy emotional climate within myself. I practice daily meditation and yoga, which brings clarity and calm even when I am sleep-deprived. Every morning I take time to remember all that I am grateful for in my life and in the wonder of the world of which we are a part. This is a part of finding happiness in life rather than settling for misery.

To prevent upset, I watch out for any tendency to unnecessarily blame myself if a client is not improving as quickly as I would prefer, or to feel annoyance or frustration at myself, and perhaps toward the client, if the client relapses or refuses to make any effort in areas explored in therapy. I make an effort to prevent weak and insufficient boundaries, and I try not to overidentify with clients' (and others') pains. I do my best to prevent distress that comes from overthinking about clients and their circumstances.

A small selection of irrational beliefs that create upset include:

- I should always excel in my work with others and always succeed in helping them achieve total happiness.
- I am a failure when clients don't improve soon enough or relapse.
- Clients should always comply with my guidance and do what I think they should do.
- I can't stand it when clients are difficult and resistant.
- I must always be there for anyone who needs me, be they family, friends, students, or clients.
- I should put the needs of others above my own.

Statements such as these can be repeated endlessly in our self-talk, and as you can see, most of these statements refer to feelings of inadequacy, a nagging belief that we should be more, and a chronic sense of self-doubt. REBT reminds us to vigorously question and dispute such beliefs, then to come up with effective rational beliefs, and to repeat them daily until we feel substantial conviction about them.

Some of the effective new beliefs that emerge, upon disputing, include:

- I intend to do the best I can in my work, but I am a fallible human and can make mistakes. When I do, I seek lessons and ways to do better going forward.
- Doing poorly does not make me a wretch or failure but a human who at times is ineffective, and at other times successful.
- I strive to unconditionally accept myself, with my flaws and vulnerabilities.
- Perfection is a self-defeating and unreachable quest. I strive to excel when possible, without needing to be perfect.
- I do my best to help clients and others and remind myself that they ultimately are responsible for their own level of happiness.
- When I choose to put the needs of others before my own, I do this from the heart and not because I think I "should."
- When I say "no" to others and set up boundaries, I can stand any rejection or displeasure they express.
- I can stand what I don't like; I just don't like it.
- I remind myself that life inevitably includes suffering, but it also contains much that is joyful and awesome.

In a loving letter to me, my beloved Al concluded by writing this: "I could go on and on about your rare ability to care for others and enjoy doing so. Quite unique, and I think it adds greatly to your life. Cherish it—but try to reduce the suffering that sometimes goes with it. That would be quite a feat. Try for it as your years go caringly on!" I also most wholeheartedly wish that for my fellow therapists.

* * *

By assuming the major share of responsibility for our clients, we deprive them of the responsibility to direct their own lives and create stress for ourselves. Reread the faulty belief statements Debbie Joffe Ellis listed, and underline any statements that might ring true for you. Do you tend to make statements like these or assume responsibility for being the "perfect" counselor? What are some examples of things you say to yourself that create stress for you? If you were able to change your thinking and become less self-critical, how do you think this would affect you?

We can change our way of thinking and our behavior patterns to reduce stressful situations and manage stress more effectively. We can discover the difference between the situations we can change and those we cannot change, and we can strive for wisdom in understanding the difference. The way we process and interpret the stress of daily living has a great deal to do with our mental attitude.

Personal Therapy as a Form of Self-Care

We would be remiss if we failed to discuss personal therapy as an invaluable form of self-care and an excellent strategy for coping with stress. We strongly endorse the value of personal therapy for counselors-in-training because it can be one of the ways to maintain self-care and competence throughout your career. Seasoned therapists often return to therapy, suggesting that this practice is critical in helping them remain competent and in coping with challenges in their professional work (Probst, 2015). Wise and Barnett (2016) reinforce our view that participating in personal psychotherapy on a periodic basis is a self-care strategy and a form of positive self-development. Experiencing our own therapy can give us a sense of what counseling might be like for clients. It provides a basis for understanding and compassion for our clients, especially when we draw on our own memories of reaching impasses in our therapy, both wanting to go further and at the same time being ambivalent about making changes. We learn what it feels like to deal with anxieties that are aroused by self-disclosure and self-exploration and how to creatively facilitate deeper levels of self-exploration in clients. We gain a greater appreciation and understanding of how challenging it is for clients to come to us and the courage it takes for them to reveal intimate aspects of their lives. Our experience of therapy is a way for us to learn how to establish and maintain a working alliance and how to deal with the challenges and uncertainties involved in therapeutic work (Ronnestad, Orlinsky, & Wiseman, 2016).

One study of personal psychotherapy among 3,995 counselors, psychologists, social workers, nurses, and psychiatrists in six English-speaking countries found that a very high percentage (87%) of their overall sample engaged in personal therapy at least once: "If there is one thing that therapists appear to have in common, it is the experience of being in therapy" (Orlinsky, Schofield, Schroder, & Kazantzis, 2011, p. 828). Benefits of psychotherapy for *therapists as people* include "positive increments in self-awareness, self-knowledge, self-understanding, self-care, and self-acceptance as well as reduction in symptoms and improved relationships and personal growth generally" (Ronnestad et al., 2016, p. 230). Personal therapy can be instrumental in increasing empathy, enhancing warmth and relational skills, expanding our awareness of transference and countertransference processes, and reducing the likelihood of burnout or unethical behavior (Orlinsky et al., 2011).

VanderWal (2017) examined the relationship between counselor trainees' personal therapy experiences and client outcomes. Her research found that clients of trainees who participated in their own personal therapy during graduate school reduced their distress more quickly than clients of counselor trainees who had no personal therapy experience or whose therapy occurred prior to training. Similarly, clients showed greater total decreases in psychological distress when their counselors reported experiencing personal therapy during graduate training compared to not attending personal therapy, or experiencing it prior to graduate training.

Perhaps you currently are or have been in personal therapy and do not need to be reminded of its value. However, not every counselor trainee or practitioner is on board with this idea. I (Michelle) recall a conversation I had with a graduate student who was so resistant to the idea of self-exploration that she complained quite forcefully about having to write more than one paper related to personal awareness and growth. She informed me that she had written a paper in another class about an area in which she needed to grow, and as far as she was concerned, she had done her work! She viewed self-exploration projects as a waste of her time. We must ask ourselves, if those in the helping professions are not convinced of the effectiveness of counseling as a means of managing stress or working through issues that cause stress, why should clients be willing to seek our services to work through their stress?

I (Michelle) tend to be open about the fact that I have done quite a bit of work and self-exploration in therapy over the years. Long before I entered the field, I found therapy to be a godsend as I addressed family issues and identity issues related to being adopted. At later points in my life, I returned to therapy to get support during challenging times, such as when my relationship with my significant partner John ended, and to process grief. I also have used time in my personal therapy to process interactions I have had with colleagues, clients, and graduate students. My time in therapy is precious to me, and I will continue to use it as a resource for both personal and professional reasons.

Promoting Self-Care Through the Practice of Self-Reflection

There are many routes to self-care. Less formal avenues to personal and professional development include reflecting on and evaluating the meaning of your work and life, remaining open to the reactions of significant people in your life, traveling to experience different cultures, engaging in spiritual activities, enjoying physical exercise, spending time with friends and family, and being involved with an avocation. Self-reflection through interaction with others is an integral aspect of many of these activities. Creating a professional network is extremely valuable. Johnson and colleagues (2012) use the term *competent community* to refer to a network of colleagues who provide valuable feedback, assist in monitoring behavior, and offer opportunities for self-reflection. Self-reflection does not come automatically; it involves attitudes and skills that must be acquired and nurtured over time. Knapp, Gottlieb, and Handelsman (2017) define *self-reflection* as "a deliberate metacognitive process involving self-observation of thoughts, feelings, attitudes, and behaviors, with as much objectivity as possible" (p. 167). They offer these insights as a route to increasing our capacity for self-reflection:

- Being a client in psychotherapy allows counselors to experience self-reflection, which is both a form of self-care and is instrumental in working with clients.
- Continuing education, especially experiential education, can be tailored to foster self-reflection. The peer review process will be most helpful if therapists approach it with a self-reflective attitude and are open to learning about themselves.
- Inviting feedback from clients or other service participants, as well as colleagues, is an excellent way to practice self-reflection and decide what behaviors might be modified.
- Expressive writing is a valuable source of self-reflection. By creating a personal journal, counselors can reflect on both their personal and professional development.
- Learning and practicing mindfulness skills have benefits in reducing stress, can increase self-awareness, and can be used for both personal and professional development.

This self-reflective stance is a pattern therapists can develop during their academic and supervisory training that they will be able to intentionally use throughout their careers. Many of the narratives by our contributors provide specific pathways to enhance self-reflection. There is no one best approach, and you may need to experiment with a variety of ways to engage in self-reflection and self-care.

Reflecting on Your Self-Care Practices

Spend a few minutes now reflecting on your present level of self-care and changes you may want to make. Ask yourself the degree to which you know your priorities and are acting on them. A good way to start is by taking this brief self-care assessment and reflecting on your ratings.

Self-Care Self-Assessment

Read each statement and rate yourself on a 10-point scale in terms of *where you are now* and *where you would like to be* with regard to achieving balance in that particular area.

1 = *Strongly Disagree*   10 = *Strongly Agree*

1. I am able to manage my time effectively in my professional life.
    ❏ 1   ❏ 2   ❏ 3   ❏ 4   ❏ 5   ❏ 6   ❏ 7   ❏ 8   ❏ 9   ❏ 10

2. I am able to manage my time effectively in my personal life.
    ❏ 1   ❏ 2   ❏ 3   ❏ 4   ❏ 5   ❏ 6   ❏ 7   ❏ 8   ❏ 9   ❏ 10

3. I regularly set aside time to meditate.
    ❏ 1   ❏ 2   ❏ 3   ❏ 4   ❏ 5   ❏ 6   ❏ 7   ❏ 8   ❏ 9   ❏ 10

4. I practice mindfulness much of the time and am satisfied with my level of presence in my daily interactions with others.
    ❏ 1   ❏ 2   ❏ 3   ❏ 4   ❏ 5   ❏ 6   ❏ 7   ❏ 8   ❏ 9   ❏ 10

5. I practice yoga, Pilates, or another form of exercise on a regular basis and can feel the benefits in terms of improved physical well-being.
    ❏ 1   ❏ 2   ❏ 3   ❏ 4   ❏ 5   ❏ 6   ❏ 7   ❏ 8   ❏ 9   ❏ 10

6. Spirituality or religion play an important role in my wellness.
    ❏ 1   ❏ 2   ❏ 3   ❏ 4   ❏ 5   ❏ 6   ❏ 7   ❏ 8   ❏ 9   ❏ 10

7. I make time to enjoy nature and appreciate its therapeutic value.
    ❏ 1   ❏ 2   ❏ 3   ❏ 4   ❏ 5   ❏ 6   ❏ 7   ❏ 8   ❏ 9   ❏ 10

8. I engage in recreational activities that reenergize me.
    ❏ 1   ❏ 2   ❏ 3   ❏ 4   ❏ 5   ❏ 6   ❏ 7   ❏ 8   ❏ 9   ❏ 10

9. Providing service to others outside of my professional work brings meaning to my life.
    ❏ 1   ❏ 2   ❏ 3   ❏ 4   ❏ 5   ❏ 6   ❏ 7   ❏ 8   ❏ 9   ❏ 10

10. My self-talk empowers me and has a positive impact on my wellness.
    ❏ 1   ❏ 2   ❏ 3   ❏ 4   ❏ 5   ❏ 6   ❏ 7   ❏ 8   ❏ 9   ❏ 10

Concluding Thoughts

We cannot eliminate all of the stressors in our life, but we can manage stress more effectively and experience more joy. Apply some of the approaches and draw upon some of the ideas described in this chapter to attain your self-care goals. It is important that you develop your own methods of self-reflection and self-care and consistently work at applying them to a variety of situations in your life. Keep in mind that you are a whole being and need to integrate your physical, emotional, social, mental, and spiritual dimensions. An effective self-care program involves reflecting on how well you are taking care of yourself in all of these areas. If you neglect any one of these aspects of yourself, you may feel the impact on other dimensions of your being. You must decide what you want and need to change in your life or lifestyle to enhance your well-being. Your self-care regimen is uniquely yours!

Chapter 6

Establishing Personal and Professional Boundaries

Effective boundaries protect the professional relationship and help us integrate our personal and professional selves. In our work as counselors, educators, clinical supervisors, and counselors-in-training, we constantly work to define and maintain clear boundaries. It is well known that boundary problems can result in harm to clients, students, and supervisees and result in distress for counselors, educators, and clinical supervisors who hold more power in the professional relationship. Boundary issues extend beyond the professional realm and can affect our personal lives too. In this chapter we focus on our successful and unsuccessful experiences setting boundaries at home and at work. Kottler (2017) notes that the personal and professional boundaries we define and enforce serve to protect both our clients and ourselves. Kottler encourages us to think about the purpose of boundaries: "We sometimes confuse boundaries with walls—that is, about the relationship designed for safety and efficiency as opposed to those artificial (and perhaps unnecessary) limits that function as armor" (p. 38). It is our hope that this discussion will inspire you to reflect on the kind of boundaries you want to establish between your work life and personal life, and between you and those you serve professionally.

Most of us are extremely busy these days, and we may feel there is not enough time in the day to accomplish even a fraction of the items on our to-do list. If you juggle the demands of a time-intensive and high-pressure job with family obligations, you know firsthand how stressful it can be. Yet we are expected to deliver both at work and at home. Some researchers have shown that balancing career and family roles introduces a high amount of stress in life (Kelly et al., 2014), We need only reflect on our own lived experiences and observe those around us struggling to balance multiple roles to understand the stress related to this balancing act. Life's demands can be taxing and overwhelming, and creating and maintaining healthy boundaries is one avenue toward practicing better self-care and reducing stress.

In recent years, technological advances have blurred the boundaries between work and personal time for many of us. Technology undeniably has enhanced our lives in many ways, but it has changed the way that many of us work. Telecommuting and flexible work hours may be quite appealing, but these changes tend to muddy the boundary between personal time and work time. It is not uncommon for people to work during evening hours, overnight, and on weekends in today's world. Moreover, being able to communicate with coworkers via email and text messaging have turned our homes, the local coffee house, or virtually any place into an office space. "The anytime-anywhere connectedness of employees to their work facilitated by modern technologies blurs the traditional boundaries that have customarily separated work from family and has changed the meaning of being at home" (Derks & Bakker, 2014, p. 413). Smartphone use can contribute to work–home interference, "a process of negative interactions between work and home domains" (p. 412), and contribute to burnout. Incompatibility between work and home demands causes strain to spill over from one domain to the other, leading to displaced stress. For example, a counselor catching up on paperwork and making phone calls to clients from home on the weekend may experience stress from two directions: (1) her children may be bickering with each other in the background or vying for her attention while she is trying to write coherent thoughts in her case notes despite feeling distracted, or (2) after ending a frustrating phone call with a passive-aggressive client, she may displace feelings of irritation onto her partner who asks for help with household tasks, potentially causing strain between them. Individuals who fail to set clear personal and professional boundaries can become overwhelmed and experience burnout if this problem is left unaddressed (Carrola, Olivarez, & Karcher, 2016).

Healthy Work–Life Boundaries

Our ability to maintain a balance between our personal and professional lives is a first-order principle of effective self-care.

Maintaining this balance enables us to put our energy fully into our work and also to be present and connected in our home life. However, achieving this balance is easier said than done! Researchers examining work–life balance among counselor educators note that budget cuts as a result of economic conditions often lead to increased workloads with fewer resources, which we have seen in recent times (Hermann, Ziomek-Daigle, & Dockery, 2014). They note that the 40-hour workweek is no longer the norm in many professions and that an academic career "mirrors larger American workforce trends" (p. 111). Whether you are counselor educators, clinical supervisors, clinicians, or graduate students, there is a high likelihood that you feel your schedule is overloaded, and a plausible reason for that is that your schedule *is* overloaded. Finding balance between our work life and our home life may seem unattainable and unrealistic, but this goal is worth striving toward. Setting healthy boundaries and striving for work–life balance are essential parts of taking care of ourselves.

Boundary issues can evolve in subtle ways, slowly eroding our well-being. We may say "yes" to projects before considering our schedules, bring case notes home from the office to catch up, work on a paper or a report during a family movie night, or go into the office on the weekend. Each of these actions separately may not threaten our personal/professional equilibrium, but when they become a pattern, counselors can become unbalanced, isolated, and fatigued. Burnout is a serious hazard of working in the helping professions, and we must be vigilant that occasional instances of burning the midnight oil do not become the norm and lead to a more chronic condition of burnout.

In "A Counselor's Journey Back From Burnout," Jessica Smith (2017), a licensed professional counselor and a licensed addictions counselor, described how her passion to help others led to burnout. She often came to work early and stayed late to meet with clients. Smith consistently rearranged her schedule to squeeze in more clients, even though she did not have the time or energy to do more. She eventually realized that she was so invested in working with clients with dire needs that she had blurred her boundaries. Her high degree of empathy and compassion for her clients resulted in losing herself in those relationships. Smith's main priority was helping others, but it came at the expense of helping herself. Because Smith's physical symptoms of burnout continued to worsen, she sought personal therapy. She resigned from her job and spent time traveling and reconnecting with herself. A highlight of her self-care journey was spending 6 days as a student at a Zen Buddhist monastery. One of the most impactful lessons she learned was that she gave much more than she received from others. Smith has this message for helpers: "We often feel it is easier to give than it is to receive, yet we need to give *and* receive in order not just to survive but thrive" (p. 50).

When defining healthy work–life boundaries, consider the many roles you play both personally and professionally, describe what an optimal work–life balance would look like in your own life, and consider how your personal values might influence your work–life balance. How involved are you in leisure or recreational activities, and what importance do you place on them? Is religion or spirituality a major part of your life and one of your core values? If so, how much time and energy do you devote to faith-based activities in a meaningful way? If you are highly invested in your children's after-school activities, how much time do you invest and what role do you play in supporting them in these activities (such as driving your child to soccer practice or coaching your child's team)? If you place a high value on advancing your career, are you willing to work overtime to achieve the level of success you desire? What other priorities compete with your career aspirations, and how can you fit them into your weekly schedule?

Adrienne Naquin-Bolton, director of a university counseling center, shares her experience with shifting priorities and finding a balance between her roles as a mother and a counselor.

Balancing Personal and Professional Roles as a Form of Self-Care

Adrienne Naquin-Bolton

I worked in the counseling field for 2 years before I had my first child. Since that time, my life has gone through a series of shifts, and my priorities have shifted as well. I fell so in love with my sweet little girl that I decided, only 2 months after returning to work, that I wanted to stay home with her. (Being in a workplace where bullying was the norm helped me make that decision.) Unfortunately, that loving feeling was short-lived and was replaced with a lack of purpose and meaning and a yearning to have my professional identity back.

I'm sure most parents can recognize this struggle for balance between two very important aspects of life: the personal and the professional. It has been, and continues to be, a learning process for me. I ask myself these questions: What is more important, my 2-year-old son being sent home from day care for vomiting or my afternoon schedule filled with clients? Can I take him with me and leave him with the secretary, confident that my thoughts won't be with him when I am in session with clients for 50 minutes at a time? Should I change career paths and accept a job with less pay and fewer benefits but that allows greater flexibility and time off?

At times I feel insecure, particularly when I struggle to make it seem like my life is all together. I am constantly confronted with difficult choices. Do I have a Pinterest-worthy birthday party for my children (who could quite honestly care less; all they want is cake and presents anyway) or pick up cake, ice cream, and generic birthday decorations the day of the party? For the holidays, do I try to compete with the impressive Christmas lights display of my neighbors, or am I satisfied with my pathetic-looking tree? I make lists of daily cleaning tasks so I don't get bogged down with a filthy house to tackle over the weekend, but by the time I get home from work, the list is already buried under a pile of mail, school art projects, and other clutter. Let's face it, writing case notes is like doing the laundry; just when you think you've caught up, another batch is waiting to be done!

So what's the solution? In my sessions with clients, I often use the analogy of a car's tires. Each tire represents an aspect of the self (physical, emotional, mental, and spiritual). Then I ask my clients to evaluate the pressure of each tire. Are some overinflated, are some underinflated, and are some just outright flat? This quick assessment gives them an idea of which areas in life need more attention and which could be put on the back burner for a while.

Today my emotional "tire" (aspect of self) is underinflated in regard to time with my children. I confess that I was the best parent . . . before I had kids. I swore that they would not watch television or spend more than 15 minutes at a time on handheld devices. Once I had kids, those ideals changed. Now I'll set up one to watch *The Polar Express* (in July!) and the other to watch Play-Doh YouTube videos while I do my own thing— guilt-free! If I am honest, a part of me feels regret that I cannot spend the time I truly would like to with my children. I reconcile these thoughts by being mindful that my sacrifice (and theirs) makes it possible for me to be fully present with another person's suffering and a witness to personal growth, and it provides financial benefits for my family. This reconciliation gives meaning to my professional and personal life.

As with all things, integrating the professional and personal aspects of life is a learning process. I am aware that I still struggle with perfectionist tendencies and with enjoying and appreciating the simple things. But when I take a step back and reflect on my life, a date night with my husband, sharing stories with coworkers, a night out with girlfriends, throwing a Frisbee with the kids on the front lawn—these are the things that matter.

• • •

Ed Neukrug, a professor of counseling and human services at Old Dominion University, shares how he has found a balance between the many roles he has assumed throughout his career. He explains his concept of living what he calls "the good life."

Balancing My Personal and Professional Life: My Self-Care "It Factors"

Ed Neukrug

Self-care, to me, morphs as we age and is critical to ensuring that our existence is meaningful as each of us defines meaningfulness. Over the years, I have settled into a unique self-care regimen that generally, but not always, works. When I'm not successful, I say to myself, "that's OK" because my personal self-care regimen is a journey—not a goal. With a bit of mindfulness, I try to remember that self-care lows and highs are road signs that remind us of how we can tweak our existence so that we are somewhat satisfied with who we are and how we behave in life. Here is a bit of history about my self-care journey.

When I was chair of our department, I had to balance my administrative duties, my writing, my teaching, and my relationships with my wife, children, and close friends. With all these roles and duties, I needed to learn how to manage the many hats I wore. I found a self-care regimen that more or less worked for me. This regimen did not appear out of the blue; parts of it were always there. But I tried to be more mindful about it and settled into it with a bit more purposefulness. Then and now, my self-care includes trying to eat well, exercising five to seven times a week, working hard and being prepared, seeing a therapist, taking breaks and vacations, and being a good husband, father, and friend. I also found that being honest with those close to me, including those with whom I worked, was critical to my balance. Secrets and deceptions are a burden on my soul. I eventually developed my unique self-care regimen. Was I perfect? Of course not. Sometimes I found myself rushing through a meeting to get back to my writing. Other times stress would get to me, and I wouldn't be as kind as I wanted to be with family and friends. Once in a while I found myself at Burger King ordering a Whopper. Sometimes, I found that I needed to purposefully find time for my wife and go away with her for the weekend. And still other times I found myself dealing with a nagging feeling about someone I cared about—perhaps a bit of anger or concern that I hadn't shared and needed to address. Generally, my self-care regimen worked, which is why I continue with it today.

A couple of years ago I had very treatable kidney cancer. I'm fine now, but it added one more piece to my regimen—to remember to love, not judge people. When I was first diagnosed, I realized that of all the things important in my life, my relationships were the most critical. And I thought about the fact that sometimes I didn't nurture those relationships as much as I could. You see, kidney cancer was a gift to me. It made me realize (or at least strongly reminded me) how important it was to love people—not judge people. I even bought a special ring that I wear on my right fourth finger to remind me to love people. I don't always wear it, and I don't always remember to love not judge, but it's there enough of the time to remind me of one more thing I have to do to keep myself in balance.

Today, trying to keep my life in balance is key to what people used to call "the good life." It includes eating well, working out, loving others, working hard, taking breaks, giving to my family and friends, continuing my personal therapy, and being real. Those are the things that seem to work for me. I call those my personal, self-care "it factors" because I believe the combination of factors that work for one person will not work for every person. I don't meditate and I don't pray, but I know that works for others. I am not a vegetarian, and I won't go sky-diving. My balance in life has to do with discovering what works for me. Have you found what works for you?

● ● ●

The Good Life

Ed Neukrug's idea of the good life includes eating well, working out, loving others, working hard, taking breaks, giving to family and friends, continuing personal therapy, and being real. I (Jude) agree with this idea of the good life but would add that for me the good life also involves being part of professional projects that give me a sense of citizenship within the counseling field. My self-care is threatened if I am feeling that I am solely working on projects for the sake of getting one step closer to tenure. I have a personal need to feel that my work can make a significant impact on the counseling field and the populations we serve, and I tend to choose projects carefully and intentionally. The good life involves sitting in my office and surveying my projects, in their various phases of completion, and knowing that I have the potential to improve my community.

In my (Michelle's) view, and at this stage in my career, the good life includes allowing myself more time to relax and incorporating more fun into my schedule. In fact, one day I would like to not have a schedule! There is never a lack of work on my plate. Even though I enjoy the various projects I work on, I recognize my need for more downtime. Like my coauthors, I derive great pleasure from the work I do. I am energized by witnessing the progress of the students I offer guidance to at the Center for Talented Youth as well as the master's students I teach in the counseling program at Johns Hopkins University. Making a positive difference in this world means a great deal to me. I want my efforts to matter, and I want to do my part to leave this world in a better place.

Jon Carlson, a legend in the counseling profession, died in February 2017. He was a leading figure in the fields of psychology, counseling, education, and Adlerian theory and practice. Throughout his life, he put Alfred Adler's idea of social interest into action as a positive force in the world. Some of Jon Carlson's accomplishments in his distinguished career included publishing 64 books, 185 articles, and over 300 training videos. Although his professional achievements were impressive, Carlson did not equate his achievements with the good life. Carlson thought it was a mistake to look at single events in judging who we are as a person. "I measure success and satisfaction on how I get along with the important people in my life: my wife, children, friends, colleagues, bosses and the students whom I teach" (Carlson as cited in Englar-Carlson & Kottler, 2017, p. 42). These words of Jon Carlson capture the essence of what holistic self-care and the good life meant to him: "I have worked hard at being physically healthy, mentally healthy, spiritually healthy and relationally healthy. You can't teach what you don't know. Our clients do not believe us when we suggest that they do things or think in ways that are not consistent with how we live our life" (p. 43).

My (Jerry's) view resonates with my colleague and friend Jon Carlson's view of putting our ideals into action with how we are living. For me, a key part of the good life is taking care of myself and expressing gratitude for the many blessings and gifts in my life. I also believe that giving back is of the utmost importance. I don't measure the good life in terms of material possessions but in terms of how I can contribute professionally. I do not have grandiose ideas about changing society, but small changes can be significant, which is why I continue to remain professionally involved. Alfred Adler's idea of social interest is a key message for me, and I do my best to share whatever talents I have in making a difference in the lives of others.

Questions for Reflection

1. How successful do you think you have been so far in establishing a healthy work–life balance through establishing and maintaining clear boundaries?

2. As you envision your optimal work–life balance, what would you need to change in your life to achieve that? Be specific. How likely are you to make those changes? Explain.

3. If you are feeling overwhelmed by work-related responsibilities or obligations in your personal life, what could you do to lighten your load?

4. What are your reactions to Jon Carlson's views of self-care and the good life?

5. What is your definition of the good life? How close are you to attaining certain aspects of your good life? What could you work on to come closer to achieving this ideal?

Gaining Support From Colleagues

Maintaining self-care by establishing a healthy work–life balance can be supported through building relationships with colleagues. Unmistakably, cultivating strong relationships in the workplace can pay big dividends, especially when times are stressful and the support of colleagues is sorely needed. We spend a large proportion of our waking hours thinking about or engaged in our work, and having dependable and trustworthy colleagues for whom we have high regard can be a lifesaver. Our own sense of well-being is influenced positively or negatively by the quality of our relationships at work. As with all relationships that matter to us, it is essential to establish appropriate boundaries with our colleagues.

My (Jude's) colleagues at Old Dominion University and I work together to support a collective healthy work–life balance. We regularly check in with each other and balance our discussion between work and non-work-related topics. My brother (Julius) and I also gain support from colleagues by creating an informal accountability group with other new professionals in the counselor education field. Connecting through group texts, emails, and video chats enables us to discuss what's happening in both the personal and professional realms of our lives. We also connect with colleagues to form writing teams, and I find that having a mutual respect for a colleague's time is essential to gaining and maintaining support regarding work–life balance. For instance, we work hard to respect each other's family time and work demands when scheduling meetings. We assign tasks and check in with each other only during our scheduled meetings and avoid putting pressure on each other. Honoring each other's time builds trust and support within our group. In addition, we help fine tune self-care plans, provide space to process experiences, and motivate each other to be healthy.

In my (Jerry's) case, colleagues are a vital source for self-care. I have always done my best to initiate contacts with many of my colleagues, whether it be meeting informally to talk about areas of common interest, working on chapters or books together, or presenting together at professional conferences. I typically have dinner with a different colleague each week when I teach each fall semester, and during our dinners we not only talk about work but also about what we want from life. Having good colleagues prevents isolation from creeping into my life. When we meet, we share our struggles in creating and maintaining the kind of boundaries we would like between our professional work and our personal life. Many of us find it difficult to turn down attractive invitations. We need to remind ourselves (and each other) that even if a project is enjoyable, it still demands our time and energy. One colleague often says, "I would love to accept your invitation if there were six of me, but I must respectfully decline because there is only one of me."

On a similar note, I (Michelle) need to accept my limits and keep reminding myself to set good boundaries in terms of taking on new projects. Although I admittedly struggle with finding an appropriate work–life balance, my immediate supervisor always reminds me to take time for myself. Like my coauthors, I enjoy collaborating with colleagues on writing projects and find support from my colleagues to be extremely important. One way that I do care for myself is through developing positive relationships with my coworkers and supervisor at the Center for Talented Youth (my day job) and with the faculty and staff in the Johns Hopkins School of Education, where I teach counseling courses as a faculty associate. I cherish these relationships and look forward to going to work because I have such wonderful colleagues.

Finding Balance After a Wake-Up Call

As a new professional and new dad, I (Julius) learned how to establish personal and professional boundaries the hard way. I accidentally dropped my 3-month-old son, Cairo Anthony, from a recliner onto the hardwood floor at home one evening after an exhausting day of work. After I lay him on my chest to burp after giving him his bottle, we both fell asleep in the recliner. I woke up to him and my wife screaming; I was confused, scared, and ashamed. I picked him up with tears running down my face as I watched his left eye begin to swell. My wife was hysterical; I had never seen her this scared and angry. We usually turn to each other in times of crisis, but I stood hyperventilating as she called the closest emergency room, our parents, and siblings. We took separate cars because I was literally frozen in place. My wife grabbed Cairo's bag, clothes, and anything else she thought he would need for the duration of his emergency hospital stay. I remember hearing my phone ring, picking it up, and hearing my wife say, "I love you, I know you didn't do it on purpose—we need you right now."

I walked into the assessment room of the hospital to see my son's smiling face and his swollen left eye. As my little family of three sat in the room, my son desperately tried to make eye contact with me. I gazed into his eyes, mouthed "Daddy's sorry," and he smiled and yelled "HEEEYYYYYYEEEEEEEEE." The doctors came in as Cairo was laughing, and they deemed him completely healthy. Cairo had a swollen eye for one day, followed by bruised skin around the eye, and absolutely no pain.

I realized that my son's fall was the result of poor boundaries between my personal and professional life. The day of this incident started at 5:45 a.m. with a steady stream of clients until 6:30 p.m. Cairo's fall truly was a wake-up call for me. In my role as a clinician, I must be present and alert for at least 7 hours of the day, giving attention to the nuances of the therapeutic relationship, client after client. In my role as a father, I want to be completely present with my son, witnessing every smile, laugh, burp, and dirty diaper. To perform these personal and professional tasks, I must be present for almost 16 hours a day, which is unrealistic. The pressure I feel to meet these unrealistic expectations shows up in my daily life. For example, in my professional life I find myself falling behind on clinical notes, isolating myself and remaining in my office even when I am not seeing a client, at times answering emails later than I would like, and committing to unrealistic writing deadlines. The unrealistic expectations are manifested in my personal life by thinking about my clients and writing projects while I am with my family, checking my email while playing with my son, and not keeping in touch with my immediate family members. In trying to attend to both my personal and professional demands simultaneously, I find that they often both suffer. I begin to feel inadequate, overwhelmed, guilty, and my self-care erodes.

Since Cairo's fall, I have implemented some strategies to help me attend to both the personal and professional realms of my life. I have made efforts to schedule office hours at the end of my day, which helps me transition from one role to the next. During the drive home, I call Jude (my twin brother) to process cases and put the day in perspective. I also listen to podcasts and audiobooks that allow me to take my clinical hat off. I try, as much as I can, to work on other scholarship projects during the weekends for a maximum of 4 hours. Taking these actions has helped me to make progress in finding a balance between my personal and professional life.

Like Julius, perhaps you have experienced a critical incident that served as a wake-up call in your life. Take some time to reflect on ways that you may push yourself beyond your own limits and sacrifice your own well-being or someone else's simply out of sheer exhaustion. What are your warning signals that you are approaching exhaustion? And to what extent do you heed these signals? What steps can you take to ensure that you don't reach a state of exhaustion or burnout?

Codependency as a Barrier to Self-Care

Many of us are drawn to the helping professions because we want to help others improve the quality of their lives and see their pain and suffering end. Sometimes our motivation to pursue this line of work stems, in part, from our own unfinished business with our family of origin. One dysfunctional pattern that some helpers report in their own families is codependency. "Codependency is characterized by a person belonging to a dysfunctional, one-sided relationship where one person relies on the other for meeting nearly all of their emotional and self-esteem needs. It also describes a relationship that enables another person to maintain their irresponsible, addictive, or underachieving behavior" (Lancer, 2016). Families vary tremendously, and we certainly don't mean to suggest that most helpers have codependent histories. Nevertheless, some do, and this can be a source of distress and emotional exhaustion. You may have counseled clients struggling with codependency issues or had coursework on this topic. Codependency themes do not define a person, and establishing appropriate boundaries with others is an important step in managing this issue. Jennifer Kordek's story illustrates how codependency can be a barrier to proper self-care for helpers if personal concerns are brushed aside or ignored.

Establishing Boundaries as a Form of Self-Care

Jennifer Kordek

As I began my education as a human services undergraduate, the term *self-care* was brought up frequently in all of my classes. I thought I had a pretty good understanding of it, but typically I related this concept to the idea that self-care meant taking a vacation or having some time to pamper myself. Both of those personal strategies are reasonable aspects of self-care, but it took me a while to understand the importance of the mental aspect behind practicing self-care.

When I entered my undergraduate program, my main motivation was a sincere desire to help others and make a difference in their lives. I prided myself on being the reliable friend, coworker, and classmate who would bend over backward to help people. In doing so, I found myself becoming mentally, emotionally, and physically exhausted. I had been in a relationship that weighed me down and left me questioning my values on countless occasions. Very early on I recognized that I had a big problem with saying "no" and establishing clear boundaries when it came to helping my significant other. There was a constant battle in my head between knowing I was doing way too much and feeling obligated to help until everything was worked out. I failed to see that I was not living a fulfilling life as long as I kept taking on his problems and making them my own.

I was mentally and physically exhausted all of the time. Quite frankly, I was completely burnt out by my significant other, but I kept telling myself that if I couldn't help him then I might not be able to help anyone. I was enrolled in a self-exploration group as part of my undergraduate program, and I finally risked opening up and took some time for myself in the group, which was freeing and healing. I spoke of how I was caring for an alcoholic and what it was doing to me. I needed and wanted help from the group facilitators, perhaps advice on what to do. Through further exploration in the group, I began to see advice from others would be of limited value and that I was in charge of my life choices. I realized that I did not have to let an unhealthy personal relationship dominate my life.

I started to look at other relationships in which I felt I was being pulled in multiple directions, and I told myself that I was going to put myself first. This was the first step in setting boundaries in my personal life. I told myself that I would still help others, but not to the extent of losing all sense of myself. Eventually I realized that others can take charge of their own lives, and I don't have to fix everything or save anyone. I learned how critical it is for me to establish healthy boundaries as a key to taking care of myself. What I needed to do was draw a clear line between what I was willing to do and not do in my personal relationships. My second step was following through with this plan. I'd be lying if I said that my follow through was flawless. There were times when I would cave in and drop what I was doing to be there for my significant other. But it became easier to say "no" and stand by my convictions when I realized that I wasn't truly helping him. I accepted that it was more important for him to see what he was doing to himself.

In my plan to successfully carry out these new boundary-setting techniques, I had to take a hard look at what I was doing to myself. I had to learn to stop being so hard on myself and, most important, change my way of thinking and learn to say "no." Learning to set and maintain boundaries in my personal life will certainly carry over into my intended professional endeavors. If I am not taking care of myself, I know I won't be of much service to anyone, or much of a friend to others.

* * *

Naomi Tapia works for a nonprofit that serves youth in the adoption and foster care system, and she has struggled with a tendency to put the needs of others ahead of her own. Naomi describes her lifelong battle to learn to take care of her own needs. Setting limits with others by saying "no" has quite possibly been the greatest challenge of all.

My Struggle in Putting Others Ahead of Myself

Naomi Tapia

I have been a caretaker for as long as I can remember, raising my siblings while my parents worked full-time jobs. From such a young age, I remember my mother constantly saying, "You have to learn to take care of yourself, if you plan to continue taking care of others." Although I heard her say these words, I never truly listened until I began seeing the physical consequences of my lack of self-care. I was diagnosed with an anxiety disorder and stomach ulcers at the age of 14, and it became clear to me that something had to be done—but I didn't know what.

When I began my undergraduate career, I learned about self-care. Despite knowing the importance of taking care of myself, I could not figure out how to begin. The only thing I thought might help was getting involved in personal therapy. Through this process of self-exploration, I began to look closely into what prevented me from taking care of myself, and I came to realize the role that guilt was playing in my life. I realized that I felt guilty and selfish when I said "no." I saw that I rarely had time for myself because I was always doing so much for others. To begin to make a change *within* myself, I had to make time *for* myself. I did so by finally learning to say "no." Unfortunately, this self-imposed boundary dissolved quickly.

During my undergraduate career, I juggled many things: being president of an organization on campus, being involved in my internship, working, and going to school full time. One of the first internships I obtained was for a nonprofit that helped homeless families find housing. As an intern, I was supposed to work 10 to 12 hours a week, but my lack of boundaries "forced me" to work more. My clients were experiencing dire conditions, such as living in their cars, tents, and motel rooms. I found myself going beyond the extra mile to help them in any way that I could. In my attempts to see how they were doing, I was constantly replying to emails and checking my voicemails outside of the office. I heard their desperate cries for help in voicemails, and I stayed up at night looking for housing for them. I sacrificed myself by not getting enough sleep because of my excessive worry about them. This failure to take care of myself took an emotional toll on me, pushing me back into the depression I had worked hard to overcome.

After months of not setting boundaries and getting lost in all that I thought I needed to do for others, I reached a breaking point. I landed back in personal therapy and on medication to control my depression. Out of my guilt over not being adequate enough for others, I had spread myself too thin. I didn't understand how to set boundaries between my personal life and work life. I had to start over and relearn how to say "no," especially to my own thoughts. I continue to practice saying "no" to the thoughts about work that pop into my head when I am with my family or friends.

Clearly, setting boundaries to ensure self-care is still a struggle for me, but I have taken significant steps in making this a part of my self-care. During my last semester in college, I left my job to take time for myself and find more balance in my life. Now, as an employee, I have learned to silence my phone when I do not need it. This allows me to be more present and centered in my personal life. To help me sleep, I jot my thoughts down on a notepad and set it aside to prevent them from clouding my relaxation. I also use guided imagery and meditation to help me "recharge." As for my physical well-being, I make it a priority to set aside time to exercise during the week, and I give myself positive affirmations. Although these are small things, they have made a huge difference. Now, when I feel that I am spreading myself too thin, I remind myself that I need to be the best version of me for my clients—and that requires me to take care of myself.

● ● ●

A graduate student's life is full of conflicting desires and obligations. Justyn Smith, a counselor education doctoral student, struggled with putting the needs of his professors, mentors, and advisers ahead of his own. He offers some practical steps that have helped him establish boundaries and prevent him from feeling overwhelmed.

Setting Boundaries and Self-Care

Justyn Smith

I believe setting self-care boundaries is all about effectively using my time to help with self-preservation. Setting boundaries helps me stay focused on reaching my goals and increasing opportunities that align with my career. To help me remain true to my boundaries, I remind myself that I am important, I have a voice, and I am allowed to set boundaries.

As a doctoral student, I quickly recognized the power differential between my professors and me. I realized that my education and career are in the hands of faculty who, at times, seem to make all of the key decisions. When this power differential is mishandled, I can feel lesser than and unimportant, and consequently I put the needs of my faculty above my own.

In the beginning of my doctoral program, I did not have multiple publications, presentations, or a full curriculum vita. I was, and still am, looking for any opportunity to gain experience, which can cause me to say "yes" to nearly everything I am asked to do. I am a bit frantic to fill my vita, and I have to remind myself to take time to think about what I want my vita to say about me. Sometimes the idea of saying "no" as a doctoral student and setting boundaries with faculty seems impossible. Many of the faculty in my program are known around the country, and some are internationally renowned. This makes it even harder to set boundaries and to stay in line with my goals. With this in mind, I devised a strategy for setting boundaries as a doctoral student that involves two basic steps:

1. *Figure out goals:* I try to visualize what I want my career to look like and the type of impact I want to make. I think about my primary reason for sacrificing the next 3 to 4 years of my life.
2. *Set priorities:* I try to organize all of my responsibilities. A couple of my projects now include working toward getting two publications before I graduate and spending time with my family.

These two steps help me use my time more effectively as I strive for success. They help me put myself first and establish self-care in my professional life. When I set appropriate boundaries, I have found that the faculty members who have my best interests in mind offer opportunities that align with my professional and personal goals. Since taking these steps, I have noticed that my work as a doctoral student has become less about filling my vita and more about making the biggest impact possible in my community and in the field.

● ● ●

Client Boundary Issues and Their Toll on Self-Care

Throughout this chapter, we have emphasized boundary issues that can be problematic for us. Our focus has largely been on setting limits in our personal and professional lives in order to strive for a healthy work–life balance and maintain some semblance of sanity! Graduate school teaches us to engage in deep introspection to work through our own boundary issues so they do not interfere with our jobs as counselors, counselor educators, and other helping professionals. We would be remiss if we failed to describe a different type of boundary issue that can occur in our line of work that can affect our sense of well-being—that of poor client boundaries. Omar De La Vega, a graduate student in a counseling program, describes how some clients need boundaries to be made exceedingly clear.

Self-Disclosure and Boundaries

Omar De La Vega

It was my first month as a trainee in practicum, and I was excited to finally begin working with clients. I was also nervous. I had taken the ethics course, and I could not help but imagine all the possible ways I might screw up. I was still trying to keep myself from literally running out of the room in terror from clients. There were just so many things to remember during an intake: the informed consent process, mental status exam, developing treatment plans, and trying not to be a robot. I am happy to report that excitement outweighed fear, but apprehension loomed overhead.

The first time I remember feeling ethical apprehension occurred during the second month at my practicum site. I was seeing an elderly client who was in great distress mentally and physically. I remember the first time I saw her. She used a cane, walked at a very slow pace, spoke in a low soft voice, and really struggled with movement. Her hair was unkempt and slightly damp, as if she had just stepped out of the shower. There was a frailty about her. She mentioned struggling with constant and severe pain for many years without respite. I remember taking a slow and empathic approach, wanting to convey the message "I am here for you." My heart really went out to her.

During our second session I felt something wasn't quite right, but I couldn't put my finger on it. I made a mental note. A quarter of the way into the session I made my first mistake. Now, I understand that self-disclosure can be therapeutic if used appropriately and if it is going to directly benefit the client. But, if I am being truly honest, I must say that I self-disclosed to this client for selfish reasons. I remember clear as day thinking, "Gosh, this poor woman is in a lot of pain. I'd really feel more comfortable if she knew she was not alone." Big mistake! As soon as I self-disclosed about my back pain, she was off and running— "Oh, you poor thing. How did you say you hurt your back?"

Then, without warning, she stood up from her chair and demonstrated the "proper" way to bend over and pick things up. Suddenly, I knew what had been bothering me; her behavior seemed seductive. Following her "demonstration," she made her way to the door and positioned herself as straight as she could against it, looked at me, and said, "This is how you're really supposed to position yourself when you have back problems." Oh, no, I thought. But I was still too new to bring into the room what I was observing. I did not want to embarrass or shame her, and I certainly did not want to be wrong in naming what I thought was transpiring. Before I knew it she was back in her chair, which was situated a short distance in front of mine. As I began to comment on her agility despite her crippling pain, I noticed her foot ever so slightly begin to slide right in between the space of where my feet were rested. No contact was made between her foot and my two feet, but without a doubt a boundary had just been crossed, and I did not know how to address it. Luckily, time was up and she was out the door. I promptly discussed my experience during supervision and the client never returned.

The best thing I can do to manage boundaries is to be mindful of borders, be aware of where they are situated, and gauge how flexible they can be. In this session, self-disclosing to comfort myself resulted in the client trying to take care of me—and probably a lot more. Although I recognize her motives likely stemmed from a deeper issue that needed to be worked through, I was remiss in blurring a boundary by self-disclosing about my own pain. This client required consistency and structure, and I learned an important lesson about setting clear boundaries and not deviating from them. Furthermore, had she returned, I would have worked closely with a supervisor to ensure that I was practicing ethically. Finally, I would make sure that my self-care is up to par. My days are not always perfect, but when I am mindful of what I need, I am less likely to cross or violate a boundary.

• • •

Honest self-reflection enhances the power of the lessons learned from our mistakes. When revealing personal life experiences to our clients, we must be mindful of whose needs are being met and the impact our disclosures are likely to have on particular clients. Although this trainee's self-disclosure was made with good intentions, it was problematic for the therapeutic relationship because it blurred an established boundary regarding sexual attractions in the counseling relationship. Herlihy and Corey (2015) emphasize the importance of consultation when sexual attractions are involved as a way to prevent inappropriate boundary crossings. "It is not uncommon for clients to develop a sexual attraction to their counselor, and it may be inevitable that most counselors will at some time feel a sexual attraction to a client" (p. 49). Nevertheless, the best interest of our clients must be foremost in our mind throughout the counseling session.

Understanding Your Limitations

Individuals experience the demands of work and home differently, and their experience is influenced by culture, social expectations, personal goals, professional goals, and family needs. It is important for individuals in the mental health field to understand when the demands of work or home are overwhelming. We cannot be all things to all people. No matter how much drive we possess or how much energy we have, there are limits to what we can do. Many of us struggle with learning the limits of our time and energy. We need to assess what we can realistically accomplish because pushing beyond our limits will result in negative consequences for our well-being.

I (Julius) take precautions to ensure that I am mentally healthy by seeking consultation, supervision, and personal therapy and staying connected with individuals who feed my soul. However, when I am overwhelmed personally and professionally, I tend to sacrifice physical health before anything else. When my physical health decreases, I become distant from my family. I constantly engage in an internal battle regarding spending time with my family versus pursuing professional achievements and the monetary security my career provides. We do not live in a perfect world, and sometimes I need to sacrifice time with my family to make sure my professional obligations are met. I cannot control when I will have more demands from the personal or professional realms of my life, but I can control how I flex and allocate my time.

As a counselor educator, I (Jude) ask myself the same questions Julius posed. During those times when I feel unbalanced, I acknowledge that I am only one person who can only do so much. I am limited by the energy I have in attending to the various demands I experience. Revising deadlines, rescheduling meetings, and prioritizing projects are ways of using my limited energy more efficiently. My self-care suffers when I have more ambition than energy and I don't respect my need to recharge.

Like Julius and Jude, I (Michelle) tend to lead an overscheduled life, and I recognize the signs when I am beginning to feel overloaded. Because so much of my work involves sitting, I notice that my back and neck tense up when I am feeling stressed and sitting too much. Having a long commute to work (a 2-hour round trip every day) contributes to my stress. In addition to physical tension, I become irritable, which I don't typically feel. When this happens, I try to remind myself to take deep breaths, which helps. Sometimes taking a brief break to step back from whatever it is I am working on helps me gain perspective when I resume the task. Occasionally I schedule an appointment for a back massage to help reduce my physical pain. I must admit, though, that setting boundaries between the personal and professional domains of my life has been one of my great challenges. As someone who has a proclivity for being a people pleaser and a perfectionist, I have room to grow in terms of learning to say "no" to projects that come my way. Even as I write this, I notice my own resistance to turning down opportunities, but I have discovered that saying "no" is sometimes a necessity.

About four decades ago when I (Jerry) was in my 40s, I faced challenges in achieving a healthy balance between my work life and my personal life. Not only was I teaching full time in human services, but I also assumed the responsibility of program coordinator for about 9 years. During summers and semester breaks, I was busy writing and revising books, conducting workshops in various states, facilitating personal growth groups, and training students and professionals in the area of group counseling. I had to learn to balance a multiplicity of professional roles, formulate long-range and short-term goals, acquire time management skills, and learn how to create some personal life amidst all the busyness of my professional life. I was doing everything I wanted to do professionally, yet I needed to learn my limitations and find a better balance with my personal life. A hard lesson for me to learn was to pause before too readily accepting an invitation for another workshop, a speaking engagement, giving a keynote at an international conference, launching a new book, or writing a chapter for a colleague. Over the years I have had to continue to remind myself that I am one person and can do only so much. I have accepted the fact that I have taken on too much at times and have difficulty saying "no." I needed to learn the value of carefully reflecting on the pros and cons of accepting invitations, no matter how enticing they appeared to be. Although I enjoyed most of what I was doing, I eventually recognized that all of this took time and energy and that my energy was not boundless.

It is more difficult now than in my younger days to meet the demands of traveling, and I have more frequently declined offers to present workshops in other countries due to the hardships associated with travel. Travel and working abroad require flexibility, and with aging I find myself more set in my ways and attached to my routines. Even with 56 years of teaching behind me and plenty of practice in self-care, I still struggle not to singularly focus on work. My projects seem to require more time these days, however, and I often underestimate how much time it takes to perform daily routines. At day's end, I am likely to say, "Where did this day go?" Taking care of myself seems even more important as I age.

We hope that you will examine your unique circumstances and acknowledge your limitations as human beings. Just as we encourage our clients and students to admit their limitations, we must do so too. Even seasoned professionals benefit from taking inventory of the ways in which their boundaries could be improved. It requires honesty on our part to recognize and accept our limitations. Sometimes our clients can give us valuable feedback that can remind us of our limitations, and thus they can be our teachers. One counselor who struggled with blurred boundaries is Jessica Smith (2017): "I pride myself of being a mirror for my clients, but the truth is that my clients are often my best mirrors and teachers—even if I don't truly want to see what they are reflecting back to me" (p. 49).

Questions for Reflection

1. How would you describe your relationships with coworkers or colleagues? To what degree are you satisfied with these relationships?
2. How would you describe yourself as a colleague? Be sure to include both positive and negative descriptors that seem relevant.
3. How can you reach out to colleagues to support your work–life balance? What would you want to ask of them?
4. In what ways have colleagues negatively influenced your work–life balance? Would you be inclined to address these issues with them? Why or why not?
5. Have you ever been involved in a codependent relationship? If so, describe the toll that it has taken on your life. How did it affect your effectiveness as a helper, and how did it affect your well-being?
6. Have you experienced clients with poor boundaries? If so, how did you handle the situation? How did your own boundaries help or hinder you in interacting therapeutically with these clients?
7. To what degree are you able to understand and accept your limitations?

Concluding Thoughts

Our self-care is influenced by how we balance and attend to our personal and professional demands. Think of work and personal life as weighing platforms on a scale. There are always demands from both of these important dimensions of our life. Strive to get a sense of when those scales are unbalanced and how you can rebalance them. Although it would be nice to be able to prescribe a formula for establishing healthier boundaries with others, it simply is unrealistic to do so. There is no single "right way" to approach boundary setting because everyone's set of circumstances and struggles vary. Each of us needs to identify what will work best for us. We hope one or more of the stories featured in these pages has sparked ideas about how you might creatively set boundaries in your own life.

We have discussed some ways to support your self-care in your profession by reaching out to others, respecting relationships, finding a balance between your work life and home life, reflecting on your boundaries, and knowing your limitations as a human being. The next chapter discusses the relationships we have with ourselves and others and how these relationships influence our self-care. Together these two chapters provide you with an opportunity to reflect on how personal and professional demands influence who you are and how they influence your relationship with others.

Chapter 7

Relationships With Self and Others

Counseling can be an isolating endeavor; to counteract that, it is important to nurture relationships in our personal and professional life. Having clear and flexible boundaries is the first step toward maintaining good relationships with yourself and others (see Chapter 6). Additional steps include self-compassion, embracing the self, finding ways to nourish oneself through solitude and connections with others, developing forgiveness for self and others, taking time to form meaningful relationships, and mentorship. Take a moment to reflect on your personal and professional relationships: Are you giving too much energy to some relationships? How do you feel about yourself as you work with clients? What do you need from your relationships to be able to take better care of yourself?

Relationship With Self

Whether you are in graduate school training to become a professional helper, are an experienced professional, or are somewhere in between in your career trajectory, you have learned that maintaining a good relationship with yourself is a crucial component of self-care. Deepening self-awareness is a core goal of any counselor training program, but maintaining a high level of self-awareness and a commitment to continued personal growth is more demanding after graduation when launching your career. With the realities of heavy caseloads, demanding clients, multiple professional obligations, and life's myriad demands, it is all too common for helpers to ignore their own needs. In fact, it will surely come as no surprise that those drawn to the helping professions often relegated their own needs in their family of origin and put the needs of others ahead of their own.

When we are no longer surrounded by professors and peers who constantly reinforce the message that we must nourish our souls and selves to be effective, we may tune out the messages warning that our own needs are not being met. Lacking self-compassion, having difficulty letting go of resentments and forgiving others, and failing to forgive ourself for perceived or actual transgressions are some of the ways we may neglect our own needs. To maintain your vitality as a helper, it is important to periodically review how well you are taking care of your relationship with the person who will be with you for the rest of your career and life—you!

Self-Compassion

Compassion is demonstrated in a genuine caring for one's self and others. To be kind to others, we must first be kind to ourselves. *Self-compassion* has been defined as being kind to oneself while having a deep awareness of and desire to relieve one's and others' suffering (Gilbert, 2010). You may be overly self-critical and wrestle with feelings of inadequacy and wanting to be different. To make changes in our way of living, we first need to accept the way we are at the present time. Personal growth is facilitated when we accept where we are now and treat ourselves with kindness. Acceptance is a process of connecting with our present experience without self-criticism or judgment, but with curiosity and kindness (Germer, Siegel, & Fulton, 2013). Learning the art of self-compassion and being accepting of ourselves is a starting point for making life changes (Neff, 2011). In their research, Patsiopoulos and Buchanan (2011) explored how the practice of self-compassion assists counselors in their daily attempts to buffer the effects of stress related to their work with others. Ariadne Patsiopoulos, a registered clinical counselor in Victoria, British Columbia, and one of the authors of this study, talks about her experience of self-compassion and how it influences her work and self-care.

My Research Interests on Self-Compassion

Ariadne Patsiopoulos

I remember one particular spring day after a difficult session with a client when I walked to a nearby park bench to reflect. While there, I noticed a seagull mechanically pecking at a crab. As I sat watching the bird's prolonged attempt to access flesh beneath the crab's shell, I also noticed my own frustration building and something tightening within me.

Suddenly, I made a connection between this spectacle and the challenging session. This uncomfortable but familiar feeling was about trying to "figure it out" and "fix it," coupled with self-judgment regarding my impasse in "solving" this puzzle of a situation with my client. I began to breathe, focusing on my heart, and sensed something tender and warm there. I allowed this felt sense to expand, visualizing it radiating throughout my body. I noticed how the pressure within was dissolving, bringing me more space, more clarity, and a return to my center.

To me, this was a moment of *self-compassion:* a gentle, loving, and sometimes fierce energy I have come to know well through various personal practices, key relationships, and pivotal life experiences. I see it as a powerful innate resource that I can choose to practice in all domains of my life, including my work in the counselling field. It is a way of being that continues to bring me to places of ever-deepening acceptance and celebration of all the facets of my unique and sacred life's trajectory: my humanity.

During my counselor training, in a very intentional way I explored self-compassion practices that would support me in being more compassionately present, attuned, and effective with myself and clients. I integrated mindful loving approaches into how I attended to my inner landscape (thoughts, feelings, and sensations) during and after sessions, interacted with others, and generally took care of myself.

I became curious about other practitioners' experiences with self-compassion and found myself broaching the topic often. A frequent reaction was along the lines of "Self-compassion? What's that?" followed by nervous chuckles and then an honest and vulnerable dialogue about various challenges in practicing self-compassion and self-care. I soon realized that what I thought was a very personal interest was, in fact, central and relevant to many. This led me to seek out and have conversations with seasoned counselors for whom self-compassion played an important role in their work and life. This became a year-long research process that affected me profoundly on multiple levels.

The stories participants in my research shared were poignant teaching tools about self-compassion as a transformative agent in their overall well-being and their capacity for self-care. Self-compassion was a vehicle that helped them navigate challenging moments within session, in training, and in the workplace. Some of their experiences echoed my own. Others helped me to clarify what self-compassion means for me and to keep building that muscle within myself. Several years prior to the start of this research, I had been on the receiving end of a painful ethical breach of trust and did not have the courage to address it with the other party. Hearing others' accounts of similar experiences led me to perceive self-compassion not just as a "gentle" act but as an empowering and self-honoring force that could assist me in future difficult professional and personal experiences.

Overall, the many dialogues I had with others about self-compassion affirmed to me how compassion and love transform and elevate us. It reinforced my belief that relating to myself with care and compassion is my responsibility to myself and, by extension, to those with whom I work and live. I have chosen to shape my life and career in ways that bring me balance, meaning, and joy—from where I live (on a beautiful island by the water), to the types of work I combine within the helping fields, to the range of activities and forms of expression I regularly integrate into my life (such as dance, meditation, writing, biking), and to the people and communities with which I engage. I identify fellow colleagues with whom I can have authentic conversations about our humanity as counselors. I am continuing to learn the value of trusting the process of acquiring compassion for self and others as a powerful avenue to self-care.

• • •

Learning about other clinicians' experiences can help us understand our own self-compassion and how to use it in therapy sessions to be more effective. Another element of building a healthy relationship with one's self is forgiveness of others and forgiveness of self, which we consider next.

Forgiveness of Others and Self

Self-compassion and forgiveness are not luxuries; they are essential values for our survival. Learning how to incorporate compassion and forgiveness into daily life is a key to healthy self-care practice. Forgiving is a willingness to abandon resentment, condemnation, and subtle revenge toward an offender and to cultivate the qualities of compassion, generosity, and even love toward that person (McConnell, 2015). Forgiving others can be releasing and freeing for those of us who have been injured in some way. Stored anger activates a state of adrenaline, which can lead to negative health consequences such as high blood pressure, depression, anxiety, and a poor immune response. Forgiveness is an important factor in facilitating our well-being (Weir, 2017). It is good for our physical health as well as our emotional well-being (Johns Hopkins Medicine, 2014). Forgiveness is a process of successive stages of healing rather than being a one-time event. Holding onto negative feelings toward those who have hurt us prevents us from clearing our mind of emotional clutter. We do not have to forget how we were mistreated, but it is important to assess the costs to us and to our relationships if we refuse to forgive.

Sometimes others are willing to forgive us for causing them hurt, but we are not willing to forgive ourselves for failing to live up to our ideals. It is not just other people that we need to forgive—we need to forgive ourselves. It is time to stop punishing ourselves and to treat ourselves with compassion, acceptance, kindness, and respect. After ending a long-term relationship with my former partner, I (Michelle) spent far too many years feeling burdened by guilt because I still loved and cared for him even though I was aware that our relationship was not healthy. We were growing in different directions, and I suspect that he was not happy with my decision to pursue a doctorate. He seemed to feel threatened by my personal growth and my professional ambitions. It became extremely painful to interact with a partner who resented me so deeply. Despite knowing that our parting of ways was probably in both of our best interests, I was the one who ultimately made the decision to leave. Being the guilt magnet that I was, I knew then that I would struggle with guilt. I had great insight into why I had difficulty letting go of my guilt and forgiving myself, but I was very slow in unburdening myself of these feelings. Today, after much introspective work, I am happy to report that I have made tremendous progress toward forgiving myself and being kinder to myself.

Our willingness to forgive others for their perceived or actual transgressions may be an equally important step in taking care of ourselves. Being trained as helping professionals does not make us immune from harboring resentments toward others or from holding onto unresolved or unexpressed anger. With a proclivity toward being sensitive and caring human beings, counselors are in an extremely vulnerable position throughout their development.

In *The Forgiving Life*, Enright (2012) develops the theme that becoming a forgiving person is part of our life and part of who we are; it is part of our very identity and our core self. Forgiveness enables us to live peacefully with others in this imperfect world, and it is "powerful medicine that can stop the ravages of resentment" (p. 14). A forgiving life can restore connections and love within the self and with others and is an ideal to strive for in life.

Forgiveness and Letting Go of Resentments

In Chapter 3, I (Jude) described some of the challenging experiences I had in my doctoral program, and as I reflect on those experiences, I still feel some anger and resentment. I began with the naïve assumption that all counselors and counselor educators are kind, self-aware, and culturally competent individuals. This left me vulnerable as a doctoral student, and I was hurt emotionally. I kept those who hurt me at a distance, which was isolating but seemed to be a useful survival tactic at the time. Learning to forgive and let go began with me embracing who I am as a result of my doctoral experience. As a counselor educator, I recognize that I still hesitate to build connections with others professionally. I am working to overcome these fears, and I make an effort to connect with colleagues in a way that feels safe for me by simply walking around our office suite and checking in with colleagues as they work. I am beginning to push myself to connect with others through mixers, dinners, game nights, and potluck gatherings. I reach out to students who I feel need more support, and I meet weekly with doctoral students who request mentorship. I make it a priority to attend students' dissertation defenses and conference presentations because I know how important the lack of this support was for me as a student. As I establish better relationships with those around me, my anger and old resentments regarding my doctoral experience are beginning to soften.

Another way I process my old anger and resentment is through keeping a journal, which I have done since my graduate school days. Reading past journal entries has helped me gain perspective on some of my graduate school experiences, and I am finding a place of forgiveness within myself. My process of journaling and reflecting helps me feel more anchored and sustains both my personal and professional self. Ashley Scott, who is working on her doctorate at Sam Houston State University, describes how she sustains herself during an experience similar to mine.

Sustaining My Professional Self

Ashley Scott

Before I began my PhD program, I considered possible challenges such as long nights, sacrifices, adjusting to new expectations, writing insecurities, lack of sleep, imposter syndrome, loneliness, financial issues, and power dynamics. However, I never considered that my identity as a Black woman would be challenged, nor could I imagine the intensity of the issues I would face and the sources of these issues. The intersection of my race and gender has been challenged in almost every aspect of my PhD process, and learning how to sustain myself professionally has been a struggle.

I am a first-generation college student, and I have often felt as if I am going through this process blind and alone. I didn't know anyone who could explain to me some of the common struggles of Black women in academia. I often feel like I don't belong because I am not like members of the dominant culture. I don't look like them, and our research interests are very different. I quickly became the "diversity person" in my cohort, the one consistently talking about Black people and multicultural issues in counseling. As I did so, I could see the annoyance and lack of care on the faces of my classmates and professors. It was as if my opinion was not important. I felt as if I was not important.

My self-care was damaged when I began to internalize and truly believe these messages. I knew there was a problem when I seriously considered taking a semester off, not because the workload was too heavy but because the struggles I was experiencing related to my identity just didn't seem worth it anymore. When I expressed these concerns to mentors and close friends, every one of them could hear the weariness in my voice and knew something had to change if I was going to complete this program.

For me, sustaining my professional self means feeding my soul. Before I began feeding my soul, I took time to write down exactly what the problems were so I could make sure I attended to them. The process of writing it down was therapeutic in itself as it was no longer all jumbled up in my mind. Overall, I knew I had to tend to my identity as a Black woman. I became very intentional in my actions in my professional and personal life. The first task was to connect with other Black women in academia, professors and students alike. I would seek them out at various professional conferences, research symposia, and universities. If I read a piece of multicultural counseling literature authored by a Black woman, I would email her and ask her specifically about her journey in academia. That is how I found my first Black female mentor in counselor education, and she has connected me with her colleagues and students. I also felt it was critical to surround myself with unapologetic Black women in my personal life. Fortunately, being a member of a historically Black sorority made this task a bit easier. But it was not enough to simply identify with them. I explained my struggles and what I needed from them, and we decided to meet via Google Hangout every week. During that time, we would affirm, uplift, empower, and encourage each other to push through all barriers, external and internal.

I also sought out spaces that affirmed my identity. I searched for literature across various professions that gave voice to Black women's experiences and attended conference sessions with content focused on Black women. In these sessions, I often heard other Black professors and students discussing the issues they have faced and how they have sustained themselves. At the Southern Association for Counselor Education and Supervision, I collected information on all the Black female doctoral students I interacted with and created a GroupMe so we could stay connected. We took a collective photo at the conference and named the group "Doctoral Sistahs Network." Simply taking the photo and naming the group was tremendously empowering and affirming. Now each of us has a safe space to find refuge on the days when we feel alone or inadequate.

Feeding my soul has truly sustained me professionally. The demands of my current endeavors weigh more heavily upon me when I am not feeding my most salient identity: being a Black woman. Self-care is a process that requires creativity and intentionality. Being intentional about taking care of myself has increased my resilience tremendously, which is key if I am going to accomplish my goals—and I will accomplish them.

• • •

Writing down your thoughts can help you clarify the issues you confront. If an individual has hurt you and you cannot forgive this action, try writing a letter—without the intention of sending it. Allow yourself the freedom to write in an uninhibited manner. You may find this exercise helps you gain clarity about the feelings and thoughts that are blocking your energy. To continue this exercise, when you are ready, draft a second letter in which you express forgiveness to that individual and clarify how it will help you to forgive him or her.

Questions for Reflection

1. How would you assess your level of self-compassion on a 10-point scale (1 = *extremely low self-compassion* and 10 = *extremely high self-compassion*)? Are there particular areas in which you tend to be more self-compassionate than others? If you are not satisfied with your current level of self-compassion, what strategies could you implement to improve this?
2. To what extent do you harbor resentment and hold on to anger toward others in your life? Do you have unfinished business with individuals that you would like (or need) to forgive in order to move forward on your own self-care journey? If so, explain.
3. How willing are you to forgive yourself when you have done something that you perceive to be wrong? What feelings are associated with this? How do you think your life would be different or how do you envision you would feel differently about yourself if you no longer carried this burden? If you find it difficult to let go of a past transgression (perceived or real), what do you think it will take to relieve yourself of this burden and forgive yourself?
4. In what ways, if any, do you struggle with embracing parts of your identity? What contributes to this? What can you do to ensure that your sense of self is being nourished?

Relationships With Others

As helping professionals, we are in the business of relating to others. We are skilled at active listening and being attentive to verbal and nonverbal gestures. It is our job to create a safe environment and a sacred space for our clients to "do their work" and explore their deepest concerns. When the deepest parts of our client make contact with the deepest parts of us, counseling is at its finest. Relating to others is not only our business, it can also be considered an art form. Helpers who counsel couples may even consider themselves to be "relationship experts." With so much "relating" going on during work hours, however, we may at times feel drained when we leave the office and go home. We may have little energy left to give to those who mean the most to us. None of us are exempt from the hazard of neglecting our own personal relationships out of sheer exhaustion from our intense focus on our work. Learning to leave our troubles and professional relationships at the office requires a good deal of work on our part (Kottler, 2017; Norcross & VandenBos, 2018). In this section, we explore how personal relationships can be affected by our work, reinforcing the importance of not only practicing self-care but also making a concerted effort to practice "relationship-care." For good reading on our relationships with self and others, we suggest *Relationships in Counseling and the Counselor's Life* (Kottler & Balkin, 2017).

Intimate Relationships With Partners

In her narrative, Ashley Scott described how her internalization of damaging messages caused her to consider taking time away from her doctoral program. She also explained how her relationships with others motivated and sustained her professional self, especially during challenging times. One of the messages I (Jude) internalize often is "I am a failure." I too make considerable efforts to sustain my professional self by connecting with others and completing tasks. It seems as though completing tasks on my to-do list is a double-edged sword; sustaining my professional self cuts into my time for cultivating healthy relationships with myself and others. During the week I was working on this chapter, I was overloaded with projects at the university including research and grant proposals in addition to my teaching and clinical responsibilities. I checked things off of my to-do list with vigor. However, as I finished my part on this chapter at 1:00 a.m., my wife looked over at me and asked if I would hold her hand. She continued by saying, "I know you are busy, but I have felt disconnected from you all week." I heard that little voice inside me whisper, "You've failed again." The challenge I face when sustaining my professional self is balancing the sustainment of my personal self as well. The most important element of my personal life is my relationship with my family, which at times is ignored because of professional demands. Kellin Murphy Cavanaugh, a doctoral student at Syracuse University, discusses how her relationship with her partner encouraged her to find a balance between her personal and professional selves, and with her relationships with others.

Balancing Care of Self With Care of Others

Kellin Murphy Cavanaugh

Entering the internship phase of my learning, I was excited, impatient, and too proud to admit to anyone that I was scared to finally begin. I interviewed for and earned my placement at a boarding school close to my home, a population with which I had always been fascinated: adolescents in a perceived purgatory. My biases about privilege, wealth, and prestige led me to expect completely different issues than the ones my first long-term client brought into session. As a random walk-in, this 16-year-old sophomore told me she was sexually assaulted by a man whom she had known for her entire life. Although I was blindsided and had to face my own sheltered life, my supervisor applauded my presence, my skills, and the interventions I would use with her over the next several sessions.

What I could not share with her or anyone else for over a year was how I was unable to be intimate with my husband for almost 2 months after hearing this client's story. Two months is not a long time in the context of our relationship, but it was incredibly taxing on how we felt about each other, on my self-esteem, and on my confidence in my ability to be an effective therapist. I kept telling myself that my skin wasn't thick enough yet, that I just needed to be exposed to even more tragedy and trauma to shed my softness and empathy and replace them with a hardened exterior.

After a few months of being at my placement, my husband told me that if I didn't find a way to separate what my clients told me from my personal life I would drive myself crazy and, ultimately, drive him crazy. I was overly focused on being an amazing counselor. It consumed me, and I was losing my awareness of my most important identities: wife, friend, sister, daughter. It was important for me to strive to be an effective counselor, but I realized it was more important to be an effective partner to my husband. Although this may seem obvious, I needed to take care of myself. The fact was, I wasn't present in my relationships, including those with my clients.

Much of the time I felt invincible from this idea of *self-care*. I didn't believe that meditating for even 10 minutes a day, or remembering to breathe deeply when feeling overwhelmed, would help me care for myself. What I decided to do was the best thing for me and it is my first piece of advice for you—I got my own therapy. Sara and I met almost every week for a year. Throughout our sessions, she shared her observations and questions with me. She also shared her own experiences with me. I had many realizations that wouldn't have been possible had I reflected on my own, the most important being that I had fallen into a cycle of caring for others because it was less challenging than attempting to care for myself.

My therapeutic process led to important lessons that positively influenced my ability to care for myself and others around me. Often, proper self-care means that it is imperative that you put yourself first. As new counselors, we acquire the ability to better sense others' anxieties.

I would often internalize the anxieties of my loved ones and colleagues. I still have to remind myself that their anxieties are not my own. In the way that we are taught to trust our client's resiliency, we must also trust in the resiliencies of those closest to us. This is my perspective on caring for myself and others. It is not always a simultaneous process, and often includes more people than two partners. Perhaps you have children, good friends, parents, and other loved ones to whom you want to demonstrate care. Remind yourself that you are trying your best to balance your new identity as a counselor and how it intersects with your sense of self and your relationships with others. My husband and I have a golden rule in our home: Saturdays are for *me* and Sundays are for *us*.

● ● ●

As counselors, we bring ourselves and our personal concerns into the therapeutic process. At times, we may experience personal crises, which have the potential to affect our professional work in both a positive and a negative manner. To continue being effective and present with clients during these times, it is crucial to be mindful of how events in our personal life can have an impact on our counseling work. At the same time, these crises can result in our becoming more empathic and connected to clients with similar issues, giving us a fuller understanding of their life situation. Aponte and Kissil (2014) believe these issues can be used as a resource to connect, assess, and intervene with clients. Robert Haynes, a clinical psychologist and former training director of the clinical psychology internship program at a state hospital, relates how he practiced self-care and worked with clients during a personal crisis.

Practicing Self-Care During a Personal Crisis

Robert Haynes

Many years ago, at a time when I was providing private counseling to individuals, families, and couples, I found myself in my own relationship crisis and eventually in the throes of separation and divorce. I truly believed I could remain focused and objective with clients who came in for marital and relationship counseling and help them sort out the values and struggles that pertained to their relationship. However, I found myself being triggered and reviewing my marital crisis as my clients talked about their problems. It was a very subtle and insidious process, and I was unaware of how it was affecting my work. I was unable to extract my own situation from theirs as I wrestled with my own desire to be a full-time father with my child and my need to seek resolution and get on with life. Although I do not believe I harmed my clients, I was unable to focus my full attention on their relationship concerns and unable to offer the best care possible for my clients at that time. Looking back on how my personal crisis clouded my ability to work effectively with some clients, I wish I had had the awareness and the humility to know that I was not able to be objective enough to work with personal problems mirroring my own life. In hindsight, it would have been beneficial for me to seek supervision and my own therapy so that I could stay more focused on the concerns of my clients.

In my book, *Take Control of Life's Crises Today: A Practical Guide* (Haynes, 2014), I discuss ways to more effectively manage life's crises. Having a general plan about what do when a personal crisis occurred in my life would have been of significant benefit to my work with clients. We can best serve our clients if we proactively develop a plan for how to proceed when a crisis occurs. That plan may include some of these elements:

- Assess and monitor your personal transitions and life crises for their potential impact on your counseling work. Practicing mindfulness and self-reflection helps us focus on our current life situation and its impact on our work.
- When a personal situation occurs, seek supervision on this matter either with a colleague or with a professional supervisor. It is good practice to continue this supervision until the personal crisis is no longer affecting your work with clients. Admitting that we don't have a handle on everything and that we need help is a huge step for many of us.
- Have a referral system for those rare occasions when you are personally not competent to work with a client. Consider how to deal with a current client if a referral is in the client's best interest. Examine the possibility of involving the client in the discussion and decision making regarding a referral.
- Consider becoming involved in your own professional counseling.
- In the event that your crisis has rendered you incompetent to work with certain clients, accurately determine when you can once again provide full attention to the counseling work.

Counselors are trained to be good listeners, to be empathic, and to respond to their clients' needs. The personal toll our professional work takes on us can be enormous. Our long-term survival as helpers is contingent upon our ability to balance a caring and empathic therapeutic style with the ability to distance ourselves from the impact of our professional life at the end of the day. The key to self-care is to be open to learn and grow from each crisis we encounter and to continue to become wiser and more resilient for our future work. This is good for our clients and for ourselves, both personally and professionally.

• • •

When we encounter clients who are experiencing a crisis, we can give the gift of presence through our words and by expressing genuine caring and a deep sense of compassion. Presence is powerful and often transcends what we can actually do to change the situation. Having an unresolved personal problem can create a rift between counselors and clients. This rift makes it difficult for counselors to connect to themselves and with their clients. Seeking supervision and consultation can improve a counselor's care for clients (Allan, McLuckie, & Hoffecker, 2016), and cultivating positive professional relationships also helps counselors maintain health and effectiveness (Rupert, Miller, & Dorociak, 2015). Jamie Bludworth, an assistant clinical professor of counseling psychology and director at the Counselor Training Center at Arizona State University, shares how his professional relationships influence his self-care.

Self-Care by Way of Relationships

Jamie Bludworth

In the course of my career as a counseling psychologist, I have held several positions of leadership and administration. In each of these positions, I have been faced with stressors ranging from clinical concerns about client safety to administrative concerns about managing the inflow of clients in systems that are understaffed and with staff who have been occasionally stretched to their limits. To be honest, self-care has never been at the forefront of my professional life and is not something in which I intentionally engage. However, when asked to write on the topic, four attitudes and activities came to my mind. As you will see, most of these have to do with relationships.

The first is an attitude that has served me well in maintaining professional energy and commitment. I find that I am most successful in managing work–life balance when I take a team approach to the work facing me. I identify the members of my team and orient myself toward them. I take time to get to know them, inviting a team member to lunch or meeting socially after work to establish a personal connection in our work together. This has helped me feel connected at work when our work so often is somewhat isolating.

The second strategy is generating close relationships with those to whom I report. I have found that the closer I am with my direct superiors, the easier my work life is. If I am able to make a human connection with my boss, then our mutual trust is enhanced when we are engaged in work in which a person's well-being may be at stake. This, of course, is dependent on the willingness of my supervisors to engage at this level, but I have not found this to be difficult, especially once we have had an opportunity to work a crisis situation together. Having a good sense of humor has helped to generate closeness in these relationships. The strength of my relationships with my superiors has significantly reduced the levels of stress I experience at work.

I show my spouse that I love her every day. I express my gratitude for our relationship and the ways in which she accepts who I am. This makes coming home after a challenging day quite rewarding and often allows me to let go of the stressful elements of work that want to attach themselves to me and follow me home. I seek her advice regarding administrative matters, and she continually reminds me of my values and commitments. Having someone who knows who I am and what I am about has kept me grounded and focused on my larger life commitments. This has, time and again, helped me to appropriately contextualize my work and allowed me to choose what importance I wish to place on a particular situation rather than automatically amplifying things to catastrophic proportions.

Finally, I have been a musician since I was a teen and have kept my love for music alive throughout graduate school and beyond. When I began graduate school, I thought I would have to give up being a musician and commit my life solely to being a student. Fortunately, I expressed my worry to a friend in my cohort who introduced me to a friend of hers who was also a musician. Through him I met other musicians and played in bands throughout graduate school (which is really the thing that kept me sane throughout the whole experience). I look forward to the creativity and comradery that comes with playing in a band and creating original music. This has been my primary, intentional form of self-care and has served me well for many years.

Over the years, I have been fortunate to have developed strategies to take care of myself that I utilize at my workplace and also outside of my workplace. Though my at-work strategies are not as obvious as taking walks or engaging in mediation or yoga in my office, they have been very effective for me and have allowed me to create professional relationships that are very satisfying and important to me. Outside of work, if I am having fun, I consider myself to be engaging in self-care, and that's good enough for me.

● ● ●

Questions for Reflection

1. How satisfied are you with the time and attention you devote to your personal relationships? If you are not satisfied, what can you do to carve out more quality time with friends, life partners, and family members?
2. If you are currently in an intimate relationship, how much energy are you able to devote to it? What are some actions or steps that you or your partner could take to improve the quality of your time spent together?
3. To what extent and in what ways does your work with clients affect your personal relationships?
4. How well have you weathered past crises in your life? Although it is difficult to predict most crises, how equipped do you think you are to handle a personal crisis? How resilient do you consider yourself to be? If you perceive that you are lacking in this area, think about ways you can foster resiliency.
5. Jamie Bludworth uses music as an outlet for self-care and enjoys the creativity and comradery that comes with playing in a band. What are your outlets for creativity? Do you engage in any leisure activities such as music, sports, or theater that enable you to bond with others?

Practicing Self-Care Within a Community

In our work as counselor educators, we each have our own ways of cultivating a community in the classes we teach. Sometimes we bring guest speakers who are experienced clinicians into our classrooms, many of whom have graduated from our programs. Students in our classes often take advantage of networking with these guest speakers when they are taking classes and also after they graduate. We also encourage our students to become active in professional organizations at the local and regional levels as well as at the national level and to network with others so they feel a sense of belongingness in the larger professional community. All four of us do this as well, regularly attending the annual conference of the American Counseling Association and using this time to reconnect and socialize with former colleagues and to meet newcomers in the field. Feeling connected to a community is a way that each of us practices self-care. In addition to joining established communities, we develop new communities or groups within communities, which can be a wonderful outlet for our personal or professional passions. Matt Englar-Carlson, a professor of counseling at California State University, Fullerton and co-director of the Center for Boys and Men, describes how he developed men's groups within his community and how that influences his self-care.

Men's Groups as a Path for Self-Care
for Male Counselors

Matt Englar-Carlson

My professional career has centered on improving the health of men and boys. I came to this focus quite naturally due to my own comfort in connecting with men, but my clinical focus developed over time. As a doctoral student, one of the pivotal experiences for me was beginning my participation in annual men's retreats, sponsored by the American Psychological Association. These were men's groups comprised of my peers—fellow students or professionals in the field, including many senior professionals whom I admired—and were places where I did not have to be the leader. I could just be a group member. I could get my own needs met, observe another skilled leader practice his craft (so I could get more ideas), and be among other men who were caring, sensitive, and willing to do personal work. Early in my career, I noticed how these retreats felt like coming up for air after being underwater for a long time. I needed the camaraderie and connection with other men, and I craved just being another group member and not being responsible for the group. I wanted to know more about group counseling with men, but the true draw was that these men's groups were powerful in sustaining my soul and deepening my own appreciation for the struggles of men. Being around courageous and supportive men inspired me to be a better man, and I developed a deeper understanding of my own masculinity and gave voice to the tender parts of me that society often shames away. Men's groups are sustaining for me, and I have worked over the years to create affirming spaces for men to connect with other men.

From my clinical and personal experiences, I knew that men have many stories to share that often go unspoken. Telling stories is a central way men build connection. There are stories of triumph and shame, and for men in the mental health field, they are often stories of being a nurturing man. Men's groups offer space for men to share these unspoken stories in the affirming presence of other men, which is not always the case in society. It feels risky for me to share sensitive information and feelings, and it is often even more difficult to allow other men to care for me through their words, empathy, and physical embraces. Yet these are the things I ask my own clients to do, and my time in groups helped me work through this in my personal life. Men's groups provide a unique window to learn about the hidden lives of men, but more important, experientially men feel a genuine connection with the other men in the group and are able to give and receive nurturing. Many men feel isolated and deeply desire a safe space to share their inner world with other men in a full and free manner. Group settings allow men to unburden themselves of the unrealistic expectation to be responsible at all times in their roles as men, work through competitiveness, and over time, listen to the playful/compassionate self. In many men's groups, cohesion gradually builds as group members navigate restrictive gender norms around building male-to-male relationships. Once some of those hurdles are crossed, however, the bonds between men in groups are often significant and unique; the relationships they form can transfer into their interactions outside of the group. When I meet other men who spend time in a men's group, the hugs easily flow, and there is often a comfort with one's vulnerability that I find inviting.

Men's groups are a wise self-care strategy for male counselors, but it can be tough to take the first step. Most male counselors were raised in a society with restrictive gender norms, and violating those norms in one's personal life can be challenging. For self-care, male counselors have to allow themselves to seek their own needs and allow themselves to be attended to by others in the group. For many men, these tasks come with layers of societal gender norms that create conflict around vulnerability and awareness of personal needs. Self-care is as loaded as any form of help-seeking, and that is often doubly the case for men. Yet beyond the fears of vulnerability, men's groups offer vast rewards that can deepen and sustain one's career and one's life as a man. For further reading on counseling men, see *A Counselor's Guide to Working With Men* (Englar-Carlson, Evans, & Duffey, 2014).

• • •

In our own community, we (Jude and Julius) have seen the benefits of having a supportive community and the strong impact it can have on an individual's well-being. After hurricane Katrina damaged the city of New Orleans and before we became counselors, we developed a summer camp for boys between the ages of 10 and 18 years old who were displaced by hurricane Katrina. We enlisted the help of many community members to provide our campers with a campus to learn information pertaining to getting a job, sexual health, physical health, nutrition, money management, networking skills, entrepreneurial skills, education on the criminal justice system, and many other issues. We called this camp the Male Apprenticeship Network (M.A.N. Camp). We developed and implemented a 2-month curriculum that included guest speakers from the community; field trips to local businesses, police stations, courtrooms, and banks; meals service by community volunteers; and community service projects. We believe this camp helped our campers feel connected to and supported by their community. Many of our campers have graduated from high school and college and are pursuing careers. This experience was rewarding but also challenging. Throughout this experience, leaning on our colleagues and community volunteers was our way of taking care of ourselves.

Although some helping professionals enjoy being their own boss and find that working independently has its plusses, working with a group of colleagues or in interdisciplinary teams can be an invaluable source of support, particularly when the nature of the work is intense. In certain clinical contexts, such as hospice work, having supportive colleagues is critical to one's wellness and is vital to one's self-care. Crissa Markow, a licensed social worker who worked for Summit View Hospice in Reno, Nevada, writes about her experience of providing hospice services and the importance of working within a supportive community.

Self-Care as a Hospice Social Worker

Crissa S. Markow

As a hospice social worker, I work closely with an interdisciplinary team to ensure the quality of life for each patient and act as a resource for the caregiver and family. I visit patients in homes or care facilities to assess needs, obtain life histories, provide counseling, connection to community resources, education on the dying process, assistance with health care directives or choosing a funeral home, support after a patient has died, or simply companionship. I've worked with patients of all ages: a child with brain cancer who had spent years in and out of the hospital, her parents also caring for her siblings and maintaining employment; a young man in his 20s who wasn't close to his family but was surrounded by a faithful group of friends; a single mother of four children, who spent her final days making legal guardianship arrangements for her kids and writing cards for upcoming birthdays and Christmases; and more typically, older people with dementia and residents of care facilities.

When I say I work for hospice, I typically get some variation of a sympathetic response: "Oh, how can you do that?" "It must be so hard to be around death all day!" "How depressing!" Actually, it is quite the opposite! An intense amount of living occurs at the end of life. It is an honor to share in people's final stages of life when they are reflecting on their past, finding closure, and developing their own understanding of death and what may come after. Working in hospice can be very life-affirming and positive, but there are also sad and difficult times that highlight the importance of healthy clinician self-care. Those in hospice work must be well-versed in self-care in order to help themselves, colleagues, and the caregivers in the home.

One of my saddest experiences was seeing a man who chose to die alone in a weekly hotel with no family or friends present. I have encountered families who are so dysfunctional I dread visiting their home. Others are determined to stay in squalid living conditions, neglect their medical needs, or live among chaos. One of the most impactful lessons I've learned is that every person who is capable of making decisions has the right to make "bad" decisions. I went into social work as an idealist but quickly learned to honor the patient's right to self-determination—one of the core values of the social work profession. As one very experienced hospice medical director liked to say, "The bed was on fire when we got there." It didn't mean ignore the issues at hand, but it is a reminder of the reasonable limits of our role. Many times remembering this one simple phrase has helped me maintain some sanity and peace about my professional capabilities.

In making daily visits, it's much too easy to overthink every interaction, wondering if I've been effective in my role. I've learned to focus on being present in each visit: where is the patient at this moment, what's important to him or her, and how can I, within reason and mindful of professional boundaries, help the patient? I rely on the interdisciplinary team for personal and professional support, and a weekly team meeting provides an opportunity to debrief and grieve the patients we've lost. Humor certainly makes its way into our staff meetings. This may sound heartless, but one can only be around sadness and heartbreak for so long without relief. Humor allows our team space to just laugh; not to take ourselves or life so seriously that it becomes a dreadful burden.

I've been fortunate to be paired with amazingly supportive fellow social workers. We've relied heavily on each other to problem solve, vent, and simply connect. Whatever your helping profession, don't underestimate the value of connecting with colleagues who are working with a similar population, share the same code of ethics, and have similar professional values. They remind you how to prioritize, problem solve, and challenge you to excel. Quite simply they get where you are coming from, and this validation can stave off burnout.

I should take steps on a personal level to practice self-care as well (if only it were so easy to follow through!). I know I am always more present and better able to handle stressful situations calmly when I am exercising, eating right, enjoying my free time, processing at the end of the day with my husband, socializing with supportive family and friends, and getting enough sleep. Regardless of your profession and the work you do on a daily basis, I encourage you to make a commitment to self-care so you can best serve your clients, colleagues, your own family and friends, and, most important, yourself.

• • •

Connecting with a community of colleagues who have professional concerns in common can help you stave off burnout. Counselors emphasize to their clients the therapeutic value of participating in a support group, but too often counselors are reluctant to seek support for themselves by connecting with colleagues. Some counselors, social workers, and other mental health professionals in private practice and agency settings, as well as some counselor educators, have found value in participating in support groups composed of members of their respective communities. Jessica Smith (2017) writes about how a few therapists in her community began a support group they call a "sangha," which meets regularly to share their knowledge and explore personal and professional concerns for the purpose of fostering awareness, understanding, and acceptance. Smith claims that participating in this supportive community "has been one of my most rewarding, nourishing and sustaining experiences, both personally and professionally" (p. 50). Each time Smith's sangha group meets, the participants comment on the ability of this group to be an uplifting and empowering resource. She encourages counselors to consider starting their own group to receive support, guidance, and compassion from other professionals.

Questions for Reflection

1. Describe the communities of which you are a part that bring meaning to your life and that offer you sustenance? What is it about these communities that nourishes you? In what ways do you provide support to members of these communities, and what impact does that have on your own sense of well-being?

2. Both Matt Englar-Carlson, who specializes in men's issues, and Crissa Markow, a hospice social worker, engage in work they are passionate about. What are your clinical or professional passions? What are ways that you have developed or can develop a sense of community with others who share these passions?

Mentorship

Mentorship can be an integral aspect of maintaining self-care throughout one's career. Perhaps you know from firsthand experience the power of mentorship from either the perspective of *being mentored* by someone who had a profound impact on your life or of *mentoring* a student or junior colleague and deriving tremendous satisfaction from that experience. Unquestionably, mentorship is a win–win arrangement when both parties are highly invested in the relationship. As the four of us are in different stages of our career, we speak about mentorship from different vantage points. Whereas Jerry and, to a lesser extent, Michelle have had more time in the field to mentor students, Jude and Julius, as early career professionals, are closer to the experience of being mentored. We share our experiences with mentorship, but first read this narrative about the art of mentoring. Brad Johnson is a clinical psychologist, professor in the Department of Leadership, Ethics and Law at the U. S. Naval Academy, and faculty associate in the School of Education at Johns Hopkins University.

Self-Care for Mentors

W. Brad Johnson

For 25 years I have been researching and writing about mentoring relationships, speaking and consulting to organizations interested in getting strong mentoring cultures off the ground, and, of course, practicing mentoring myself. Here is one consistent truth I've discovered over all of that time: Everyone in an organization or institution seems to quickly figure out who the great mentors are, and those folks tend to be in high demand! In fact, great mentors can easily become overcommitted, overwhelmed, fatigued, and, ultimately, less effective in the mentor role if they are not careful to set some limits and engage in thoughtful self-care.

Read most anything about mentoring relationships (mentorships) and you might notice the nearly maniacal cheeriness with which people discuss mentoring. I predict you will encounter purely positive assessments of the impact of mentoring in the lives and careers of mentees; the benefits to organizations, business, and universities that facilitate strong mentoring; and even the psychological and career benefits for mentors themselves. Although it is very often true that good mentorships do result in profoundly positive outcomes for all parties involved, too often we fail to acknowledge that there are *costs* associated with deliberate and thoughtful mentorship of a junior person. Specifically, mentoring costs a mentor time and energy, and mentoring can take a significant toll on the mentor's own well-being in a number of ways.

Research on the characteristics of great mentors shows that they are often high on scales of other-oriented empathy and caring for others. Although caring and empathy are wonderful mentoring attributes, they heighten the risk of compassion fatigue and eventual burnout. The highly compassionate professional can easily assume some of the distressed mentee's emotional burden. It is my own observation that younger professionals (such as early career counselors or new professors) are more vulnerable to some measure of emotional entanglement with mentees and subsequent exhaustion if several of their mentee's are emotionally demanding. Personally, I've learned the hard way that setting limits on the number of students and junior professionals I mentor is just as important as setting limits on the number of clients I am willing to see. Sure, it can be a nice stroke to the ego when aspiring mentees cue at one's door, but failing to set limits on the volume of people you mentor is destined to lower the overall quality of your mentoring work. Mentorships are relationships and therefore more interpersonally demanding for those of us on the introverted end of the personality spectrum. As an introvert by nature, I need time to recharge—usually with the office door closed, a cup of coffee, and something interesting to write—quietly, alone (this is why the academic life so agrees with me).

Here is an important lesson about the art of mentoring: one of a mentor's most solemn and essential obligations to a mentee is to serve as an intentional role model for what it means to be a professional. With self-awareness and forethought, the excellent mentor is deliberate about not merely "telling" mentees how to be competent, ethical, and balanced but also "showing" them how to be these things. In a real way, failing to overtly model self-care for my mentees is to let them down. For me, self-care consists of a number of important elements, including daily exercise, time with friends and family, reading for pleasure (primarily good fiction entirely unrelated to my work), and sampling interesting new craft beers with a few good colleagues from work now and then. I often share some of these details with my mentees. I schedule our meetings around my exercise time during the day, talk about a fun novel I am reading, or reflect on some interesting place my wife and I explored over the weekend. I tell my mentees who my closest colleagues are and how I rely on them for support, friendship, and monitoring of my well-being. The beauty of giving mentees an open window into my ongoing efforts at self-care is the fact that it naturally opens the door to conversations about how they themselves are faring in their efforts to balance work/school and life.

Let me conclude with the honest admission that I don't always get self-care right as a mentor. Even after all these years, I still have trouble saying "no" to prospective mentees, even when I know that I should, and sometimes a junior colleague might walk by my office and see me working at my computer late in the evening. On such occasions, I try to make my own slip a teachable moment and share the bitter truth with my own mentees that I am human and highly fallible. Good self-care takes a village, and even our own mentees can help us to better see when we are veering away from work–life balance.

• • •

For Brad Johnson, the art of mentoring means serving as an *intentional* role model for what it means to be a professional. When we take proper care of ourselves physically, emotionally, socially, and spiritually, we may feel better equipped to model the best versions of ourselves for those we are mentoring as well as for our clients and students.

Johnson and Smith (2016) describe an excellent mentor as having self-awareness, emotional intelligence, relationship know-how, and a genuine desire to see a good person thrive in his or her career. Effective mentors encourage mentees to increasingly embrace the *possible self,* an image of what they can become in life and in their profession. Johnson and Smith state that outstanding mentors communicate high expectations and confidence that mentees can deliver. Although effective mentors encourage striving for excellence, they challenge the notion of perfectionism. Mentors serve a key role in showing mentees that competent people are not perfect.

Our Reflections on Mentoring and Being Mentored

Michelle's Reflections on Mentoring Students

I (Michelle) derive great pleasure from being a positive role model for the students I teach. At least I hope I am a positive role model! I certainly try to be. Years ago, as an undergraduate student in the human services program at California State University, Fullerton, and later in my graduate studies both at Northwestern University and the University of Iowa, I was fortunate to have a few superb mentors who modeled being authentic and compassionate counselor educators. Although I attribute my professional development in part to the knowledge I gained through coursework, I do recognize that more than *what* my professors taught me was *how* they taught me, and how they mentored me. Some of these mentors taught me about the importance of being real, having a sense of humor, giving myself permission not to be perfect, and many more priceless lessons by modeling this behavior. On a similar note, my doctoral adviser, Nick Colangelo, taught me other useful lessons such as how to keep my composure under pressure and how to deliver a message effectively, simply by modeling this behavior. As I transitioned from being a doctoral student to an early career professional, I often reflected on the lessons I had learned from my mentors by remembering how they handled situations.

Now that I am in the position to mentor counselor trainees, I am mindful not just of *what* I am communicating to them but *how* I am communicating my messages. It is of the utmost importance to me to model being authentic, compassionate, and empathic. My hope is that those who consider me a mentor experience me as a positive role model.

Jude's Reflections on Developing a Community of Mentors

I (Jude) have developed a community of mentors—a mixed group of counselor educators of various ethnicities, ages, professional focuses, and experiences—that I feel I can go to at any moment for support. Being mentored was of paramount importance in my personal and professional development, and my mentoring experiences continue to demonstrate that I am not alone. As a counselor educator new to the profession, I have already begun the process of mentoring many of my students. I hope to pass along to my students some of the strategies I used when developing my community of mentors.

Personal needs assessment. I developed my community of mentors around a central question, "What do I need?" My most vital needs as a new professional are strategies for navigating the unique issues African American men face in the counselor education profession, finding a balance between work and personal life, and obtaining tenure.

Recruiting mentors. Once I was able to pinpoint my needs as a mentee, I actively searched for individuals who could provide mentorship to meet my specific needs. I looked at websites of CACREP counseling programs for African American male faculty members. I attended the ACES and ACA conferences and looked for presentations by African American male counselor educators. I attended their presentations and exchanged contact information. I followed up with these presenters via email and made an effort to maintain a connection with each of them. I also reconnected with past faculty members and engaged them in discussions about how they were able to balance work and life. I then actively searched for tenured faculty members with research interests similar to mine.

Forming community. One of the most influential decisions I made when forming my community of mentors was the recognition that I wanted to reach out to others for help. I looked for mentors who would enable me to feel safe enough to be myself. I chose mentors who would be willing to be vulnerable and share with me both their mistakes and their successes. I did not expect to find a mentor who could support all of my needs. I go to some mentors when I am experiencing something related to my culture, to others when I feel unbalanced, and to others when I need to talk about my career plans.

Maintaining mentorship community. To maintain this community, I try to communicate with my mentors at least two to three times a month. I call or write an email, or we have group video meetings. I attempt to maintain a network of mentorship by introducing others to my group of mentors. I do my best to connect with my mentors at regional and national conferences.

Impactful mentorship experience. One of the most influential mentorship experiences in my life is my relationship with Ty Leonard. What made this relationship so impactful was his expression of love, patience, and genuineness toward me from the moment I met him. My first interaction with him was during my interview for the counseling graduate program at Mary Hardin-Baylor University. During that interaction, he jokingly told me that my brother (Julius) was accepted into the counseling program, but I was not. My last interaction as his student was on graduation day when he explained that my doctoral program was going to try to change me, and he made me promise to contact him if I felt that my identity was being threatened. From my first to last interaction as his student, Leonard acknowledged my culture and gave me space to express it in class and in the counseling room. He saw within me something greater than I saw in myself, and he pushed me to grow into that potential. He created safety, which allowed me to explore my identity as a counselor. He encouraged me to learn from my mistakes, and oftentimes he owned his own mistakes. He taught me how to be a counselor and helped me find my voice and integrity as a professional. He has seen me grow from my first counseling session to my first keynote speech. He seamlessly transitioned to being a colleague and friend; his presence and caring remain steadfast.

Julius's Reflections on Mentoring

My (Julius's) thoughts on mentoring were highly influenced by the careful stewardship of my mother and father, Lorraine and Jude Austin Senior. In a recent conversation with my mother, she told me that in raising my brother, sister, and me it was important to control who and what influenced our development. My mother strategically and carefully planned the schools and extracurricular activities and sports we were involved in with the hope that we were in a safe enough environment to learn, grow, make mistakes, and be challenged. Being mindful of who influenced my development is a notion that has been carried over as I matriculated through undergraduate and graduate school, as well as in my personal and professional life.

I share Jude's sentiment about having a community of mentors from which to draw support. These are individuals I trust with my personal and professional development. It is important that I invite mentors into my life who challenge my thinking, allow me to be vulnerable, and confront me when I am not meeting my potential. I gravitate toward members of the profession I respect and who are genuine and humorous. One of the most important aspects to choosing a community of mentors is diversity among backgrounds. I need mentors who offer knowledge based on different educational and personal backgrounds from me as well as wisdom from having longevity in the helping profession. Now, as counselor educators, both Jude and I make ourselves available as mentors for minority students within and outside our programs, and both of us are active members in diversity dialogues and committees on our respective campuses.

Mentoring is a multifaceted relationship encompassing career, personal life, and key life transitions such as beginning a new job or starting a family. It is important for me to choose mentors who can support my development through these life transitions. An example of this is my relationship with Linwood Vereen, whom I consider a mentor and a friend. We do not speak with each other every week, but I always feel rejuvenated after our conversations. The last time we spoke, our conversation revolved around fatherhood, conference presentations, journal articles, marriage, work–life balance, the tenure process, and transitioning into new positions. This relationship allows me to test ideas with a more experienced counselor educator, to express myself in ways I cannot with other colleagues, and to gain meaningful fellowship. Our relationship is sound enough to incorporate working together on writing and research projects, which adds a mutually beneficial aspect to the relationship.

In mentoring my students, I strive to replicate this relationship. I hope to genuinely support my students' professional development and encourage them to take risks and to be vulnerable. Although I am not a mentor to every student, I do try to support each student to the best of my ability. Mentoring, like any other relationship, takes effort and commitment and shifts over time. To echo

Michelle's reflections on mentoring students, my hope is that those who consider me a mentor will experience me as a positive role model who demonstrates genuineness, the willingness to be imperfect, and, most important, the ability to be present in relationships.

Jerry's Reflections on Mentoring

I (Jerry) recognize the influence mentors had in encouraging me to strive for my professional goals. Having a community of people who believed in me gave me a sense of hope when I felt discouraged. I remember how much I valued my mentors' belief in me and their encouragement to persist, especially when my self-doubts could have gotten the best of me. Passing this belief on to many of my students is one of the most rewarding aspects of mentoring and teaching for me.

Over the years I have made it a priority to include friends and colleagues in many of my projects, which have become joint ventures instead of solo endeavors. I see a good deal of power in the collaborative approach, and I have consistently included colleagues when writing books and articles, creating educational video programs, coteaching a variety of courses, giving workshops, and giving presentations at professional conferences. By striving to be inclusive, these projects become more meaningful to me. Mentoring is a venture that can benefit both the mentee and the mentor. I have gained much from initiating these relationships with colleagues and students, and those whom I have been fortunate enough to mentor often have become important sources of mentoring for me.

Mentoring is an advocacy process that involves helping mentees discover their own voice, which can result in empowerment. In my mentoring relationships, I try to do more than advocate *for* mentees. My goals are to teach those I mentor to think for themselves and to speak for themselves. I want to empower individuals to eventually mentor themselves so that they can create the kind of professional life they have envisioned.

Questions for Reflection

1. What kind of support system do you have to help you stay focused on your academic and career aspirations? What steps can you take to create a support system?
2. Are you willing to ask for the help you need?

3. Can you identify one mentor who inspired you to pursue your dreams? How has this individual had an influence in your life?
4. Are there any particular words of wisdom or principles taught by influential people in your life that you can look to for inspiration to help you maintain self-care practices?
5. What are some specific ways you have dealt with roadblocks to achieving your goals?
6. What kind of mentor(s) do you most want?

Ways to Benefit From Mentors

Above all, find your passion and have the courage to pursue your goals. Find mentors who can help you translate your dreams into reality. Here are a few thoughts about making mentoring a meaningful experience:

- Don't strive to copy anyone else's style; experiment and create your own unique style of helping that fits you.
- Pursue your own passions and dreams rather than living by another's design for you.
- Mentoring can help you to find your passion, but you have to take the steps that translate this passion into accomplishing your goals.
- Although you may learn lessons from your mentors, faculty, and supervisors, put these lessons through your own filter.
- Reflect on interpersonal qualities modeled by your mentors, such as displaying empathy, compassion, and authenticity.
- Be open to assistance from many different sources. Seek multiple sources for mentoring, including your peers, friends, and family members. Don't underestimate what you can get from others in your program.
- Find a group of supportive people to offer you encouragement when you are inclined to give up.
- Regardless of where you are on your academic or career path, look for ways to teach others what you have learned.
- Network with peers, reach out to instructors and supervisors, and make connections that can lead to internship placements and jobs.
- Give thought to what kind of mentoring you want for yourself and the kind of mentor you want to be to others.
- Learn how you can get involved in research projects, writing, or coteaching with mentors.

Concluding Thoughts

This chapter explored how relationships with self and others influence counselor self-care. We shared our experiences regarding self-compassion, forgiveness of self and others, and embracing one's self. Professionals in the field revealed how personal issues or crises influenced their work, how relationships influenced their self-care, how connecting with others within their respective communities enhanced their self-care, and how mentors need to practice self-care too.

We encouraged you to seek mentors to assist you in reaching your personal and professional goals. It is extremely important that you ask for what you need from your faculty and peers to feel cared for and to care for yourself throughout the graduate student process. It is also important that you recognize when you are not getting what you need from your program. Reflect on personal and practical lessons you have learned from your association with mentors. Consider how you can build on what you have learned from mentors in developing a better relationship with yourself and also with others.

Our relationships with ourselves, our constant internal dialogue, our beliefs about ourselves, and how we respond to our circumstances influence our self-care and our effectiveness in our professional roles. Caring for others is a major emphasis in counseling, supervising, and teaching, yet our ability to care for others will be limited if we neglect to care for ourselves. The individuals we choose to have in our lives will have a profound affect on our worldview and on our work with clients. Establishing relationships that are fulfilling and supportive can positively influence self-care for mental health professionals. We hope this chapter helps you gain an appreciation for how your relationship with yourself and others influences your practice of self-care.

Chapter 8

Finding Meaning in Life

We exist on this earth for an undetermined period of time. What we do with that time has the potential to bring great meaning to our lives or, conversely, to leave us feeling unfulfilled and our lives void of meaning. Meaning in life is found in many ways, such as through work, loving others, engaging in new adventures, engaging in self-reflection, and by serving others. During difficult times, meaning acts as a compass to help us find our way out of feelings of hopelessness and despair. Thinking holistically—aligning and reflecting on the physical, emotional, intellectual, social, and spiritual aspects of living—can help us gain clarity about our purpose in this unpredictable world and improve our overall wellness. Identifying what brings meaning to our lives can be a useful resource when developing a self-care plan.

Researchers have found a significant relationship between meaning in life and psychological well-being (García-Alandete, 2015). In addition to having significant benefits for well-being, meaning can enhance physical health, increase happiness, and reduce depression, anxiety, and suicidal ideation (Waytz, Hershfield, & Tamir, 2015). To live without meaning gives rise to considerable distress. In this chapter we discuss the relationship between meaning in life and counselor self-care. One prominent theme is discovering actions each of us can take to place greater attention on what is most important to us in our own lives. Our guest contributors describe specific ways they create meaning for themselves and how this is connected to self-care.

Finding Meaning in the Midst of Self-Doubt

Finding meaning through our work is something that all four of us have in common, and it is something that many helping professionals experience. A major impetus for people who enter the mental health field and other counseling specialty areas is to make a positive difference in the lives of people who are struggling. Although earning a decent wage is important, financial gain is not the most important motivating force for people who enter the helping professions. There is much riding on our perceptions of our own level of competence in helping others in bringing us meaning. This can be problematic for those just starting their training who may be plagued with self-doubts about their helping skills.

When I (Jude) was a graduate student learning basic counseling skills in my program's community clinic, oftentimes my sessions ended with me feeling unhelpful. My clients' frustration with their lack of progress mirrored my own throughout the counseling process. My early experiences with counseling clients led to self-doubt about my effectiveness. The more times I left feeling confused and hopeless, the more my self-care was affected. I felt rudderless. I did not have faith in my competence as a counselor, and I began to contemplate whether counseling was what I was supposed to be doing with my life. I did not give up, and I found that creating meaning in life demands courage. The road is not smooth and persistence is key.

In "Facing the Fear of Incompetence," Kathleen Smith (2017) suggests that a counselor's self-doubt is linked to the fear of incompetence. She reports that self-doubt among counselors tends to be associated with higher levels of stress, burnout, depression, career changes, and ethical misconduct. However, some research suggests there is value in a counselor embracing self-doubt. Counselors who are not overly self-confident and have some degree of self-doubt are able to recognize their shortcomings and are likely to reflect on their work, which Smith indicates can aid in establishing a quality therapeutic relationship. Smith believes that "self-doubt often nags at the minds of counselors, but the practice of vulnerability might offer both a powerful antidote against unrealistic expectations and a prescription for forming stronger connection with clients" (p. 28). Counselors who view clients as having a significant role in creating change are able to be realistic about what can be accomplished. Self-doubt decreases when counselors are able to share the division of responsibility for therapeutic progress with clients. Counseling practitioners who depend on their professional work to provide them with meaning in life are vulnerable if their feelings of incompetence get the best of them.

Philosophical Perspectives on the Meaning of Life

Humans have struggled to answer the question, "What is the meaning of life?" This question has inspired philosophers and religious leaders alike and has been the subject of debate for centuries. The answers to this question have ranged from optimistic to hopeless. In this section, we highlight the teachings of the ancient Cyrenaics and Mohists, who held contrasting philosophical views about what brings meaning to life.

The Cyrenaics were founded around 400 BCE by Aristippus, one of Socrates's students. This group believed that to find meaning in life one should pursue pleasure from moment to moment. One's own pleasure should take priority over the pleasure of the community. According to Cyrenaics, finding meaning in life involves ignoring the restraints of social conventions and doing what is most pleasurable in the moment (Lampe, 2014).

Around the same time as the Cyrenaics were establishing themselves in Greece, Mohism emerged in China. According to Mohist teachings, meaning in life can only be achieved when everyone shows an equal amount of care and attention to everyone; no one person's needs are valued above another's. In contrast to the views of Cyrenaism, Mohism stressed the importance of community and helping all people achieve their goals (Zhang, 2016). It is interesting to consider how these early ideas still have relevance in today's world and in the counseling field. As helping professionals who embrace a multicultural perspective, we must always consider balancing the needs and desires of individuals with the needs and desires of the community. As we help our clients explore meaning in their own lives—identifying what matters most to them while taking into account the needs and expectations of those in their communities—we have the opportunity to engage in this same type of introspection about what brings us meaning. Should we seek pleasure in the moment as did the Cyrenaics, or are we better served by taking a community perspective as did those who subscribed to Mohism? Or does the answer lie somewhere in between?

We know that people feel a greater sense of meaning in life when they understand themselves, the world around them, and their fit within the world (Steger, Kashdan, Sullivan, & Lorentz, 2008). Seeking meaning and purpose in life is a core aspect of human existence. It is the result of active thinking and choosing; it is not automatically bestowed upon us. We need clear ideals to which we can aspire and guidelines by which we can direct our actions. Creating meaning in life is a lifelong process. Influential leaders in the psychotherapy field have emphasized the concept of meaning in life as an existential theme with which we all grapple.

Key Figures in Existential Psychotherapy

Existential psychology offers a foundation for finding meaning in life, and this therapeutic approach is directly linked to self-care. We briefly consider a few key figures in the existential movement, with emphasis on understanding how the search for meaning is central to human existence. Some psychotherapists who made pioneering efforts in understanding what it means to be human are Viktor Frankl, Rollo May, Irvin Yalom, Alfred Adler, and Jon Carlson.

Viktor Frankl and the Search for Meaning

Viktor Frankl, a European psychiatrist, dedicated his professional life to the study of meaning in life. A key pioneer in the field of existential psychotherapy, Frankl (1963, 1965, 1967, 1969) made significant contributions to the development of a conceptual foundation for meaning in life. The approach to therapy that he developed is known as *logotherapy*, which means "therapy through meaning" or "healing through meaning." Frankl believes that what distinguishes us as humans is our search for purpose. A central concern for humans is to discover meaning that will give our life direction, so the search for meaning is a primary motivational force. On the basis of his clinical work and study, Frankl contends that a lack of meaning is the major source of existential stress and anxiety. Frankl (1963) notes that "everything can be taken from a man but one thing: the last of the human freedoms—to choose one's attitude in any given set of circumstances, to choose one's own way" (p. 104). Frankl believes that people who confront pain, guilt, despair, and death can effectively deal with their despair and thus triumph. Logotherapy provides inspiration to continually seek the meaning that is necessary to live in authentic ways. This idea is captured in an adage that can be found in a church in Hawaii: "Who you are is God's gift to you; what you make of yourself is your gift to God."

Drawing on his experiences in the death camp at Auschwitz, Frankl believes that inmates who had a vision of some purpose or task in life had a much greater chance of surviving than those who had no such sense of hope. We have many opportunities to make choices, and the decisions we make or fail to make shape the meaning of our lives. Frankl identifies philosophical and clinical implications regarding the finding and loss of meaning in one's life. A theme of his writings is that we can find meaning in life through work, through loving, through suffering, or through doing for others. The central motivation for living is the will to meaning; we have the freedom to find meaning in all that we think; and we must integrate body, mind, and spirit to be fully alive. Frankl's writings reflect the theme that the modern person has the means to live but often has no meaning for which to live. Frankl's (1963) compelling book, *Man's Search for Meaning*, has been a bestseller around the world.

Rollo May on Freedom, Responsibility, and Meaning in Life

Rollo May, a key figure in contemporary existential psychology, made major contributions to the profession by highlighting the central role of freedom, responsibility, and meaning in life in the psychotherapeutic process (see May, 1950, 1953, 1961, 1969, 1981, 1983). May's many books have had a significant impact on existentially oriented practitioners, and his writings helped translate key existential concepts into psychotherapeutic practice in the United States and Europe. May was convinced that psychotherapy should be aimed at helping people discover the meaning of their lives and should be concerned with the problems of *being* rather than merely be aimed at solving problems. It takes courage to "be," and our choices determine the kind of person we become. Questions of being address how we deal with intimate relationships, growing old, facing death, and taking action in the world. May believes that confronting death in later life is essential to promoting creativity and meaning. According to May, it is the task of therapists to help individuals find ways to contribute to the betterment of the society in which they live.

Irvin Yalom: Pioneer in Contemporary Existential Psychotherapy

Irvin Yalom, a leading figure in the development of existential therapy in the United States, is in his mid-80s and continues to contribute to the profession through his prolific writings. His pioneering work, *Existential Psychotherapy*, written in 1980, is a classic and authoritative textbook on existential therapy. Yalom developed an existential approach to psychotherapy that addresses four "givens of existence," or ultimate human concerns: freedom and responsibility, existential isolation, meaninglessness, and death. These core existential themes deal with our existence, or being-in-the-world. Yalom believes that how we address these human concerns and existential themes greatly influences the design and quality of our lives. It is the therapist's task to be a fellow traveler with clients and facilitate their exploration of existential concerns so that they might make life-affirming choices. Yalom frequently talks about the value of personal therapy for students, trainees, and therapists. He sees personal therapy as an opportunity to explore key existential concerns and as a way to examine the quality of our lives as a route to finding deeper meaning in our lives. For Yalom, personal therapy can be a key resource for self-care, which can enhance our personal life and our effectiveness in carrying out our professional roles.

Yalom's (2008) book, *Staring at the Sun: Overcoming the Terror of Death,* is a treatise on the role of death anxiety in psychotherapy, illustrating how death and the meaning of life are interrelated themes associated with in-depth therapeutic work. Confronting death allows us to reenter life in a richer and more compassionate way. The reality of death is a catalyst for finding meaning in life. Our mortality can motivate us to reflect on what we are doing, how we are living, and what changes we want to make to be able to live more mindfully. Rather than being preoccupied with the fear of death, an awareness and acceptance of death can provide the foundation for a meaningful life. If we accept that we have only a limited time in which to live, we can make the most of the time we do have by doing our best to live each day as fully as possible.

Kottler and Carlson (2016) explore the notion of therapists finding meaning in life through their work and by leaving a legacy. They remind us that we are all dying and that our days are numbered. "And all of us, at least those who practice therapy, wish to leave behind something meaningful and poignant, something that makes a mark, something that means something to the world and the loved ones we leave behind" (p. 195).

Facing death can provide the motivation for us to take advantage of appreciating the present moment. Corey, Corey, and Muratori (2018) write, "If we are able to confront the reality of death, we can change the quality of our lives and make real changes in our relationships with others and with ourselves" (p. 382). If we defend ourselves against the reality of our eventual death, life becomes meaningless. This reality can provide the impetus to search for our own answers to questions like these: "What is the meaning of my life?" "What do I most want from life?" "How can I create the life I want to live?"

Alfred Adler: Social Interest and Wellness

Another major figure with an impactful philosophical perspective on self-care through finding meaning in life is Alfred Adler, who is considered a forerunner to the existential approach that focuses on internal determinants of behavior such as values, beliefs, attitudes, goals, interests, and the individual perception of reality. He was a pioneer of an approach that is holistic, social, goal oriented, systemic, and humanistic. Adler emphasized that all behavior is purposeful and goal oriented and that we can be best understood by knowing the goals and meanings toward which we are striving. The future is more significant than our past. Looking at the direction in which people are moving reveals their meaning and purpose in life. Adler's notion of social interest is vitally related to wellness. Social interest requires that we have enough contact with the present to make a move toward a meaningful future, that we are willing to give and to take, and that we develop our capacity for contributing to the welfare of others and strive for the betterment of humanity. Adler believed that contributing to the welfare of others was a sign of mental health.

Jon Carlson: A Contemporary Leader of Adlerian Theory and Therapy

A major contemporary figure in Adlerian therapy, Jon Carlson devoted his professional life to helping his clients and students find meaning in their lives by doing what they could to help others. Carlson was named a "Living Legend in Counseling" by the American Counseling Association in 2004. Carlson faced some major health crises and battled a rare form of lymphoma for 6 years before his death in February 2017. Carlson had an adventuresome personal and professional life and practiced many forms of self-care including rigorous exercising, jogging, hiking, meditation, and engaging in holistic health practices. Carlson found meaning in life by packing his life with memorable experiences, including travel to many parts of the globe. Even after his illness and treatment, he continued seeing clients, doing workshops, teaching, writing, and traveling. Englar-Carlson and Kottler (2017) said, "Jon had an adventurous spirit that was evident not only in his life journey, but also in his many contributions to our profession" (p. 43). His passion for serving others was the centerpiece of his self-care, and it is what gave meaning to his life. Asked when it was time to quit practicing, Carlson wrote: "I'm 70 years old and have already been written off as a dead man several times. . . . I suppose that's why people keep asking me why I'm still working. I almost have to apologize for still wanting to help people, still serving others" (Kottler & Carlson, 2016, p. 48). Carlson's last book was *Adlerian Psychotherapy* (Carlson & Englar-Carlson, 2017). Indeed, Jon Carlson did not simply talk about social interest, his life was a testimony to putting his existential values into action.

Questions for Reflection

1. At this time, what are some of the main sources of meaning and purpose in your life?
2. In what way does the reality of mortality relate to your finding meaning in life?
3. How do you view living with meaning and purpose as an aspect of self-care?
4. What importance do you place on serving others? To what extent do you think you will be able to focus on service to others if you are not practicing self-care?

Jerry Corey's Reflections on Existential Themes

When I (Jerry) am asked what my theoretical orientation to psychotherapy is, my response is the existential approach. Although I favor an integrative approach to therapy, existential concepts form the foundation of my counseling orientation. Existential writers such as Frankl, May, and Yalom have greatly influenced my thinking, both personally and professionally. In all honesty, I cannot say that my self-care plan includes embracing death as a way to savor life. I do struggle with death anxiety even though I believe that accepting my limited time spurs me to make the most of this time. I realize that I have many more years behind me than I have ahead of me. I have lived for a half century more that Jude and Julius and for 30 years more than Michelle. One hopes that with age comes wisdom, but I am not sure! I am aware of how fast time goes by, and it does not seem to slow down as I age. I recall both my 60th and 70th birthday parties as if they were yesterday, yet I recently turned 80. Where did those two decades go, and will I still be hiking mountain trails at 100? The inevitable loss of family members and close friends is a sobering reality. My mother died when I was 60, and her presence is sorely missed by all our family. We visited her almost every week and treasured our time with her. She maintained an interest in daily life until she left us at age 94. Our daughters were very close to her, and we all often wish that she could have met her great-grandchildren. She taught me many lessons in life, and I would do well to spend some time reflecting on her advice. I have lost several close friends in the last decade, which makes me realize that time is precious. Many friends I used to hike with are now barely able to walk, which is a sobering thought. I would like to believe that my body will keep on functioning at peak levels in the coming years, and I practice self-care to ensure that I keep on keeping on!

I don't live in terror of the limitations of my remaining years, yet it does nudge me into assessing what I am doing with my life. I have excellent health and a good life in so many respects, which allows me to continue in my pursuit of meaningful goals. Each day I reflect on many of the things for which I am grateful. In Marianne's and my personal life, we have been blessed to have friends who represent different worldviews, and our friendships with people from diverse segments of society have injected vitality into both our personal and professional lives. Much of what I have achieved professionally is the result of collaborations with colleagues and friends in the profession, and I expect that these relationships will continue in the years ahead.

From the beginning of my career, I have been motivated by a desire to make a difference. My most meaningful work has been helping my students achieve their goals on their personal and professional journeys. Getting my students to challenge themselves by questioning life and stretching their personal and professional boundaries has always been more significant to me than merely presenting academic knowledge. My work does not end with me but continues through my students as they accomplish goals they never imagined possible.

I have always admired and respected Carl Rogers as a person and for his revolutionary contribution to the counseling profession. Rogers faced the prospect of his death by reflecting on following his passion for making a difference and realizing that his ideas would continue to live on long after his death. He believed he would remain alive in spirit as long as his life's work continued to help others (Rogers, 1980). I appreciate Rogers's notion of living on through the clients, professionals, and students who are able to profit from our contributions. I do hope my professional endeavors extend beyond my lifetime.

Each year, at the American Counseling Association conference, Jamie Bludworth (also known as "Stan" in one of our educational videos) and I give a presentation for graduate students and new professionals on "Becoming a Professional Counselor." Jamie and I share our professional experiences and encourage those who attend to reflect on the kind of professional counselor they want to become. A theme of our presentation is finding ways to maximize our abilities to take an active role in creating a meaningful career, which will translate into having a meaningful life. We emphasize that the true reward for a meaningful career is making the fullest use of the unique gifts we each possess. Each of us has special talents, and we will all touch the lives of many people. If you hope to retain your vitality and stamina in carrying out your mission, it is essential to have a self-care plan in place.

Meaning and Counselor Self-Care

Although existentialism is not my approach to counseling, when I (Jude) was a counselor-in-training, my clients' existential concerns in session mirrored my own concerns as a counselor. I had a clearly defined plan for my life: I loved sitting in the counselor's chair; I loved the spontaneous moments of creativity, embraced the ambiguity, and dove deeply into the therapeutic process. However, having a plan does not equate to having meaning in life for me. In fact, my plan felt hollow and without meaning. As a counselor-in-training, I did not have a clearly defined approach to counseling, and my work was less impactful. A client's decision to attend counseling is courageous and requires sacrifice, and I need to honor their sacrifice by providing the best service possible. My clients needed more than I felt capable of giving them. Containing my self-doubt became more difficult, and I began to question how my plan brought meaning to my life and whether it stymied my client's growth.

This doubt had a negative effect on my self-care. My sleep was disrupted, I felt unmotivated, and I was constantly anxious, both inside and outside of sessions. A supervisor suggested that I try the Gestalt perspective in session. I began to read Gestalt literature and to think about myself through the Gestalt lens. After making many technical mistakes and seeking an enormous amount of supervision, I became aware of the value of connecting deeply with others, which had implications for a meaningful life.

Up until that point, my meaning in life had mainly involved achievement and survival: "In order to survive, I must achieve."

Those of you who have gone through the process of becoming a counselor know that some early experiences are filled with failure and disappointment and others with triumph and growth. My early clinical experiences threatened the fabric of what, at the time, brought substantial meaning to my life plan. By doing my own personal work to clarify my definitions of *surviving* and *achieving*, I was able to develop a new message and apply it to the physical, emotional, social, and spiritual dimensions of my life: "In order to live, I must connect." This gave my plan weight and helped me work on a deep level with clients. I began to engage in other activities that brought me closer to others. I spent more time in the counseling clinic watching my colleagues work and processing their experiences. I engaged with my clients by prioritizing connection rather than focusing only on achieving treatment goals. This feeling of connection to others and having a different way of measuring my success as a counselor drastically improved my self-care and self-efficacy.

Most counselors enter the field because they believe their calling in life is to help others, and their meaning in life is connected to their work. We have witnessed colleagues who have lived fulfilling lives in the service of others as well as colleagues trapped in a vicious cycle in which the very thing that brings meaning to their life prevents them from enjoying life. Wardle and Mayorga (2016) explained that counselors often overextend themselves at work, leading to poor self-care and eventually to empathy fatigue or burnout.

A number of our contributors expound on the theme of finding meaning in their work and how a purposeful life is a centerpiece of self-care. We hope you will reflect on ways to find meaning through work without allowing work to consume your life. Michael Morgan, a professor in the counselor education program at the University of Wyoming, explains that connection and empathy are among the most meaningful things in his life, yet he needs to remind himself that there is a price to be paid for caring for clients.

Put Your Energy Where Your Heart Is

Michael Morgan

By the fifth week of my internship at a community mental health agency, I knew something was off. We talked about self-care in my master's program, but I had never really thought I needed to do anything. I was active, had a family, loved what I was doing, and felt great. I didn't need a new self-care plan to nurture my own wellness—

or so I thought. I had adjusted fairly well to the demands of graduate school. Practicum was over, and although I knew I still had much to learn, I felt good about my clinical skills. I was excited to accelerate my learning and ready to see more clients each week with greater autonomy through my internship experience.

My caseload quickly built beyond the two to three clients a week I saw in practicum. By the 5th week, I began seeing the signs. I wasn't as excited about seeing clients anymore, and I sometimes celebrated secretly when a client canceled. I was overwhelmed by the breadth and depth of clients' concerns, felt insecure about my ability to help, and missed the supervision I had received in practicum. Worse, I was taking my clinical worries home with me. I was becoming impatient with family and found that I didn't want to hear about others' problems. I was not very compassionate. I began noticing these things after 5 weeks, but it took considerably longer to recognize that taking care of myself would require intentional change on my part, and longer still to know what I needed to do.

Such early compassion fatigue and self-doubt worried me. A central part of how I find meaning in life is linked to understanding and empathizing with others. I believe this is central to helping others transcend their challenges and grow. This belief is deeply rooted in my faith tradition and a number of experiences from my personal history. It's how I want to be in the world, and it is one of the things that drew me to counseling as a career. But here I was, barely halfway through my master's program and already losing the desire to be compassionate that was so important professionally and personally.

I decided I was investing too much energy in empathizing with clients and not getting enough downtime away from the challenges of clinical work. I focused on carefully guarding my efforts to understand and empathize. I made changes to bring more relaxation, comfort, and happiness into my life. And it helped a little. These can be important aspects of self-care. But I was still not quite myself and was guarded with my compassion, especially at home (I gave at the office!).

Over time I came to realize what many of you probably already see. Pulling back from the very things that bring deep meaning to my life didn't really help. Gradually I discovered that the more experiences I had outside the clinic that invited me to understand and empathize with others, the more understanding and compassion I had in all areas of my life. For me it's a little like a long-distance bike ride. I love going the distance, and although I am tired at the end, I am also energized and revitalized—it becomes a flow experience. Connection and empathy are among the most meaningful things in my life. If I pull away from them, my capacity to draw on them diminishes. If I intentionally cultivate them, I'm more compassionate with clients, family, and the other people in my life. I'm more who I want to be.

I like to nurture these qualities by getting close to the human experience, opening myself to understanding, and finding examples of kindness and compassion. Good literature, film, and art do this for me, and I naturally enjoy these. Taking time to serve others or for solitude and reflection, which I don't enjoy as easily, also nurture me.

Make no mistake, I still enjoy mindless movies and books or video games with my adult children, and sometimes I am impatient with clients and family or bring my work worries home. But I know that part of my self-care has to include regularly seeing compassion at work around me, and I need to let compassion work in me outside of my professional responsibilities. When I do this, I come away revitalized and a better person.

What worked for me may not work for you, although maybe it will. But I do believe we're better counselors and humans when we actively nurture the things that are most meaningful to us. I hope you'll spend time figuring out what that is for you and commit to making it a regular part of your life.

● ● ●

If you find meaning through understanding and empathizing with others, integrating a variety of ways to understand and empathize with others outside of your clinical work may help you take care of yourself. In the following narrative, Jessie Darkis, a doctoral student in the counseling and counselor education program at Syracuse University, discusses how he puts his energy into a passion that was once close to his heart and how that experience has influenced his self-care as a counselor.

Meaning of Life and Self-Care

Jessie Darkis

Making meaning of my life has been a continual process for me, and as I continue to grow, develop, and learn, my understanding of the world is constantly evolving. Accepting the fluid nature of life has better prepared me to understand myself, which has given me a deeper appreciation of how to truly engage in self-care.

I clearly remember learning about the importance of self-care as a master's student in counseling. The list of self-care activities seemed contrived and cumbersome—I recall wondering how I would ever be able to find the time to do these things. As I continued my education, it became even more challenging to engage in self-care. During my final semester as a master's student, in an effort to complete all of the necessary hours for my internship experience, I faced the harsh reality that I was not taking care of myself.

One evening, during the height of my internship experience, I came home and spilled the weight of my day onto my roommate's shoulders.

She listened attentively, and then I began apologizing, explaining that I greatly appreciated her support but needed to find a self-sustaining way to take care of myself. Considering other ways to engage in self-care was painful at first. For as long as I could remember, the most meaningful and effective way for me to take care of myself was to spend time with horses, which my time and resources did not allow. I wondered how anything could ever replace the emotional and spiritual depth I felt when I connected with horses.

A week or so later, after a busy morning at my internship site, I decided to walk to lunch. Outside a café sat an old, repurposed piano in a community garden. I had practiced as a child but had never prioritized playing as an adult, and certainly not in a public place. People bustled about the city streets during the lunch hour rush, and before I could stop myself, I sat down and touched the yellowed ivory keys, giving myself permission to play. I did not know how long I stayed there, who was or was not watching, or what it sounded like. What I knew was that my heart felt full and my head felt clear.

As a first-year doctoral student, I am still learning how to manage and balance my time, but I now recognize the importance of incorporating self-care into my everyday life. I relish a 5-minute break to brew coffee with members of my cohort, an afternoon walk with my dog through the streets of Syracuse, a phone call home to my parents, or an evening at home with my partner. In opening my heart to the world and to my life, I have started to appreciate all of the things that are ready and waiting to help me take care of myself.

● ● ●

Many of us come to the counseling field carrying experiences that can enable us to get through difficult times. These resources can be found in obscure places from our past. Take a few moments to reflect on the experiences that brought you joy as a child and how these experiences and events relate to your self-care now as a counselor. Andy Felton, an assistant professor in the Rehabilitation and Counseling Department at the University of Wisconsin–Stout, explains how the things that bring meaning to his life also sustain his self-care as a counselor.

Wholesome Health

Andy Felton

Wellness is regularly reinforced in training programs and in the counseling field. A balance of mental, emotional, behavioral, and physical well-being is something we strive for in ourselves and promote in others. Part of the challenge is that there is no algorithm for maintaining our well-being.

Through my wellness journey, I have identified five concepts that have served me well. These interconnected themes of enjoyment, connection, creativity, growth, and moderation have all played a role in my wellness.

Enjoyment: Enjoyment is a rather simple concept that tends to be overlooked. The more I relish what I am involved in, the more satisfaction I have throughout the process and in the final product (if there is one). I fully acknowledge that I sometimes engage in activities that seem tedious or mundane, but it is in those moments that enjoyment is even more vital. Finding ways to appreciate the challenges allows for greater levels of motivation and helps me develop a greater connection to my experience.

Connection: When I talk about connection, I mean it in every sense of the word, connections with myself, with others, and with my world. Practicing mindfulness helps us fully integrate our thoughts and our experiences, but I believe we must go a step further and allow the mind and body to be fully engaged. Inviting all of myself to be a part of and connect with the world around me requires patience, vulnerability, and openness. However, when I strive for such connection, I tend to enjoy the experience and learn more about myself, about others, and recognize my true passions.

Creativity: Creativity reinforces enjoyment and connection. Creativity invites and strengthens catharsis, divergent thinking, and integration of self. In addition, creativity is much more of a process— being aware of my experience in the moment—than a product. I exert effort to include creativity in many aspects of my life. In my leisure time, for instance, I have found that painting, drumming, and photography challenge me, peak my interest, and allow me to be fully immersed in the moment. Creativity is also extremely helpful in the healing process, especially when experiencing catharsis and gaining new insights about myself. As a clinician, I have witnessed the benefits for my clients as they gained new insights and growth through creative methods. In the classroom, I put effort into finding unique ways of teaching material to further help students engage in their learning and think about material in a different way. Creativity keeps my experiences enjoyable and integrates multiple parts of the brain to assist in development, problem-solving skills, and emotional release. With such knowledge, it seems only appropriate to find creative ways to better ourselves and work on maintaining our wellness.

Growth: Expanding from creativity, growth is about challenging myself in order to become a more well-rounded person. Acknowledging that I have much to learn, practicing new skills, and facing the limits of my comfort zone help with my personal growth. Art and music foster such growth; however, I notice my greatest development through my travels and meeting new people. Having a genuine curiosity and openness toward others while exchanging stories with them helps me recognize my personal views, understand the perspectives of others, and enhances my ability to empathize. Such levels of growth require self-awareness and a willingness to take risks. I recognize that everyone may not be able to travel; however, all of us can find ways to challenge ourselves. By permitting myself to take risks, I have learned more about how to be patient, self-compassionate, and empathetic toward others, and I have seen how resilient people can be.

Moderation: Wellness often requires some level of balance. Efforts to address the mental, emotional, physical, and behavioral aspects of life can be demanding. It is not uncommon to focus solely on one aspect of ourselves and ignore the rest. No matter how you approach wellness, moderation will help assure that you are better able to address the complexities of maintaining your well-being.

• • •

Forming a philosophy of self-care can be especially difficult for beginning counselors. The narrative by Kent Becker, dean of the College of Social Sciences at Saybrook University, describes how he compartmentalized different aspects of his life and handled existential angst as he transitioned from one role to the next in his career as a counselor educator.

Trust, Truth, Beauty, Compassion

Kent Becker

I often tell my wife that I am a simple man, and I am. As the world around me becomes increasingly complex, I find that I must increasingly position myself within a set of core beliefs that are, in my opinion, timeless.

Trust in self: I have gone through multiple transitions since beginning my academic career: from teaching on campus to teaching off campus; from teaching in a physical classroom to teaching in a virtual classroom; from teaching undergraduate students to teaching graduate students; from working in a master's level program to coordinating a doctoral program; from being unpublished to being published; from being nontenured to being tenured: from serving as a faculty member to serving as a department chair; from serving as a department chair to serving as a dean. Each transition brings excitement and more than a healthy dose of anxiety.

When I get anxious, I make lists. I make lists before I start the new role. I make lists once I begin the new role. I make lists of what I need to do. I make lists of what I need to learn. I make lists of who I need to meet. I make lists of lists. Although these lists do not actually help me accomplished much, they do seem to bind my anxiety and help me to feel a bit less incompetent as I venture into the unknown. Each time I seem to convince myself that my next professional step will require an entirely new set of skills, unique knowledge, and unfamiliar competencies. And (thankfully) each time I finally realize that what has helped me to succeed in the past will help me to succeed in the present and in the future too.

It is at this point that I start to breathe, relax, and engage my work with creativity and focus. Yes, I still make lists, but they are less about what I am not and more about what is possible.

Truth and beauty: Several years ago I spent some time reflecting on what is important to me, my personal mission statement. I found myself landing on two words: truth and beauty. When I am seeking to center myself or when I am struggling with a decision, I often come back to these two words and reflect . . .

- Am I speaking my truth?
- Am I inviting others to speak their truths?
- Am I creating the space for others to share their truths?
- Am I adding beauty to the world?
- Am I open to seeing the beauty that exists within all beings?
- Am I creating the space for others to share their beauty?

These two words, simple as they may be, resonate with me. I have found a home within them. What are your words?

Compassionate presence: The ability to be truly present in the life of another is how I understand compassionate presence. To be fully present as a husband, father, teacher, and administrator is a daily journey. I fail often. I also surprise myself from time to time. It is in these moments that humanity lives. It is in these moments that understanding unfolds. It is in these moments that healing thrives. Regardless of role, it is in these moments that I genuinely surrender and connect as a human being. It is in these moments that I truly feel that I am of service.

• • •

Questions for Reflection

1. If you are a student, how do you expect that being a counseling professional will contribute to the ways you find meaning in life?
2. In what ways does your self-care plan align with activities that bring meaning to your life?
3. What difficulties, if any, do you have in balancing your time between your work life and your personal life? To what degree are you satisfied with the way that you are incorporating self-care in your daily life?

Religion/Spirituality and Meaning in Life

Some form of religious faith or personal spirituality can be a powerful source of meaning and self-care for counselors. Johnson (2013) believes therapists would do well to spend time reflecting on their own spiritual identity and journey, especially on experiences that were emotionally intrusive and fostered reactivity. If therapists understand and have worked through their spiritual emotional baggage, they can listen to their clients without becoming emotionally reactive or trying to impose their personal agenda on clients. Johnson contends that a client-defined sense of spirituality can be a significant avenue for connecting with the client and can facilitate the therapeutic change process. According to Leppma and Young (2016), counseling students who practice loving-kindness meditation can increase their feelings of wellness and empathy toward their clients. There are many more examples of how connections to a religious community or to spiritual activities such as meditation and mindfulness can improve your meaning in life and self-care (Coleman, Martensen, Scott, & Indelicato, 2016).

According to Francis (2016), clients' core beliefs and values are often used as ways of coping and gaining support in times of challenge. "These beliefs and values are part of what makes up the cultural picture of the client and can be used by the skillful and sensitive counselor to help the client navigate the counseling process toward healing and wholeness" (p. 563).

Although some clients do not talk explicitly about spirituality, existential themes often emerge in therapy. Therapists need to listen for the existential concerns of their clients regarding meaning, values, mortality, and being in the world. It is important to attend to how clients define, experience, and access whatever helps them stay connected to their core values and their inner wisdom. If counselors have explored the meaning and purpose of living themselves, they are more likely to be able to facilitate exploration of clients' meaning and purpose. If we are able to access the sources of meaning in our life, we have a way to connect with our clients on their journey in creating a meaningful life.

Adrienne Naquin-Bolton, the director of the University Counseling Center at Nicholls State University, explains how she finds meaning and takes care of herself through spirituality and faith.

Finding Meaning Through Spirituality and Faith

Adrienne Naquin-Bolton

Growing up in south Louisiana along the banks of Bayou Lafourche where Roman Catholicism is nothing short of a spiritual powerhouse, my exposure to various faith practices has been slow in coming. I am a practicing Catholic and have always credited the traditions of my faith to be major factors in my own spiritual development. However, I have come to realize that I have been utterly naïve about these traditions and practices as well as those of other faiths.

I can recall my first experience with someone who had different spiritual beliefs and core values than my own. In that instance, I took on the role of a student and encouraged the client to educate me about his values and the meaning they provided for his life. It was a wonderful learning experience as it helped me to overcome my initial fear of how to make the therapeutic relationship work.

My current work as a director of a college counseling center also brings me in touch with young adults who question their core beliefs and values. My university is in rural, southeast Louisiana, but my students are not immune to exploring spiritual beliefs outside of those with which they have been indoctrinated. Distancing themselves from these oftentimes forced beliefs results in students asking themselves existential questions: What am I doing here? What is my purpose? What do I have to contribute to this world? I experience these questions as being very spiritual in nature. I believe that spiritual matters lie at the heart of many problems that lead clients to seek therapy. I also ask these questions of myself, particularly during times of significant life changes and in response to hearing the struggles of clients. I ponder these existential questions when passing or visiting cemeteries in my community. I often wonder about the struggles of those individuals during their lifetime. How much importance was placed on them, and what did it matter in the grand scheme of things? These questions have been helpful in placing my own struggles into perspective.

My spiritual beliefs and practices have helped to provide a unique balance to my experiences as a counselor. I find it difficult to hear stories of suffering day in and day out. I am aware that this difficulty, if not regulated, can cause me to feel like I am losing faith in humanity. My faith helps to provide a sense of hope in what I believe is a flawed world. I find meaning in my clinical work, which gives me a real-world avenue to extend love and compassion to my clients, which are fundamental tenets of my faith. I also extend mercy to those who otherwise feel judged for their decisions.

Our role as empathic, nonjudgmental counselors is a far cry from the rest of the world, which I perceive as screaming blame and shame. I will truthfully admit that I have my own struggles with critiquing, passing judgment, and gossiping about other people in my personal life. Nevertheless, I find that I have no struggle being open and merciful with my clients because they are coming to me in a state of extreme vulnerability, often telling me things they have not told their closest acquaintances. I realize that any hope of developing a therapeutic alliance would be dashed immediately if I did not convey empathy and nonjudgmental acceptance to my clients.

I find meaning through a spiritual connection when viewing a magnificent sunset, a mountainous expanse, or a powerful thunderstorm. That feeling also is present for me when hearing a baby laugh, watching a kitten play, or seeing two people in love. I believe this connection can be present in the counseling office as well.

Allowing clients to experience their deepest, rawest emotions and be in a place of extreme vulnerability gives me an opportunity to practice unconditional acceptance. As a therapist who adheres to humanistic approaches, I appreciate the here-and-now focus of the session and witnessing as the client strives toward self-actualization. Empowerment is a key focus in my work, and I can only hope to help each client reach his or her fullest potential.

● ● ●

Faith provides a sense of hope in what we can all probably agree is an unfair world. We have worked with clients, students, and supervisees who face extremely difficult challenges in life. We are often left in awe at the resilience of these individuals. Part of trusting the therapeutic process is having faith in a client's, student's, or supervisee's will to meaning. Shana Gelin, a doctoral student in the counseling and counselor education program at Syracuse University, shares her experience of using spirituality and faith to attend to her self-care.

Finding Peace in the Midst of Personal Stress

Shana Gelin

"All great spirituality is what we do with our pain." This quote by Richard Rohr, an ordained friar and spiritual writer, captures the very essence and core of spirituality and faith for me. It defines these concepts as tools to deal with discomfort. I use spirituality and faith to balance my clients' narratives, graduate school workload, and personal stressors.

For me, spirituality encompasses my belief in a higher power or a driving life-force. Faith is knowing my purpose in life, and putting trust in that driving life-force. I use both concepts to find meaning in life and to develop a deep sense of self-awareness. Faith and spirituality are my sources of strength and courage when fighting through adversity during the trials of my life that Richard Rohr refers to as "pain." The pain, frustration, and exhaustion of a graduate student in a counselor education program is quite taxing. Having the roles of a counselor, supervisor, researcher, graduate assistant, and student makes self-care a must for me. In a counseling setting, I find meaning through spirituality and faith by understanding that I have the ability to serve others.

As a graduate student, I wear many hats, and my meaning of spirituality and faith is a guide to doing what I'm supposed to do in each venue. I've realized that my spiritual practices took a back seat to my studies and my stress levels became stronger. I was tired, pulled in so many ways, and feeling guilty about taking time for myself. In understanding who I am, I then knew that the missing link to intrinsic internal peace is my spiritually. I socialized with other people in my cohort, thinking that was what I needed, but I was still left empty. One day I found myself stopping all the work I had to do to pray. This gave me the strength I needed to move forward and believe in the work I was doing.

As a counselor, I've realized that I was not prepared enough for sessions with clients. I would be physically present but found myself asking clients to repeat themselves because of my lack of concentration. I was preoccupied when meeting with clients, thinking about all of the other responsibilities I had as a doctoral student. I needed an outlet before sessions, and my spiritual practices provided the sense of peace I needed. Saying a prayer reminded me of my purpose to serve and to be present with all of my clients.

Finding my own spiritual path is helping me to understand clients who practice other ways of finding meaning, such as mindfulness and yoga. I view spirituality as a tool to better conceptualize my clients and understand the world in which they live. Spirituality affects the way I approach treatment plans, crisis prevention plans, safety plans, and other forms of client care. Sometimes clients have expressed feeling safe talking about spirituality in sessions with me when they have not felt safe doing so with other therapists. Attending to a client holistically makes this process of counseling a unique and fulfilling journey.

For clients that consider faith and spirituality a part of their lives, I ask them how their spiritual practice is going. Oftentimes, the more stressful life gets (for some) the more their spiritual or faith practices take a back seat. The same has been true in my own life. As a graduate student and counselor, I needed to find peace in the midst of the stressors of life. Now I know that bringing peace into my life is what allows me to be the best emerging counselor educator that I can be.

● ● ●

What are some of your ideas regarding how you can increasingly bring peace into your daily life?

Questions for Reflection

1. What role, if any, does religion or spirituality play in your life? If applicable, does it play a role in your work or service to others?
2. To what degree does your religion or spirituality assist you in better understanding the meaning of life?
3. How do you envision that your religious beliefs and spirituality will affect your life and well-being in the future?

Cultural Influences on the Meaning of Life

Religion or spirituality has a powerful influence on the ability of some counselors to find meaning in life and be well. For others, cultural influences can be just as influential. Self-care, as it is viewed in the counseling literature, was not emphasized in my (Jude's) family. My parents, like their parents, sacrificed, struggled, and worked hard so that the next generation had just a few more opportunities than the one before. Who and where I am now is the result of generations and generations of sacrifice, struggle, and hard work. I sometimes see my sacrifice, struggle, and work through a cultural lens as just the price I have to pay for the next generation to have more opportunities than I have. From time to time in this early stage in my career, it feels as though that price is higher than I can pay.

As I reflect on my cultural influences, I notice that my self-care works in two ways: (1) when I take specific steps to ensure than I enjoy my life, and (2) when I hold onto cultural principles that have been passed down from generation to generation in my family. Here are a few core intergenerational principles that I value most when I focus on finding meaning in life and the need for self-care.

Principle 1: Squeeze the tomato, but don't let the juices fall. This is a saying my late grandpa told me when I was a kid. In every stage of my life (high school, college, and being a professional athlete), this saying has taken on a different meaning. At this early professional stage of my life, I take away a couple lessons from this principle: (a) squeezing the tomato means getting the most I can out of life, and (b) don't let the juices fall means being mindful of the sacrifices I make now. I see the tomato as life, something delicate and easily bruised or ruined. I see squeezing the tomato as my attempts to get the most out of life (tenure, healthy relationships, boundaries, success, peace, children, and making an impact). I see trying not to let the juices fall as my attempts to limit the messiness of life or the negative consequences. This principle challenges me to think about those before me and what happens after me; it puts my existence into perspective. It also sparks an internal debate regarding the sacrifices I am making today to squeeze what I can out of life while I am here. For example, I want tenure but am not willing to sacrifice the relationships with my family to achieve this. At times my goal to get tenure gets the best of me and I stay up late, jot down research ideas while I am supposed to be spending time with my family, and talk excessively about my projects when I meet with loved ones. As much as I can, I try to remember this principle, check in with myself, and weigh my options.

Principle 2: Go slow and use both hands. This is a saying my dad repeatedly told me, especially when I was around power tools. Even as I write this piece, I hear my dad's voice saying, "Just take your time son, go slow." As a kid, my dad would have my brother and me do chores that involved some form of picking up several heavy things and moving them a yard or two to the side. My brother and I would try to find ways of easing the load. We would try to figure out a shortcut that took hours to set up, yet we eventually failed when determined hard work would have succeeded. My dad would check in on us hours later and say, "Just take your time boys, go slow, and use both hands." Now, as I look at my to-do lists, I fight down feelings of being overwhelmed. I remember this principle and take my time, use everything I have at my disposal (myself, colleagues, friends, and family), and one by one move these items a yard or two to the "task completed" side.

Principle 3: Remember I am loved. My mom said this to me before every major event in my life: my first professional soccer try out and game, my first Olympic developmental team try out and game, and my dissertation defense. When my self-care is failing, I find that I judge myself harshly and my self-worth gets attached to my achievements. As a new faculty member who is close in age to some of my students, I sometimes experience feelings of being an imposter. These emotions cause me to think that I have not done enough, not won enough awards, and not published enough. They hinder my creativity and distract me from doing my best work. I catch myself waiting for my department head to call me in his office and say, "We've finally noticed that you were faking it Jude, nice try, we'll take over from here." Being mindful of my mom's wise saying helps me realize that my self-worth is not connected to my achievements. I work hard to stay connected with my family. These connections to my wife, parents, and siblings recharge me.

Using a combination of these principles to take care of myself has kept me grounded and motivated. Taking care of myself in this early stage of my career entails honoring the sacrifices made by others on my behalf, being intentional regarding the sacrifices I make, being patient and determined in completing tasks, and looking to my family's love for me as the source of my self-worth. When my self-care is protecting me, I have the freedom to seek out opportunities that fit my passions, I am willing to try new things, I am not stopped by a fear of failing, and I am able to learn from my mistakes without too much self-judgment. Above all, I make time to nurture my personal and professional relationships, which are of paramount importance to me and are a deep source of meaning in my life.

Concluding Thoughts

Finding meaning in life is a process unique to each of us. Our life experiences, culture, spiritual or religious values, and many other influences determine what brings us fullfillment. In this chapter we highlighted a variety of approaches to finding meaning in life and how our philosophical views contribute to counselor self-care. Key existential figures have contributed to our understanding of how awareness of death can motivate us to live more fully and meaningfully. Take some time to review the themes in this and previous chapters and identify those that give your life a sense of meaning and purpose. In the final chapter we provide suggestions for further development of self-care strategies and discuss the importance of designing a realistic action plan to enhance your self-care practices.

Chapter 9

Creating a Realistic Self-Care Plan

After reading the narratives of our many contributors as well as our personal successes and struggles with self-care, we hope you are inspired to create or reexamine your own self-care plan. If you have a self-care program, take some time to evaluate your plan and consider revisions that complement your current lifestyle. In this chapter we focus on how to put your personal self-care plan into action. Contributors with various levels of experience in the counseling field share ways they motivate themselves to actualize their dreams and personal goals. Self-care is an ethical mandate and a bulwark against burnout; none of us can afford to set self-care as a low priority. The most challenging aspect of putting a self-care plan into action often is taking that first step and initiating a change in your life.

How Change Happens

Whether we like it or not, change happens, sometimes gradually in small steps and at other times all at once. We see our clients, colleagues, supervisees, and students resist change all the time, and sometimes we resist change too. Change can be unsettling, and we may experience setbacks along the way. Change requires us to venture outside our comfort zone, and most of the time we have mixed feelings about making significant changes. It is important to celebrate your successes one step at a time and to be aware of any unrealistic expectations. Be patient with your process, and practice self-compassion. It is critical to be kind to yourself and to reach out to others when you need help.

Kottler (2014) reminds us that significant change is a response to our chosen attitudes, beliefs, and perspectives. There are good reasons for us to avoid change because change involves surrendering something familiar and comfortable. If we refuse to make changes in our life and lifestyle, our self-neglect may catch up with us and diminish our quality of life. If we resist change and do not attend to our physical, psychological, emotional, or spiritual needs, our bodies, minds, and souls will likely pay a steep price—one that we cannot afford. Our clients will suffer from our self-neglect too!

Reluctance to make life changes is so common that Prochaska and Norcross (2018) described a change model that outlines five identifiable stages of change. In the *precontemplation stage*, the individual has no intention of changing a behavior pattern in the near future. In the *contemplation stage*, the person is aware of a problem and is considering overcoming it, but he or she has not yet made a commitment to take action to bring about the change. In the *preparation stage*, the person intends to take action immediately and reports some small behavioral changes. In the *action stage*, the individual is taking steps to modify his or her behavior to solve a problem. During the *maintenance stage*, the individual works to consolidate the gains made and to prevent relapse.

We do not pass through these five stages in a linear fashion, and our readiness can fluctuate throughout the change process. If change is initially unsuccessful, we may return to an earlier stage. You may want to change certain patterns because they are no longer serving you, but you may be reluctant to leave familiar patterns. You may be afraid of the unknown or feel that the stakes involved in changing are too high. It is important to find an inner source of motivation that will enable you to challenge your reluctance to make life-affirming choices. The process of change begins when we are able to recognize and accept certain aspects of ourselves.

Questions for Reflection

1. At this time, where do you see yourself in this stages of change model regarding your self-care action plan? To what degree are your satisfied with your present plan? If you are not satisfied, what will help you to become more *ready* to implement changes to your self-care plan?
2. What price is involved in making changes in your life, and what is the cost of refusing to make changes you deem desirable?

3. Generally, how much action do you take in making changes in the way you are living? How accepting are you of those aspects of reality that you cannot change?
4. To what degree do you understand the difference between the things you have control over and the things that are beyond your control?

Creating an Action Plan for Self-Care

Robert Wubbolding, an internationally known teacher, author, and practitioner of reality therapy, believes it is necessary to develop action plans if we are serious about making changes. Self-care plans are built on an honest evaluation of current choices. As you read this narrative, imagine creating an action plan to take care of yourself and others that includes both short- and long-range goals.

WDEP: We Definitely Endorse Planning for Counselor Self-Care

Robert E. Wubbolding

"To fail to plan is to plan to fail." Personal success—in business, promoting products or services, achieving a degree or credential, or maintaining or improving your personal health and self-care—does not happen automatically. Planning is central for any achievement. The same is true for personal well-being such as gaining more skill in interpersonal communication, increased self-esteem, parenting skills, more satisfying relationships with peers, or even becoming a more spiritual or religious person. These accomplishments do not occur automatically as we grow through developmental stages. Formulating specific plans and implementing them facilitate success.

Effective plans have several characteristics that can be summarized in the acronym SAMIC[3]. A results-centered plan is not complicated; it is simple. To achieve the desired result, the plan must be attainable and realistically doable. It is measurable, answering the question, "precisely when will I follow through on my plan?" "I" stands for immediate. The plan maker implements the plan as soon as possible, without delay. The most effective plan is one controlled by the planner and not dependent on other individuals or outside circumstances. Ideally, the counselor, choosing a self-care behavior, makes a firm commitment to implement the plan. A consistent plan, repeated regularly, is required to achieve your goals, but a plan performed a single time is better than no plan. For a more in-depth discussion of making an evaluation of current behavior and creating an action plan for change, see my latest book, *Reality Therapy and Self-Evaluation: The Key to Client Change* (Wubbolding, 2017).

A vital part of counselor self-care is the objective of more effective communication with colleagues, friends, and family. Fulfilling this objective begins with a genuine self-evaluation of current interpersonal relationships, such as assessing the manner of communication and deciding whether it is helping or hurting interpersonal relationships. The desired result is the formulation of planned behavior that is more respectful, considerate, and even assertive when necessary. Self-care plans are built on an honest evaluation of current choices. Subsequent plans might include spending time together, listening to each other's hopes and dreams, respecting the other person's needs, and being mindfully aware of the other person.

In my personal and professional life, I implement the SAMIC[3] model as a way to keep myself focused and to consistently evaluate what I am doing each day and how this behavior is affecting my life and my relationships with significant others. My professional work is enjoyable and meaningful, but it is demanding. I present workshops both nationally and internationally, and this takes energy. One fun activity I have done for many years is read books on history and current events. I am firmly committed to my cardio exercise program, and my wife, Sandie, and I enjoy it together. My personal relationships (especially with Sandie) are a source of nourishment for me, ensuring that I have the stamina I need to effectively engage in teaching, supervising, and doing workshops. I take making action plans for both my personal life and my professional work seriously; applying planning principles enables me to successfully achieve most of my goals. I am convinced that having a vision alone will not result in meeting my life goals; it is creating and carrying out realistic plans that provides a pathway to success.

In my classes, I suggest that students clarify what they want in their careers and take realistic steps to fulfill their desires. I stress the necessity for students and counselors to attend carefully to their own needs: self-preservation, belonging, inner control or power, freedom, and fun. And, most important, I encourage them to find purpose and meaning in their work and in their life, which I do my best to model. I suggest focusing on activities that improve their minds and emotional lives. Satisfying the need for belonging by spending quality time with family and friends prevents counselor burnout. If counselors choose to spend quality time together with family and friends, they will develop topics for conversation that are life-giving and uplifting, not energy-draining. Finally, I believe that good humor and fun times lie at the heart of mental health. I spend a few minutes each day reflecting on several enjoyable experiences I have had, and I recommend this practice to my students.

• • •

Wubbolding demonstrates that positive change in self-care practices does not happen automatically. How can you apply the specific steps he suggests to your self-care plan? Designing and implementing a self-care action plan begins by making an evaluation of what you are doing. Self-evaluation, which is the cornerstone of reality therapy, is basic to planning for change. Others cannot make this evaluation for you. Key questions that should be included in your self-evaluation are:

- Is what I am doing helping or hurting me?
- Is my current behavior satisfying or unsatisfying to me?
- To what degree is what I am doing enhancing my relationships?

It is crucial to assess what you are doing, where you are presently, and where you want to go. This evaluation involves honest reflection on how you are currently acting. If you decide that what you are doing is not in your best long-term interests, and that you are not meeting your needs, you are in a good position to develop specific plans and implement them to make behavioral changes.

Effective Planning for Self-Care

Wubbolding (2017) uses the acronym SAMIC³ to capture the essence of a good plan: **S**imple, **A**ttainable, **M**easurable, **I**mmediate, **C**ontrolled by the planner, **C**ommitted to, and **C**onsistently done. We gain more effective control over our lives with plans that have these characteristics:

- Good plans are realistically doable, positive rather than negative, and dependent on you rather than on others. Although plans need to be specific, concrete, and measurable, they should be flexible and open to revision.
- Plans involve process-centered activities such as writing a letter to a friend, taking a yoga class, beginning meditation, substituting nutritious food for junk food, devoting 2 hours a week to volunteer work, or taking a vacation.
- Good plans describe a positive course of action or specify what actions you are willing to take. Even small plans can help you take significant steps toward desired changes.
- Plans are carried out as soon as possible: "What are you willing to do today to begin to change your life?"
- Plans can be revised. After you have implemented your plan, it is useful to evaluate it and make any revisions that you deem necessary.

How might you be able to apply the characteristics of a good plan to your own life? Evaluate your present level of self-care, and consider specific changes you most want to make. Ask yourself, "What plans can I make now that will result in a more satisfying life?" After identifying what you want your self-care program to look like, devise a plan to help you attain the results you want. Refer to the self-care assessment at the end of Chapter 5 and answer these questions: Where are you now on various aspects of your self-care plan? Where would you like to be? What can you do to improve designing and carrying out your self-care action plan?

Mike Aldrich, a marriage and family therapist trainee, took an honest inventory of his health and behavioral patterns and realized that excessive drinking, use of drugs, poor eating practices, and lack of exercise were not conducive to achieving success in his graduate program. Mike's self-care plan was effective because of his willingness to engage in a self-evaluation process that convinced him that he would have to make some major changes in his behavior if he hoped for success as a graduate student.

The Practice of Patience With Self-Care

Mike Aldrich

For the majority of my life, I have struggled to take proper care of myself. I was an active member of a fraternity on campus as an undergraduate; in that culture binge drinking and drug use were not only accepted, they were encouraged. I was drinking heavily 4 nights a week and smoking marijuana more days than not. For brief periods I was eating well and exercising, but I would quickly nosedive into longer periods of lethargy and fast-food binges.

When I entered my graduate program, I knew my habits would need to change for me to be successful. However, during my first year of graduate school I still engaged in many of the behaviors that I thought I could extinguish. It was not until my third semester in the program that I took an honest inventory of my self-care habits and how they would affect not only my personal life but my professional career as well.

I heard about self-care in many of my classes, but I did not think it was critical enough to be included in the ethics code. Then I began to hear my peers saying that self-care is an ethical mandate. This was a vital wake-up call for me. It was at that point that I decided to make some drastic changes in my life.

My first task was to take an honest inventory of my current self-care practices and to measure their impact on my professional work. For example, I enjoy playing videogames (and I do consider them to be a form of self-care), but this activity is much less important to my self-care than a balanced diet and a good exercise regimen. Therefore, I made the decision to cut back on this hobby to create more time to prepare fresh food and go to the gym.

To practice self-care effectively, I needed to look at all the activities I enjoy and prioritize those that will benefit me most. One of the major changes I made was to put my new habits into my calendar and create to-do lists. I started to schedule when I would go to the grocery store and when I would workout. By having these activities on a list or calendar, they felt more like permanent parts of my schedule and less like items I could just brush off. I also enlisted the help of those around me. I started going to the gym with my roommate, who would push me off the couch when I tried to avoid exercising. I joined a weight-loss competition at my office, and the weekly weigh-ins and money incentives helped propel me to exercise more frequently and for longer periods of time. Surrounding myself with people who motivate me has been instrumental in keeping my commitment to my self-care action plan. As a part of my self-care plan, I radically reduced the amount of alcohol I was drinking so I could function more effectively.

In addition to the physical dimension of self-care, I began to embrace some of the spiritual aspects of self-care that I had been neglecting. I have enjoyed the benefits of meditation and prayer for many years. However, like exercising, these practices went through periods of frequent use and then stagnation. It was important for me to set realistic and attainable goals for myself to balance and integrate these activities into my life. Instead of trying to meditate every day, I decided to try and meditate three times a week. I also used to think that I needed to pray every night to take care of myself. I now pray when I find it helpful and necessary, which is usually when I am struggling and need to reach out to my Higher Power for assistance.

After integrating these changes in my life, I was stunned at the results. In 7 months I lost 18 pounds, I feel happier and more energetic, and I am more spiritually grounded and connected to those I care about. I have been able to manage this lifestyle for a longer period of time than I ever have before.

My best advice regarding implementing a self-care plan is to embrace the occasional "cheat" on your plan. I realized that I relapsed so often because I relied on an all-or-nothing mentality. If you want to take self-care seriously, you have to be kind to yourself and occasionally indulge in some of your less beneficial behaviors. Don't be afraid to take one day off to grab a beer and a burger with a good friend.

• • •

The Challenge of Maintaining Your Self-Care Plan

Staying the course and making necessary changes is fraught with difficulty, and you may well encounter setbacks in moving through your plan. Kottler (2014) put it well: "Change almost never occurs in a predictable, incremental, and progressive trajectory. There are a few steps of progress forward, and then a slip or slide backward" (p. 307). Kottler identified a host of reasons for the failure of changes and recommended developing skills for coping with lapses while remaining on a meaningful course. These lapses remind us that there are many challenges not only in making life changes but also in maintaining them. By not demanding perfection, we can credit ourselves with any movement that brings us closer to our self-care goals.

Alyssa Theis learned the value of practicing compassion toward herself when she did not meet her expectations. She built accountability into her plan by recruiting family members and friends. Although she faces challenges in putting her plan into action, Alyssa continues to learn the importance of involving others in helping her stick to her plan.

Building Accountability Into My Self-Care Action Plan

Alyssa Theis

Creating a plan for self-care has been both a challenging and a rewarding experience for me. As a graduate student, life can be chaotic and busy. Finding the time to sit down and create a change plan is hard enough, let alone actually sticking to that plan once it is created. My commitment to self-care has slowly developed over the years I have been involved in the human services field, but it was not until I started my master's program that I really began to develop a plan.

When I began graduate school, I made a conscious decision to implement a self-care plan as soon as possible. I was first introduced to the concept of self-care while working as a case manager a couple of years before starting my master's program. My workplace educated me about the importance of this practice, but I never took the time to sit down and come up with a plan for myself. As a result, I burned out quickly and struggled to manage the demands of my position. Going back to school gave me the time I knew I needed to really sit down and figure out what it was that my personal self-care plan would look like. My school's counseling program was critical in helping me develop my plan because every class placed a heavy emphasis on self-reflection and putting our goals into action.

I have come to realize the crucial role of accountability in carrying out my plan, as doing this is challenging for me. I have asked my family members and friends to help me stick to my commitments, and involving them as much as possible has greatly increased the odds of sticking to my plan. One part of my self-care plan involves staying physically healthy in a fun way. To accomplish this, I joined a rock climbing gym with my husband about 6 months ago. He and I agreed to go at least twice a week, and I am really proud to say that we have stuck with it.

Involving him in this part of my plan has increased my accountability, as he pushes me to go on days I do not feel up to it, and it has given us a new fun activity to do together. We also committed to having at least one camping trip or weekend getaway planned at any given time, although this can be hard to do with my busy schedule.

Despite my successes in sticking to my plan, maintaining it requires major effort. Eating healthy and maintaining my exercise goals are difficult when running around between work, school, and practicum. Some days I just do not wake up early enough to both prepare my meals for the day and make it out the door on time. Other times, I feel too tired to focus on being mindfully present at home (another goal of mine) after I have had a long week of clients, paperwork, and studying. I've learned to include self-compassion as a part of my plan, and I remind myself that I really am doing the best I can; sometimes it is OK for that to be enough. Although this has helped me get through those days when I am hard on myself, I definitely need to continue to work on this area.

Like many people in the counseling field, I prefer taking care of others to focusing on myself. The self-reflective activities and assignments in my master's program have really helped me to develop and commit to a specific plan of action. The more closely I am able to follow my plan, the better I am able to be present with my friends, family members, and clients. Practicing compassion toward myself when I fall short of my own expectations is just as important as following my plan. Most of us can easily create a safe, warm, and compassionate environment in which our clients can experience the successes and failures of committing to their change plans. I consider it my ethical responsibility as a counselor to practice that same care toward myself.

* * *

Practicing self-compassion can strengthen your resolve to be accountable. Amanda Johnson, a graduate student in counseling, accepts the reality that she will not be perfect in implementing her action plan, but she stays focused on building on her strengths.

Weaving Self-Care Into My Daily Routine

Amanda Johnson

Learning to incorporate regular self-care into one's life is not always easy, but I view it as a necessity to be able to function optimally, in both my personal life and my graduate work. Making time for myself can be difficult, but I believe I am more successful in my endeavors when I take the time to care for myself. My self-care plan incorporates strategies for wellness in all aspects of my lifestyle. I have noticed that the more self-care I weave into my daily routine, the more I am able to fulfill my other obligations and commitments in life.

Self-care is both a cognitive and a behavioral process, and I have found different paths for caring for myself when stress is getting the best of me or I feel overwhelmed. One simple approach I use is to live mindfully. The simple act of paying attention to my breath and body for a moment can calm me down during times of stress. Taking a minute to absorb the sights and sounds around me creates a moment of tranquility in a stream of chaos. But mindfulness is just the beginning.

This year I made a sincere effort to incorporate more ways to better care for myself, such as good nutrition, exercise, and yoga. At the beginning of the school year, I started walking with another mom in the mornings. I quickly realized how much having a workout partner could hold me accountable. It works both ways in fact; we each hate having to cancel on the other, so at least 3 days a week we walk/jog in the mornings after dropping our daughters off at school. Incorporating regular exercise into my routine has prompted a heightened awareness of what I choose to eat and put in my body as well. Once I implemented a few self-care tactics, others seemed to follow as a continuation. My once a week yoga session gives me the chance to listen to my body and strengthen my core, and it feels like a refresh button for my body and mind. I enjoy spending time with my family and friends, and I make sure to include some pampering when my budget allows. My self-care plan allows me to be a devoted mother of two, a dedicated graduate student, a loyal daughter, a thoughtful friend, and an ethical counselor.

Researchers talk about stages of change and the need for maintenance and routine when incorporating something new into daily life. I am realistic enough to know that relapse happens and that I may return to old behaviors at times. I try not to be overly self-critical when my plan is not working well. A very important aspect of implementing self-care for me means being forgiving of myself. I realize that everyone makes mistakes, and it is imperative that I accept my imperfections and use them to build on my strengths. Some weeks I feel on top of the world and get everything done with time to spare and a smile on my face. Other times, I feel more like a robot, just going through the motions and getting through the day. When I incorporate healthy behaviors during those sad times, I find myself living more of the positive life I enjoy.

When I schedule activities that keep me well, it becomes part of my daily routine. Whether my schedule is busy or not, I am convinced that I consistently need to stay focused on goals that contribute to my wellness. When life is chaotic and I feel overwhelmed and pulled in different directions, I try to remember that taking care of myself is absolutely essential if I hope to take care of others.

• • •

All three of the graduate students' stories speak to the ethical imperative of taking care of oneself as a prerequisite to taking care of others. They all emphasize the importance of having a personalized self-care plan that they use in many aspects of their daily life. They give themselves room to feel pride in what they *are doing* rather than dwelling on what they *are not doing*. Dana Blake, who recently graduated with an undergraduate human services degree, realizes that she needs to make taking care of herself a priority to be able to provide quality service to others.

Self-Care That Works

Dana Blake

I married when I was young, raised three children, and divorced after 24 years of an emotionally abusive marriage. I returned to school during my divorce and began working as an assistant in special education. I am currently working toward my special education teaching credential. I also intern as a small group leader. My goal is to obtain a master's degree in counseling and then to become a licensed marriage and family therapist in private practice.

I feel passionate about self-care. In my current work with children with mild to moderate disabilities, my role as a small group facilitator, and my future work with my counseling clients, my ability to be patient, present, and authentic is essential to my effectiveness. I must bring my best self into the room. My students, group members, and future clients require and deserve that from me. To bring my best self into my work, it is critical that I take care of myself outside of work. At age 46, I am just beginning a career path that I hope to continue for a long time. Taking care of my overall health is a major factor in being able to maintain my professional edge now and as I get older.

Motivation alone is not enough when it comes to practicing self-care. My specific plan for self-care has evolved over the last few years. It includes the elements of physical, spiritual, mental, and emotional health. My plan for physical health includes eating clean, practicing yoga, running, and getting good sleep. I care for myself spiritually by having a daily quiet time to read and pray while I enjoy my morning coffee. I am in recovery for emotional abuse through a 12-step group, which is how I am currently caring for my mental and emotional health. I also make time to spend with family and friends each week. I mark the elements of my self-care plan on my calendar in the same way I plan my work, school, and other responsibilities. I have a very full schedule: I work full time, take 15 units at school, have an internship, and maintain personal relationships. At first glance, it would seem that I don't have time for self-care. By making the time and prioritizing the elements of my self-care plan, I am so much more efficient and effective that self-care is actually the key to accomplishing all that I do.

An effective plan for self-care must be practiced and maintained, and this can be challenging. I have developed strategies to help keep me on track with my plan. However, the most important part of maintenance is being flexible and not beating myself up when I mess up! Maintaining my self-care plan is a balance between having boundaries with myself and others and being flexible and making allowances. Having boundaries with others is an area of particular struggle for me. I had to learn to say "no" to spending time with a significant other so I can practice yoga and get a good sleep. I had to risk his negative response to care for myself. I have learned that I can choose to care for myself first and survive someone else being temporarily upset about it. This area of personal growth has been a by-product of my desire to implement my self-care plan.

By practicing self-care, I am able to reduce my anxiety and to be present for my students, group members, and future clients. I am able to be more authentic working with others when I am following my own path toward becoming the person I want to be. I understand personally the challenges and obstacles that get in the way of making healthy changes in the way I think and live. It is a constant and ever-changing process that will continue throughout my life. Ultimately, the most important thing I will bring to my professional work is myself! My presence, spirit, and my connection with my clients is the foundation for the work I hope to accomplish. To be of highest service to others, I must make myself and my own health a priority.

● ● ●

Questions for Reflection

1. When your self-care plan is not working well, are you committed to sticking with your action plan? What would a relapse mean to you, and how would you recover from it?
2. What have you learned about working with barriers to self-care that you can apply to your life?
3. Motivation to change alone is not sufficient to bring about desired changes in self-care. What do you need besides motivation to experience success with your self-care plan?
4. What challenges do you expect to encounter in designing and maintaining a self-care plan? How could you address each of these challenges?
5. Is it essential to practice self-care as a prerequisite to taking care of others? How convinced are you that you cannot afford to neglect caring for yourself if you are interested in effectively serving others?
6. The importance of relationships with others and recruiting family members and friends in implementing a self-care program has been a common theme of contributors. What personal relationships can you use as resources for carrying out your self-care action plan?

Consistency in Implementing Your Self-Care Plan

Talk is cheap; putting our words into action is the hard part. Reflect on your own tendencies and consider what you would need for your self-care plan to be successful. Of course, what constitutes *success* is open to interpretation. You might be content with achieving minimal or moderate growth in a positive direction, whereas someone else might view anything less than perfect compliance with the plan to be a sign of failure. How much improvement do you need to make in your practice of self-care to feel satisfied? What could help you achieve consistency in putting your self-care plan into action?

We have isolated five factors that help people to consistently implement their plans and take action. These essential factors are self-discipline, motivation, accountability, the ability to cope well with setbacks, and presence of a strong support system. Evaluate yourself on these factors to assess your likelihood of making consistent progress in your self-care plan. On a scale of 1 to 10, rate yourself on the following factors:

1 = *Extremely Low*   10 = *Extremely High*

1. Your level of *self-discipline* in committing to your self-care plan:
   ❏ 1   ❏ 2   ❏ 3   ❏ 4   ❏ 5   ❏ 6   ❏ 7   ❏ 8   ❏ 9   ❏ 10

2. Your level of *motivation* to practice good self-care:
   ❏ 1   ❏ 2   ❏ 3   ❏ 4   ❏ 5   ❏ 6   ❏ 7   ❏ 8   ❏ 9   ❏ 10

3. Your ability to hold yourself *accountable* for the self-care goals you set:
   ❏ 1   ❏ 2   ❏ 3   ❏ 4   ❏ 5   ❏ 6   ❏ 7   ❏ 8   ❏ 9   ❏ 10

4. Your ability to *cope well with setbacks* in your self-care regimen and to get back on track after you have relapsed:
   ❏ 1   ❏ 2   ❏ 3   ❏ 4   ❏ 5   ❏ 6   ❏ 7   ❏ 8   ❏ 9   ❏ 10

5. Your *level of support* from family members, friends, and colleagues in maintaining good self-care practices:
   ❏ 1   ❏ 2   ❏ 3   ❏ 4   ❏ 5   ❏ 6   ❏ 7   ❏ 8   ❏ 9   ❏ 10

After assessing yourself on these factors, which of them, if any, are of most concern for you? For example, if you know you have difficulty holding yourself accountable for maintaining an exercise program and rated yourself on the lower end of the accountability scale, what could you do to boost your rating? Would building some incentives into your program or asking a friend to help you boost your rating? Although we might very well make progress in meeting some of our goals, there is a good chance that we will not implement our self-care plans perfectly. Indeed, just when we think we have perfected our self-care regimen, something is liable to happen to remind us that nothing is perfect or lasts indefinitely. In emphasizing this message, we hope to encourage you to persist in your self-care program, even when you cannot implement it perfectly.

Our Reflections on Writing *Counselor Self-Care*

The process of writing this book has been a fascinating journey for us individually and collectively. We have learned much about ourselves, each other, and the topic of self-care by reflecting on the themes introduced in each chapter and by reviewing the narratives our many contributors so generously provided. This book would not be complete without adding our own reflections on how we have been affected by working on this project.

Jude's Personal Reflections

Earlier in this book I referenced the counseling adage, "You get the clients you need." This adage can be modified and applied to my experience in this collaboration, "You get the projects you need." While working on this book, it was necessary for me to confront my relationship to self-care. Reading the stories from our guest contributors, discussing this project with my coauthors, and genuinely sharing my experiences was a source of self-care for me this year. Inviting others to contribute to this book and discussing their narratives and experiences kept me in contact with peers and colleagues. I felt less alone in my own self-care process as I read the contributors' pieces. I was humbled by the many stories shared by individuals I admire both personally and professionally. On the surface, these individuals appear to have everything put together. Reading about their challenges regarding self-care caused me to reflect on how my students might perceive me. I am challenging myself to be more transparent regarding my self-care process and to be curious about theirs, especially with doctoral student mentees. When students ask me how I am doing, I appropriately share my feelings of exhaustion or anxiety about certain projects and events. I make sure to follow this up with an explanation of what I am doing to take care of myself. Essentially, immersing myself in this process has encouraged me to be more open about self-care with myself and others.

Writing this book also gave Michelle, Jerry, Julius, and me the opportunity to discuss difficult topics such as maintaining professional boundaries, finding meaning in life, and nurturing relationships. I enjoyed talking to my coauthors on a frequent basis and learning from them. Having these conversations as a doctoral student would have better prepared me for becoming a faculty member. Through this writing process, I learned the art of self-care, which for me has less to do with planning and more to do with adapting. Like the old boxing adage—"Everyone has a plan until they get punched in the face"—this writing experience has punched me in the face a couple of times. Managing my other research projects, settling into a new home, and juggling my other personal and professional responsibilities have caused me to push the boundaries of my self-care. My self-care plan had to be adapted to my circumstances, and I rolled with the changes.

Working on each chapter taught me something about surviving in this profession. Chapter 2 helped me to see my career as a marathon, not as a sprint. Chapter 3 helped me to understand how important self-care is now that I am no longer a student, but a new professional. I feel I now have more empathy for my students who may be facing obstacles to which I am not always aware. Chapter 4 helped me think about the relationship between my personal and professional life and how these parts of me interact with each other. Chapter 5 provided some unique approaches to self-care that I had not considered. Chapter 6 caused me to reflect on the boundaries in my life and how they influence my self-care. Chapter 7 helped me understand how my responsibilities and projects have influenced my relationships with myself, friends, family, and colleagues. Chapter 8 pulled together the themes from previous chapters and helped me see how I gain meaning in life through self-care.

Lessons Learned

Working on this book has made me confront my values as a counselor educator. When I was a doctoral student, my thoughts of what I would do as a faculty member to support my students and take care of myself were somewhat naïve. Becoming a faculty member has alleviated some financial stress, which greatly improved my sense of well-being, but this position also presents challenges for me. One challenge is learning how to tap into my own creativity to find better ways to support my students.

Reading contributed pieces from counselor educators, I was reminded that a counselor education faculty is made up of people who have a great deal of responsibility for their students, communities, colleges, and universities. Increased research pressure and other factors can cause faculty members to be less present for their students. In our haste to accomplish everything required of us, we may miss the mark on helping trainees buffer themselves against the hazards of burnout by failing to adequately emphasize self-care in our classes.

In reflecting on the number of students who graduate from counseling programs each semester, my colleagues and I wonder what percentage of those students are healthy or unwell. How many of those students will cause harm to their clients? How many of those students have the capacity to do deep, meaningful work with their clients? How many of those students will cause harm to themselves due to the stress inherent in the work we do? Our answers to these questions, along with the experiences shared in this book by students, have inspired me to make self-care an essential part of my courses and more of a priority in my life.

Julius's Personal Reflections

I feel fortunate to be writing a book at this point in my career, but even luckier to be writing this book with kind, caring, genuine, and humorous coauthors. Michelle, Jerry, and Jude have made the process of being vulnerable at different stages of the book so much more bearable. We have gone through personal shifts and changes together, and I thank my coauthors for accepting me and being patient with me throughout this writing process.

The hardest parts of this collaboration have been the balancing act between our personal and professional lives and juggling the differing schedules and time zones in which we live. Due to the number of clients I see daily, I did most of my writing on weekends. I am grateful that my family allowed me to carve out time to complete writing assignments. I appreciate that my writing team acknowledged the many hats that we all had to wear through this process and trusted me to make time for this book.

Lessons Learned

The most interesting aspect of this book for me is that the student contributors have come from such varied educational backgrounds. Some unifying themes among them are stress, frustration, perfectionism, hope, anxiety, self-compassion, and acceptance, which my current students experience as well. I teach beginning counselors who feel an immense amount of pressure and responsibility toward me, their clients, and themselves. I want to increasingly reflect on how my presence can contribute to my students' self-care. Working on this book has compelled me to ask myself two key questions: "In what ways am I influencing my students to care for themselves?" and "How can I emphasize the importance of self-care in my classroom?" After much reflection, I have reached the conclusion that one way I can promote better self-care among my students is to incorporate this discussion in the structure of my classes.

Graduate students usually have high expectations for themselves, are highly motivated, and sometimes are their own harshest critics. A unique aspect of a classroom is that it is a microcosm of the outside world. By cultivating an environment in my classroom that this is a safe place for students to check in with each other, to be vulnerable, and to evaluate each other and themselves, I can incorporate self-care and make sure everyone feels welcomed and connected. Many of my students are making transitions from being at work or tending to their personal lives to attend my graduate classes. I want to be intentional about the way we care for ourselves as we transition into the learning environment. It is important to spend the first 10 to 20 minutes of each class checking in with each other. I also think it is important to carve out 1 or 2 days in the syllabus as designated "work days" in which students come to class and work on a major course assignment. These work days provide a break from course material; students are able to work on assignments in class and receive clarification if needed. I think these additions to the structure of my courses will help relieve some of the academic pressure students are under and promote better self-care.

Michelle's Personal Reflections

When Jerry proposed the idea of coauthoring this book, I wondered whether I was the right person for the job. Although I have long been aware of the importance of practicing good self-care, I admittedly struggle with it. Having known Jerry for many years and being in awe of his physical fitness and knowing that Jude and Julius were former professional soccer players, I questioned whether I would have anything of substance to contribute. After all, there were days when the most physical activity I participated in was walking to and from the parking garage at my workplace and taking an occasional walk around the fifth floor in my office building. I know physical activity is only one dimension of self-care, but in all honesty I did not do a marvelous job of tending to my self-care in other ways either. As I contemplated the idea of working on this book, I had the insight that my key contribution could be writing about those obstacles to self-care that so many of us face and sharing the personal challenges I encounter in practicing self-care. I am so glad I challenged my self-doubts and undertook this project because it has been a rewarding experience. After reviewing and editing the contributors' personal narratives about their unique experiences with self-care, I felt the sense of "universality" that Irvin Yalom speaks about as a therapeutic factor. Reading about others' struggles with self-care (including those of my coauthors) reinforced my suspicion that it is probably more common to struggle than not to struggle with self-care. Knowing that I am not alone in practicing self-care *imperfectly* has helped me to accept my limitations. In fact, in line with the paradoxical theory of change, by accepting myself as I am—rather than trying to be someone or something I am not, namely, a person who is great at self-care—there is a greater likelihood that I will actually implement some changes in my self-care regimen. Truth be told, I have already begun to do so.

Just as we have urged you to take an honest inventory of your self-care habits (both positive and negative), I have felt compelled to examine my own self-care shortcomings and successes while working on this book. I know, for instance, that I would feel better if I exercised on a regular basis and adopted better dietary habits. I am satisfied with some areas of my self-care such as making sure I get adequate sleep at night. I would like to increase my participation in some activities that I currently enjoy, such as carving out time for massages or manicures/pedicures, watching movies or TV programs, and attending concerts with friends. I also recognize that I do need to make more of an effort to incorporate "fun" in my life. My father's death and the month from hell leading up to his death, which transpired while we were working on this book, reminded me of the importance of finding joy in the small things in life, such as enjoying a beautiful bouquet of flowers or a picture-perfect sunset (but not a sunrise—I am not an early riser!). Largely as a result of that ordeal and my involvement in writing this book, I have made a concerted effort to reflect more often on what I am grateful for in my life and to practice self-compassion.

Lessons Learned

I have always talked with students about the importance of being kind to themselves and giving themselves a break (advice I needed to heed in my own life), but this project led me to give more serious thought to other ways I could incorporate self-care in my classes.

I am a big fan of group work and often include check-ins and small group activities in my classes. I could easily give students the prompt during class to talk about aspects of their self-care—both what they are doing well and what they struggle with today. I could challenge them to create their own self-care plans and to take time in class to develop them. Practicing self-care is one of their ethical obligations and a buffer against experiencing burnout, so I think that would be time well spent.

I truly enjoyed my conversations with Jude, Julius, and Jerry in putting this book together. One might say that these conversations, in and of themselves, were a form of self-care. Major stressful events occurred in my personal life and in the world during the writing of this book, which made the task of writing about self-care a timely gift. As Jude noted in his personal reflections, perhaps we do get the projects we need. For that I am grateful.

Jerry's Personal Reflections

Although I am not new to writing textbooks, working with three coauthors on a brand new book was stimulating. We drafted the proposal collaboratively, completed the first draft, and exchanged ideas on how we could reach our audience with the message "Counselor, Take Care of Thyself!" We invited a wide range of students, counselor practitioners, and counselor educators to share their self-care stories, and I was impressed with their level of honesty and their courage in disclosing their struggles and sharing the action plans they devised to treat themselves with increased kindness and compassion. Despite the obstacles they encountered, their stories are filled with their hopes and visions for the future. Many themes were explored, including not demanding perfection in taking care of themselves, continuing to strive to do better despite occasional setbacks, asking for the help they needed, and recognizing that consistently practicing self-care is essential if we are to competently serve others.

Of course, working with 52 guest contributors was a catalyst for me to reevaluate my own self-care program. I certainly don't need to increase my commitment to exercise, but other aspects of my plan have room for improvement. Instead of being caught up in communing with nature when walking on a mountain trail, I am often on my antiquated cell phone talking to friends, family members, colleagues, or my coauthors. These talks can be productive, but they are not exactly mindfully walking in nature! As I walked along a trail talking one day,

I encountered a rattlesnake, and I jumped straight up in the air! I told myself I would be more mindful after that, but I have failed to carry through with my intention. It is a challenge for me to keep from getting swept up in intense activity and tasks to be done. One area I would like to build into my daily self-care practice is some brief time for mindfulness meditation and quiet self-reflection, but I tell myself that I am too busy to "just do nothing." Now what would I say to someone who says, "I don't have time to exercise"?

Lessons Learned

To apply what I have learned through this process to my professional life, I intend to continue to create space in the classes I teach for discussions around self-care. Focusing on some aspect of self-care in each class session might be as simple as taking a few minutes for a guided imagery or a few quiet moments of transition from the outside world to being fully in the class experience. I am likely to invite former students, including some who are guest contributors in this book, to come to class to share their unique self-care journeys as a form of inspiration and empowerment. Perhaps I will ask students to design a personal self-care action plan during the semester and encourage them to use each other as a support system in implementing some aspect of their plan. In short, I intend to find ways to bring many of the messages in this book into the courses I teach because self-care is an essential part of every counselor's professional and personal life.

Key Messages in the Book

As we conclude *Counselor Self-Care*, we turn our attention back to you and ask you to reflect on the key messages in this book. We hope we have inspired you to move forward with your own self-care plans and that you persist in striving for what you want and need. Here are some key messages that we gleaned from working on this project:

- Strive to do your best, but do not let perfectionism dominate your life and immobilize you. It is perfectly all right to practice self-care imperfectly! Doing some self-care is better than doing no self-care.
- Recognize your fears, doubts, and negative self-talk and be willing to challenge what might hold you back from achieving your self-care goals.

- Take an active role in reflecting on how you can incorporate self-care principles and practices in your life, even if your graduate program does not provide this encouragement.
- Remain open to asking for the help you need, not only in graduate school but throughout your professional journey. We encourage clients to do this, and we should practice what we preach and be willing to reach out to others when we need support.
- Create and maintain appropriate boundaries with clients and others; setting clear boundaries provides the opportunity to fully participate in self-care.
- Realize that there is no one right self-care plan. Design a plan that fits you and provides motivation for you to take care of yourself on all levels.
- Develop self-discipline, be willing to work hard, and don't give up when the road is rough. Don't let discouragement get the best of you.
- Think of ways you can be accountable to yourself in carrying out your plans. Devise ways to monitor your self-care practices.
- Don't equate making mistakes with being a failure. Be open to learning from mistakes.
- Say "yes" to opportunities as often as you can, especially early in your education or career, but try to avoid becoming overwhelmed. Once you are established in your career, you may need to be more selective about the opportunities you choose to take.
- If you lose your way in your journey toward self-care, don't lose hope for you will find the path again.

If you commit to a self-care program at an early stage in your professional development and career, maintaining your self-care program as you get older and prepare for retirement will come easily for you. The earlier you start, the easier it is for self-care to become a part of your lifestyle. But don't despair if you have waited until you reach a more advanced season in your life and career. It is never too late to make positive changes in your life. After all, as counselors and helping professionals, we are in the business of helping people of all ages and circumstances to improve their lives. We (Michelle, Jude, Julius, and Jerry) deserve the same opportunity to get the most out of our lives—and so do you!

References

Allan, R., McLuckie, A., & Hoffecker, L. (2016). *Clinical supervision of psychotherapists: A systematic review.* Retrieved from https://www.campbellcollaboration.org/media/k2/attachments/Allan_Clinical_Supervision_Title.pdf

Aponte, H. J., & Kissil, K. (2014). "If I can grapple with this I can truly be of use in the therapy room": Using the therapist's own emotional struggles to facilitate effective therapy. *Journal of Marital and Family Therapy, 40*(2), 152–164.

Austin, J. T. (2016). *Helping counseling students develop therapeutic presence: A modified Delphi study* (Unpublished doctoral dissertation). University of Wyoming, Laramie, Wyoming.

Bamonti, P. M., Keelan, C. M., Larson, N., Mentrikoski, J. M., Randall, C. L., Sly, S. K., . . . McNeil, D. W. (2014). Promoting ethical behavior by cultivating a culture of self-care during graduate training: A call to action. *Training and Education in Professional Psychology, 8*(4), 253–260. doi:10.1037/tep0000056

Barnett, J. E., Baker, E. K., Elman, N. S., & Schoener, G. R. (2007). In pursuit of wellness: The self-care imperative. *Professional Psychology: Research and Practice, 38*(6), 603–612.

Barnett, J. E. (2017). An introduction to boundaries and multiple relationships for psychotherapists: Issue, challenges, and recommendations. In O. Zur (Ed.), *Multiple relationships in psychotherapy and counseling: Unavoidable, common, and mandatory dual relations in therapy* (pp. 17–29). New York, NY: Routledge.

Carlson, J., & Englar-Carlson, M. (2017). *Adlerian psychotherapy.* Washington, DC: American Psychological Association.

Carrola, P. A., Olivarez, A., & Karcher, M. J. (2016). Correctional counselor burnout: Examining burnout rates using the Counselor Burnout Inventory. *Journal of Offender Rehabilitation, 55*(3), 195–212.

Coker, A. D., & Bryant, R. (2016, April). *Courageous conversations with women of color in counselor education.* Association of Multicultural Counseling and Development [Webinar series]. Retrieved from https://youtu.be/MqlRt-ETGYE

Coleman, C., Martensen, C., Scott, R., & Indelicato, N. A. (2016). Unpacking self-care: The connection between mindfulness, self-compassion, and self-care for counselors. *Counseling & Wellness: A Professional Counseling Journal, 5.*

Corey, G., Corey, M. S., & Muratori, M. (2018). *I never knew I had a choice* (11th ed.). Boston, MA: Cengage Learning.

Dalai Lama. (2001). *An open heart: Practicing compassion in everyday life.* Boston, MA: Little Brown.

Dattilio, F. M. (2015). The self-care of psychologists and mental health professionals: A review and practitioner guide. *The Australian Psychologist, 50,* 393–399.

Derks, D., & Bakker, A. B. (2014). Smartphone use, work–home interference, and burnout: A diary study on role recovery. *Applied Psychology, 63,* 411–440.

El-Ghoroury, N., Galper, D. I., Sawaqdeh, A., & Bufka, L. F. (2012). Stress, coping, and barriers to wellness among psychology graduate students. *Training and Education in Professional Psychology, 6,* 122–134. doi:10.1037/a0028768

Ellis, A., & Ellis, D. J. (2011). *Rational emotive behavior therapy.* Washington, DC: American Psychological Association.

Englar-Carlson, M., Evans, M. P., & Duffey, T. (2014). *A counselor's guide to working with men.* Alexandria, VA: American Counseling Association.

Englar-Carlson, M., & Kottler, J. (2017). In Memoriam—Jon Carlson: A positive force in counseling, psychology and the world. *Counseling Today, 59*(10), 42–43.

Enright, R. D. (2012). *The forgiving life.* Washington, DC: American Psychological Association.

Felix, E. D., & Afifi, W. (2015). The role of social support on mental health after multiple wildfire disasters. *Journal of Community Psychology, 43*(2), 156–170.

Francis, P. C. (2016). Religion and spirituality in counseling. In I. Marini & M. A. Stebnicki (Eds.), *The professional counselor's desk reference* (2nd ed., pp. 559–564). New York, NY: Springer.

Frankl, V. (1963). *Man's search for meaning.* New York, NY: Washington Square Press.

Frankl, V. (1965). *The doctor and the soul.* New York, NY: Bantam.

Frankl, V. (1967). *Psychotherapy and existentialism.* New York, NY: Simon & Schuster.

Frankl, V. (1969). *The will to meaning: Foundation and applications of logotherapy.* New York, NY: New American Library.

Fried, A. L., & Fisher, C. B. (2016). Moral stress and job burnout among frontline staff conducting clinical research on affective and anxiety disorders. *Professional Psychology: Research and Practice, 47*(3), 171–180.

García-Alandete, J. (2015). Does meaning in life predict psychological well-being? *European Journal of Counselling Psychology, 3*(2), 89–98.

Geller, S. M. (2017). *A practical guide for cultivating therapeutic presence.* Washington, DC: American Psychological Association.

Geller, S. M., & Greenberg, L. S. (2012). *Therapeutic presence: A mindful approach to effective therapy.* Washington, DC: American Psychological Association.

Germer, C. K., Siegel, R. D., & Fulton, P. R. (Eds.). (2013). *Mindfulness and psychotherapy* (2nd ed.). New York, NY: Guilford Press.

Gilbert, P. (2010). *The compassionate mind: A new approach to life's challenges.* Oakland, CA: New Harbinger Publications.

Gutierrez, D., Conley, A. H., & Young, M. (2016). Examining the effects of Jyoti meditation on stress and the moderating role of emotional intelligence. *Counselor Education and Supervision, 55,* 109–122. doi:10.1002/ceas.12036

Gupta, N., & Irwin, J. D. (2016). In-class distractions: The role of Facebook and the primary learning task. *Computers in Human Behavior, 55,* 1165–1178. doi:10.1016/j.chb.2014.10.022

Hales, D. (2017). *An invitation to health: Build your future* (17th ed.). Boston, MA: Cengage Learning.

Haynes, R. L. (2014). *Take control of life's crises today: A practical guide.* Chula Vista, CA: Aventine Press.

Herlihy, B., & Corey, G. (2015). *Boundary issues in counseling: Multiple roles and responsibilities* (3rd ed.). Alexandria, VA: American Counseling Association.

Hermann, M. A., Ziomek-Daigle, J., & Dockery, D. J. (2014). Motherhood and counselor education: Experiences with work-life balance. *Adultspan Journal, 13,* 109–119.

Hollis, R. B. (2016). Mind wandering, control failures, and social media distractions in online learning. *Learning and Instruction, 42,* 104–112.

Jacobs, G. A., Gray, B. L., Erickson, S. E., Gonzalez, E. D., & Quevillon, R. P. (2016). Disaster mental health and community-based psychological first aid: Concepts and education/training. *Journal of Clinical Psychology, 72*(12), 1307–1317.

Johns Hopkins Medicine. (2014, Summer). The healing power of forgiveness. *Health,* 6–9.

Johnson, R. (2013). *Spirituality in counseling and psychotherapy: An integrative approach that empowers clients.* Hoboken, NJ: Wiley.

Johnson, W. B., Barnett, J. E., Elman, N. S., Forrest, L., & Kaslow, N. J. (2012). The competent community: Toward a vital reformulation of professional ethics. *American Psychologist, 67*(7), 557–569.

Johnson, W. B., & Smith, D. (2016). *Athena rising: How and why men should mentor women.* Brookline, MA: Bibliomotion.

Kabat-Zinn, J. (1990). *Full catastrophe living.* New York, NY: Delacorte.

Kabat-Zinn, J. (1994). *Wherever you go, there you are: Mindfulness meditation in everyday life.* New York, NY: Hyperion.

Kampfe, C. M. (2015). *Counseling older people: Opportunities and challenges.* Alexandria, VA: American Counseling Association.

Kelly, E. L., Moen, P., Oakes, J. M., Fan, W., Okechukwu, C., Davis, K. D., . . . Casper, L. M. (2014). Changing work and work-family conflict: Evidence from the work, family, and health network. *American Sociological Review, 79*(3), 485–516.

Killen, A., & Macaskill, A. (2015). Using a gratitude intervention to enhance well-being in older adults. *Journal of Happiness Studies, 16,* 947–964.

Kottler, J. A. (2014). *Change: What really leads to lasting personal transformation.* Oxford, NY: Oxford University Press.

Kottler, J. A. (2017). *On being a therapist* (5th ed.). Oxford, NY: Oxford University Press.

Kottler, J. A., & Balkin, R. (2017). *Relationships in counseling and the counselor's life.* Alexandria, VA: American Counseling Association.

Kottler, J. A., & Carlson, J. (2016). *Therapy over 50: Aging issues in psychotherapy and the therapist's life.* New York, NY: Oxford University Press.

Knapp, S., Gottlieb, M. C., & Handelsman, M. M. (2017). Enhancing professionalism through self-reflection. *Professional Psychology: Research and Practice, 48*(3), 167–174.

Lampe, K. (2014). *The birth of hedonism: The Cyrenaic philosophers and pleasure as a way of life.* Princeton, NJ: Princeton University Press.

Lancer, D. (2016). *Symptoms of codependency.* Retrieved from https://psychcentral.com/lib/symptoms-of-codependency/

Leppma, M., & Young, M. E. (2016). Loving-kindness meditation and empathy: A wellness group intervention for counseling students. *Journal of Counseling & Development, 94,* 297–305.

Luke, C. (2016). *Neuroscience for counselors and therapists: Integrating the sciences of mind and brain.* Thousand Oaks, CA: Sage.

Lyubomirsky, S. (2013). *The myths of happiness.* New York, NY: Penguin Press.

Marchant, J. (2017). Think yourself healthy. *Prevention, 69*(1), 28–31.

May, R. (1950). *The meaning of anxiety.* New York, NY: Ronald Press.

May, R. (1953). *Man's search for himself.* New York, NY: Dell.

May, R. (Ed.). (1961). *Existential psychology.* New York, NY: Random House.

May, R. (1969). *Love and will.* New York, NY: Norton.

May, R. (1981). *Freedom and destiny.* New York, NY: Norton.

May, R. (1983). *The discovery of being: Writings in existential psychology.* New York: Norton.

McConnell, J. M. (2015). A conceptual-theoretical-empirical framework for self-forgiveness: Implications for research and practice. *Basic and Applied Social Psychology, 37*(3), 143–164.

Millegan, J., Delaney, E. M., & Klam, W. (2016). Responding to trauma at sea: A case study in psychological first aid, unique occupational stressors, and resiliency self-care. *Military Medicine, 181*(11), 1692–1695.

Moate, R. M., Gnilka, P. B., West, E. M., & Bruns, K. L. (2016). Stress and burnout among counselor educators: Differences between adaptive perfectionists, maladaptive perfectionists, and nonperfectionists. *Journal of Counseling & Development, 94,* 161–171.

Mullenbach, M., & Skovholt, T. M. (2016). Burnout prevention and self-care strategies of expert practitioners. In T. M. Skovholt & M. Trotter-Mathison, *The resilient practitioner: Burnout and compassion fatigue prevention and self-care strategies for the helping professions* (3rd ed., pp. 231–254). New York, NY: Routledge.

Myers, S. B., Sweeney, A. C., Popick, V., Wesley, K., Bordfeld, A., & Fingerhut, R. (2012). Self-care practices and perceived stress levels among psychology graduate students. *Training and Education in Professional Psychology, 6*(1), 55–66.

Neff, K. (2011). *Self-compassion: Stop beating up on yourself and leave insecurity behind.* New York, NY: HarperCollins.

Norcross, J. C., & VandenBos, G. R. (2018). *Leaving it at the office: A guide to psychotherapist self-care* (2nd ed.). New York, NY: Guilford.

Orlinsky, D. F., & Ronnestad, M. H. (2005). *How psychotherapists develop: A study of therapeutic work and professional growth.* Washington, DC: American Psychological Association.

Orlinsky, D. E., Schofield, M. J., Schroder, T., & Kazantzis, N. (2011). Utilization of personal therapy by psychotherapists: A practice-friendly review and a new study. *Journal of Clinical Psychology, 67*(8), 828–842.

Passmore, J., & Oades, L. G. (2015). Positive psychology techniques—Random acts of kindness and consistent acts of kindness and empathy. *The Coaching Psychologist, 11*(2), 90–92.

Patsiopoulos, A. T., & Buchanan, M. J. (2011). The practice of self-compassion in counseling: A narrative inquiry. *Professional Psychology: Research and Practice, 42,* 301–307.

Prabu, D. (2015). Mobile phone distraction while studying. *New Media, 17*(10), 1661–1679.

Probst, B. (2015). The other chair: Portability and translation from personal therapy to clinical practice. *Clinical Social Work, 43,* 50–61.

Prochaska, J. O., & Norcross, J. C. (2018). *Systems of psychotherapy: A transtheoretical analysis* (9th ed.). New York, NY: Oxford University Press.

Rogers, C. R. (1980). *A way of being.* Boston, MA: Houghton Mifflin.

Ronnestad, M. H., Orlinsky, D. E., & Wiseman, H. (2016). Professional development and personal therapy. In J. Norcross, G. R. VandenBos, & D. K. Freedheim (Eds.), *APA handbook of clinical psychology* (Vol. 5, pp. 223–235). Washington, DC: American Psychological Association.

Rupert, P. A., Miller, A. O., & Dorociak, K. E. (2015). Preventing burnout: What does the research tell us? *Professional Psychology: Research and Practice, 46*(3), 168–174.

Scherger, J. E. (2016). *Lean and fit: A doctor's journey to healthy nutrition and greater wellness.* Author.

Schueller, S. M., & Parks, A. C. (2014). The science of self-help: Translating positive psychology research into increased individual happiness. *European Psychologist, 19*(2), 145–155. doi:10.1027/1016-9040/a000181

Seppa, N. (2015, March). The mess that is stress: Chronic angst triggers a slew of changes that harm long-term health. *Science News Magazine, 187*(5), 18–23.

Siegel, R. D. (2010). *The mindfulness solution: Everyday practices for everyday problems.* New York, NY: Guilford Press.

Silva, A. E., Newman, D. S., Guiney, M. C., Valley-Gray, S., & Barrett, C. A. (2016). Supervision and mentoring for early career school psychologists: Availability, access, structure, and implications. *Psychology in the Schools, 53*(5), 502–516.

Singh, R. (2007). *Inner and outer peace through meditation.* Lisle, IL: Radiance.

Skovholt, T. M., & Trotter-Mathison, M. (2016). *The resilient practitioner: Burnout and compassion fatigue prevention and self-care strategies for the helping professionals* (3rd ed.). New York, NY: Routledge.

Smith, J. (2017). A counselor's journey back from burnout. *Counseling Today, 59*(10), 48–51.

Smith, K. (2017). Facing the fear of incompetence. *Counseling Today, 59*(10), 28–32.

Stebnicki, M. A. (2008). *Empathy fatigue: Healing the mind, body, and spirit of professional counselors.* New York, NY: Springer.

Stebnicki, M. A. (2016). Military counseling. In I. Marini & M. A. Stebnicki (Eds.), *The professional counselor's desk reference* (2nd ed., pp. 499–506). New York, NY: Springer.

Stebnicki, M. A. (2017). *Disaster mental health response: Responding to trauma in a multicultural context.* New York, NY: Springer.

Steger, M. F., Kashdan, T. B., Sullivan, B. A., & Lorentz, D. (2008). Understanding the search for meaning in life: Personality, cognitive style, and the dynamic between seeking and experiencing meaning. *Journal of Personality, 76*(2), 199–228.

Troisi, J. D., Leder, S., Steigler-Balfour, J. J., Fleck, B. K. B, & Good, J. J. (2015). Effective teaching outcomes associated with the mentorship of early career psychologists. *Teaching of Psychology, 42*(3), 242–247.

VanderWal, B. L. (2015). *The relationship between counselor trainees' personal therapy experiences and client outcome* (Doctoral dissertation). Retrieved from http://scholarworks.wmich.edu/dissertations/

Walsh, R. (2011). Lifestyle and mental health. *American Psychologist, 66,* 579–592.

Walsh, R. (2014). Contemplative psychotherapies. In D. Wedding & R. J. Corsini (Eds.), *Current psychotherapies* (10th ed., pp. 411–460). Belmont, CA: Brooks/Cole, Cengage Learning.

Wardle, E. A., & Mayorga, M. G. (2016). Burnout among the counseling profession: A survey of future professional counselors. *i-Manager's Journal on Educational Psychology, 10*(1), 9.

Watkins, P. C., Grimm, D. L., & Kolts, R. (2004). Counting your blessings: Positive memories among grateful persons. *Current Psychology, 23*(1), 52–67.

Waytz, A., Hershfield, H. E., & Tamir, D. I. (2015). Mental simulation and meaning in life. *Journal of Personality & Social Psychology, 108*(2), 336–355.

Weir, K. (2017). Forgiveness can improve mental and physical health. Research shows how to get there. *Monitor on Psychology, 48*(1), 31–33.

Wise, E. H., & Barnett, J. E. (2016). Self-care for psychologists. In J. Norcross, G. R. VandenBos, & D. K. Freedheim (Eds.), *APA handbook of clinical psychology* (Vol. 5, pp. 209–222). Washington, DC: American Psychological Association.

Wise, E. H., Hersh, M. A., & Gibson, C. M. (2011). Ethics and self-care: A developmental lifespan perspective. *Register Report, 37,* 20–29.

Wise, E. H., Hersh, M. A., & Gibson, C. M. (2012). Ethics, self-care and well-being for psychologists: Re-envisioning the stress-distress continuum. *Professional Psychology: Research and Practice, 43*(5), 487–494.

Wubbolding, R. E. (2017). *Reality therapy and self-evaluation: The key to client change.* Alexandria, VA: American Counseling Association.

Yalom, I. D. (1980). *Existential psychotherapy.* New York, NY: Basic Books.

Yalom, I. D. (2008). *Staring at the sun: Overcoming the terror of death.* San Francisco, CA: Jossey-Bass.

Zhang, Q. (2016). Equality and universal love: Human dignity in Mohism. In *Human dignity in classical Chinese philosophy* (pp. 143–172). New York, NY: Palgrave Macmillan.